DATE DUE

Witness to a Generation

Witness To A Generation

Significant Writings from

Christianity And Crisis (1941-1966)

Edited by Wayne H. Cowan

With a preface by Herbert Butterfield

The Bobbs-Merrill Company, Inc.
A Subsidiary of Howard W. Sams & Co., Inc.
Publishers   Indianapolis   New York   Kansas City

The editor acknowledges with gratitude the permission to reprint "A Protestant Looks at American Catholicism" by John C. Bennett, originally published in *Facing Protestant-Roman Catholic Tensions*, edited by Wayne H. Cowan, Associated Press, New York: 1960; and "The Gospel According to Saint Hereticus," from *The Collected Writings of Saint Hereticus*, edited by Robert McAfee Brown. Westminster Press, Philadelphia: 1964.

Designed by Martin Stephen Moskof
Printed in the United States of America

Dedicated
to
Reinhold Niebuhr
who founded *Christianity and Crisis* and
made it a journal of prophetic Christian realism
and to
John C. Bennett
who sustained it by his sensitive, balanced
and penetrating insights.

Preface

The region which once was Christendom, and which for centuries was the carrier of modern civilization, has come to seem a small affair in the global balance of power. Its own lengthy history has come to be regarded as in a way a drag upon it, a thing which disqualifies it for the role of leader any more. Yet only the other day its cultural influence came to a culmination, as its science, technology and organizational methods—even its political ideals and its Marxism—spread over the face of the wide world.

Never since the very earliest centuries of its history has Christianity been confronted by a challenge like the one now presented by this secular civilization which seems to be fundamentally the same in one country as in another. The cultural forces at work in this new kind of world seem to tend to the dissolution of those older religious systems, which perhaps were really politico-religious in character—a great bloc of Islam over one part of the map, a big slab of Christianity over another part— as though faith itself were regional in character, and creed an hereditary affair. Some of the traditions of the older Christian system (which we might describe as "historical Christianity") make the situation in certain ways more difficult for us today than for our predecessors who confronted the civilization of the ancient Roman Empire. The very memory of the days when Christianity was allied with power still provokes both the resentment and the suspicion of non-believers and is sometimes responsible for a certain steeling of the heart. The remaining strength of the traditions themselves sometimes hampers the attempt to achieve a radical kind of re-thinking in the Churches. No longer can religious conformity draw strength from the alliance with political authority and current conventionalities. That is why it is harder to be a Christian today, but the challenge is greater, as it often requires a higher and perhaps more authentic decision.

The challenge comes to Christians at a time when the developments in the world's thought—men's notions about the universe in general, for example, but also the current attitude to human history—create the need for some hard meditation on the very nature of religion. We need much of the kind of thought which gets behind the popular philosophies of the day and the fashionableness, the plausibility of scientism. We need also further reflection on the drama of human life under the sun as exhibited in a few thousand years of history. Above all, the Christian needs to go back to the original fountain of the faith—holding fast to what has proved the permanent basis of a spiritual life: the attachment of simple men to the risen and living Christ. Those who hold fast to this can afford to be flexible about everything else in the created universe.

Indeed, it is precisely in respect of the relations between Christianity and the world of human affairs that every age needs to do some re-thinking. Today a special problem has become particularly urgent: how to find the procedures of the spiritual life—the technique of a deep internal life—in an age and a world in which secular duties, secular considerations, go beyond all precedent in the colossal compulsive demands they make on everybody. But even in what concerns the realm of mundane affairs it is open to the Christian to show that he has at least one advantage over the mere secularist. He will be less likely to make gods out of the things to which so many people seem ready to bow and abase themselves, less prone to turn the immediate object into an absolute end, less a victim of the superstitions of the secularist. It is true that certain combinations of religion and worldly-mindedness have at moments given almost a diabolical character to political conflict. But a Christianity that is separated from ecclesiastical interests can still be in touch with the hard earth, and can be the way to a clearer, cleaner kind of worldly wisdom.

In this whole realm in which Christianity mixes with human affairs, one has to meet questions as they arise, feeling one's way and threshing out the problem as each new thing turns up. Essays such as those in the present volume have a special relevance for this reason. They meet issues while they are still alive—they catch the moment, catch the bird while it is still on the wing. Here is the important contribution which Christianity *and* Crisis *has been making now for a good run of years. The essays are calculated to lead to further thought, for in discussing the Christian attitude to problems as they emerge, they raise that larger question, still not entirely clarified: what are to be the relations between religion and mundane society in our kind of world? The present is not a moment in which all Christians will be agreed on all concrete issues. We ought to analyze to a great depth the places where we differ from one another, for here may be the key to a real advance.*

We are faced with serious moral paradoxes in a world where vast human conflicts may involve imperfect but well-meaning men on both sides; a world where what we might almost call little sins sometimes have vastly disproportionate consequences, and an object that is initially (or even inherently) good may be transmuted into evil if it has to be achieved by too great an exercise of power. Unselfish men who love one good thing too much may wreak appalling havoc in a country. Though Churches have sometimes intervened in public affairs with too great partisanship, there is a charity which can give release to imaginative sympathy and may equip the Christian in particular for the comprehension of the people not like-minded with himself. Perhaps it needs much science and a capacious kind of charity to disentangle one's duty in our kind of a world: and the Christian ought not to rely on mere good intentions but to carry his thought and his studies to some depth.

Peterhouse
Cambridge, England

Herbert Butterfield

Contents

Introduction

THE year was 1940. News from Europe grew more ominous with each passing month. The Nazis overran the Netherlands and Belgium in May and June; the British were driven from the Continent at Dunkirk. Before the end of July the French had capitulated. In October the Balkans were added to the Nazi trophies. Fighting against overwhelming odds, the Royal Air Force won the Battle of Britain in late summer and early fall.

Across the Atlantic, the United States lay almost inert. Americans preferred to debate the matter at a distance; the war was not their affair. An unholy alliance developed between pacifists and isolationists as Senator Burton K. Wheeler, Colonel Charles A. Lindbergh and the America First Committee worked closely with pacifist clergymen. The latter were the product of an older perfectionism that was affronted by the horrible international reality produced by the Treaty of Versailles. Not even their idealism could lead them into battle again "to make the world safe for democracy." Polls indicated that the alliance held the upper hand as they argued for neutrality and non-intervention. They sought to convince the nation that the United States was not in peril of invasion and that Latin America would not fall under German domination if the Axis won. There were plans to establish "peace through mediation," and an aura of holiness attended their position of neutrality between the belligerent and "evil" nations. Their utopian efforts to keep the nation untainted in the face of the Nazi threat ignored the fact that, while guarding our virtue and maintaining our purity, they were irresponsibly ignoring the dangers facing the nations of Europe.

Hindsight makes all wisdom commonplace, and all of this may seem quite academic in the year 1966. But it was frightfully real to much of the world community and to a small group of Protestants, led by theologian Reinhold Niebuhr, who met in Manhattan throughout 1940 to discuss the founding of a journal that would counter this essential irresponsibility. On February 10, 1941, these words appeared in the lead editorial of a new bi-weekly publication called *Christianity and Crisis:*

> The tragic irony of the hour is that so many of the men in America whom this revolt against Christian civilization most concerns seem to be least aware of its implications. The freedom of these men to speak and write depends upon the existence of a certain type of civilization. Yet they talk and act as if they believed that, whoever wins, religion-as-usual, like business-as-usual, will be the order of the day. . . . The choice before us is clear. Those who choose to exist like parasites on the liberties that others fight to secure for them will end by betraying the Christian ethic and the civilization that has developed out of that ethic.

Thus began a witness to a generation that needed to be shaken loose from its faith in historical progress, its cherished belief that history itself is redemptive. The calamitous events of the last twenty-five years were far more effective in destroying this faith than any words in this or any other journal. But the influence of this publication in its interpretation and understanding of the meaning of Christian faith for these events—in the Protestant community, at least—was not insignificant. The major motifs of the thought of Reinhold Niebuhr (complexity, paradox, irony, the mixture of man's motives and the entangling jumble of good and evil that mark all human actions) appeared again and again in its pages as he established the journal's image of Christian realism and did battle with American (and Russian) self-righteousness and the sentimentalism that seemed almost endemic to American Protestantism.

Perhaps the most obvious way this journal of opinion did this was by refuting what it considered to be erroneous answers offered by Christians to the problems that confronted the generation. One of the most basic sources of confusion was the simple assumption that "Christianity's contribution to politics consisted purely in the demand that men and nations should love one another." *Christianity and Crisis* pointed out that religious men—by distorting the experience of men and nations throughout history and attempting to by-pass the unending struggle for justice—were merely confusing the conscience of the nation where they might have enlightened it.

This was true not only in 1941 but also as the peace approached and visionaries set forth in all directions with their distressingly naive proposals for world government. It was seen again in the early postwar years when "misguided or self-deceived idealists" failed to recognize that "self-interest corrupts even the most ideal motives" and that the Russian regime, though in theory an almost complete contrast, was frightfully like that of the Nazis.

Lest the reader conclude that *Christianity and Crisis* represented the hard-headed military on its knees, let evidence be quickly entered into the record that it dissociated itself from the concept of a "holy war" in its first issue, that it criticized the conduct of the war (the relocation of loyal Japanese Americans, obliteration bombing and our demand of "unconditional surrender") not infrequently.

Its opposition to the dangers of McCarthyism started early in 1950, and its critique of crude, jingoistic anti-communism continues to this day. As Russian communism showed signs of evolving from its revolutionary stage, this journal—thanks in good part to the keen insight of Editorial Board Co-Chairman John C. Bennett—was one of the first to recognize and give attention to this fact and to welcome the break-up of the Communist monolith.

The journal's focus has not always been on issues of war and peace. Through much of its first decade this was in fact the case, though throughout this period a deep and abiding concern for the ecumenical movement and the world church was also in evidence. During most of this period the circulation of the journal remained low, at no time approaching 10,000. And financial crisis was every bit as real as the many-faceted crisis to which the editors sought to bring the light of Christian understanding. This was true despite the fact that the Editorial Board served without payment of any kind and that no honoraria were given for articles until 1963. Almost annually the Board of Sponsors was confronted with the question of whether the journal had not served its purpose and should cease publication. This question was last raised in 1954 when circulation hovered near 4,000 and the treasurer's books showed a deficit of almost $2,000. At that point an appeal was addressed to the subscribers, which said in part:

> We do not promise or threaten to go on forever. We merely desire to serve the Church and our generation as long as a sufficient number of friends regard our services as worthwhile.

They did, and very gradually, over the next years, the situation improved. The journal broadened its perspective to give more attention to "culture" (the modern novel, the contemporary theater, the mass media of radio, television and cinema). It moved beyond the plain eight-page format of the first thirteen years to 12–24 pages of a still simple but more inviting format. As it did so, it rallied and gained new readers; by the twenty-fifth anniversary in 1966 the circulation was approaching 20,000.

From its early days *Christianity and Crisis* recognized that a prime function of the religious journal is to carry on a dialogue with the modern world, a dialogue marked by openness and sensitivity to insights from sources—secular and religious—outside Christian faith. Such a dialogue leads to the discovery of those relevant insights common to both the Christian and non-Christian. Because of its drive to explore the common and uncommon resources of our civilization, the journal has not rejected wisdom that did not bear a "Christian" or "Protestant" label. To an extent that is rare for a religious publication, its editors, through close contact with the broader world, have allowed themselves to be instructed by its insights.

Lewis Mumford, Arnold Toynbee and Hans Morgenthau have made significant contributions to crucial questions in *Christianity and Crisis*. At the twenty-fifth anniversary colloquium on "The Crisis Character of Modern Society," such persons as Hannah Arendt, Herbert Blau, Richard Goodwin and Gerald Holton served as members of the panels and as prime discussants of the theme.

Thus, it is not surprising that critics have frequently charged that the journal spoke more of crisis than of Christianity. One reason for this may be that this is, as someone has said, the "crisis century" rather than the "Christian century," as some believers in progress thought fifty years ago. A more adequate reason—and one that reflects more realistically the approach of the editors—was noted recently by William Arthur, the editor of *Look* magazine. After reviewing a number of Protestant publications, he concluded that religious magazines frequently overemphasize the reader's Christian obligations, testing his faith every few paragraphs, and that their efforts to bring together the material and spiritual are usually self-conscious and self-defeating. In *Christianity and Crisis,* he said, "the application of the Judaeo-Christian ethic to the problems of our time is implicit in [its] philosophy but it is not reiterated in almost every paragraph." Nonetheless, Martin Marty is undoubtedly correct when he writes of the journal in *The Religious Press in America:* "it would hardly be recognizable as a Protestant organ in many a faithful upper midwestern congregation."

Because of its positions on church-state questions and its basic openness to Roman Catholicism, some critics have maintained that the journal has "sold out" and is "soft on Catholicism." But this was the price of dialogue; and once it had been entered into honestly there began the process that Robert McAfee Brown has called "caricature assassination." Thus, well in advance of John XXIII and Vatican II, *Christianity and Crisis* had moved from moderate anti-Catholicism to a recognition that the Roman Catholic Church was not a monolith forever frozen against change and that it was, in fact, in ferment from top to bottom. Articles by the late Gustave Weigel, S.J., William Clancy, Daniel Callahan, John Leo, James Finn and other "aggiornamento" Catholics frequently appeared, setting forth firsthand evidence of post-Tridentine Catholicism.

Christianity and Crisis has had to face criticism from another corner as it has sought to answer the question—Does Christian faith offer a unique answer to the questions raised by life in the modern world? Some Christians certainly think so, and they give the journal a low score for not elucidating this answer in unequivocal terms. A great deal of underbrush must be removed, however, in order to get at the heart of the question.

That Christian faith has guidance to offer is the premise upon which the journal was founded. But this has never been taken to mean that there is a Christian answer to every problem that arises. Matters of social policy may involve Christian judgments, but they are more likely to involve preeminently technical and other judgments based upon somewhat hazardous predictions regarding the impact of any given policy on society itself. And even where Christian faith can offer clarity of insight it may well be, as in the case of the conflict between the Jews and the Arabs in Palestine, that there can be no just solution since two or more acknowledged Christian objectives may be in conflict. This difficulty has been reflected in the pages of the journal not only in the disagreements within the Editorial Board on the Palestine question but also in the lack of consensus in the Suez Crisis, to mention just two. In all these matters *Christianity and Crisis* has been at pains to point out the need for perceptive judgment in relating gospel absolutes to challenges of justice, order and peace.

Nevertheless, the journal has always insisted that there are specific Christian insights and it has sought to discern and interpret their meaning for each issue it has taken up. Its concern for the exploited and the neglected has led it to give strong support to the racial revolution and to interpret the nature of the "third world" and its revolution of rising expectations. Idolatry, whether national or international, has always been fair game in its editorials and articles.

By the time *Christianity and Crisis* celebrated its twenty-fifth birthday the configuration of forces in the world and our nation had changed to such an extent that Dr. Niebuhr could write in the anniversary issue (February 21, 1966) that "the problem of indiscriminate pacifism . . . has given way to the problem of curbing pure force in the international realm. Thus we seek to persuade our nation that Chinese communism cannot be contained or restrained purely by military violence, particularly when we regard ourselves as the appointed saviors of the world and do not consult the consensus of the nations." A companion editorial by Dr. Bennett in the same issue was entitled "From Supporter of War in 1941 to Critic in 1966." The entire Editorial Board joined in signing an editorial in the following issue, "We Protest the National Policy in Vietnam," which concluded:

> The threat of this moment is a preoccupation with the enemy that destroys our society's power to understand itself or its foes. In such a time the greatest service to the society comes from those voices— in church, politics and press—that risk the displeasure of the powers that be in order to challenge dogmatisms that imperil ourselves and our world. To these voices we again add our own.

Vice President Hubert H. Humphrey in addressing the anniversary banquet concluded his remarks by declaring that the need for this journal would continue "because two things are not going to go away: the claims of social justice and the complexities of politics. . . . *Christianity and Crisis* as a Christian journal must by definition have a perspective as wide as humankind and one eye on eternity. It cannot afford to reflect parochial nationalism or a short-run outlook. A journal like that, a perspective like that, is the requirement of our time."

But it is Reinhold Niebuhr who best suggests the journal's witness to future generations when he says:

> The moral crisis is ever changing, but all changes reveal one constant factor. The moral life of man is continually in the embarrassment of realizing that the absolutes of biblical and rational norms —which enjoin responsibility for the neighbor's welfare—can never be perfectly fulfilled, either by the use of or abstention from any of the instruments of community or conflict. Therefore, religious and moral guides must teach the necessity of discriminate judgment. As long as this journal combines moral imperatives with moderate moral discrimination, it will have a creative future in both Church and Nation.
>
> (issue of February 21, 1966)

A final word about the volume itself. One does not put together a book like this with anything less than a strong sense of discomfort at the recognition of how much important thinking and good writing must be left out. That many deserving articles on important subjects are not included in this collection will be as immediately apparent to the close reader as is the fact that the work of many longtime contributors is also missing. Nevertheless, I hope the material brought together here captures the journal's characteristic flavor and gives some indication of its breadth and depth.

The articles appear here almost precisely as they were originally published, with virtually no editing and only a few changes of title. By and large the material has been arranged with an eye to the internal consistency of the book rather than chronologically, though the date when each article appeared has been noted for the reader's information.

A word of appreciation is due to a number of persons: to the various members of the Editorial Board and contributing editors who through the years have given unstintingly of themselves without remuneration to produce the journal; to my colleague and associate editor Frances S. Smith who delayed her departure for Geneva and her new position with the World Council of Churches to help make this volume an early reality; to Dr. Roger L. Shinn for his advice and counsel in the most trying and difficult problem of making the selections (though the editor alone is responsible for the final choices); to Arthur J. Moore and other editors who contributed ideas and suggestions along the way; to Lawrence Grow of Bobbs-Merrill for his guidance and calm reassurance at a number of points; to my secretary, Mrs. Ed P. Sanders; and to my wife, Ruth, who had the hardest job of all in trying to keep up with our two-year-old son, Kristor, while his father absented himself to work on this book.

Valley Cottage, N.Y.   Wayne H. Cowan
July 7, 1966

The Immediate Crisis

I

The Christian Faith and the World Crisis

❧

Reinhold Niebuhr

IT IS OUR PURPOSE TO DEVOTE this modest journal to an exposition of our Christian faith in its relation to world events. This first article will seek, therefore, to offer a general introduction to the faith that is in us. We believe that many current interpretations have obscured important elements in that faith and have thereby confused the Christian conscience. This confusion has been brought into sharp relief by the world crisis; but it existed before the crisis, and it may well continue after the crisis is over. We therefore regard our task as one that transcends the urgent problems of the hour, though we do not deny that these problems are the immediate occasion for our enterprise.

At the present moment a basic difference of conviction with regard to what Christianity is and what it demands runs through the whole of American Protestantism and cuts across all the traditional denominational distinctions. There is, on the one hand, a school of Christian thought that believes war could be eliminated if only Christians and other men of good will refused resolutely enough to have anything to do with conflict. Another school of thought, while conceding that war is one of the most vivid revelations of sin in human history, does not find the disavowal of war so simple a matter. The proponents of the latter position believe that there are historic situations in which refusal to defend the inheritance of a civilization, however imperfect, against tyranny and aggression may result in consequences even worse than war.

This journal intends to express and, if possible, to clarify this second viewpoint. We do not believe that the Christian faith as expressed in the New Testament and as interpreted in historic Christianity, both Catholic and Protestant, implies the confidence that evil and injustice in history can be overcome by such simple methods as are currently equated with Christianity. We believe that modern Christian perfectionism is tinctured with utopianism derived from a secular culture. In our opinion this utopianism contributed to the tardiness of the democracies in defending themselves against the perils of a new barbarism, and (in America at least) it is easily compounded with an irresponsible and selfish nationalism.

We intend this journal to be both polemic and irenic, as far as human frailty will permit the combination of these two qualities. It will be polemic in the sense that we shall combat what seem to us false interpretations of our faith, and consequent false analyses of our world and of our duties in it. It will be irenic in the sense that we shall seek to appreciate the extent to which perfectionist and pacifist interpretations of Christianity are derived from genuine and important elements in our common faith.

Perfectionists are right in their conviction that our civilization stands under the judgment of God; no one can have an easy conscience about the social and political anarchy out of which the horrible tyranny that now threatens us arose. But they are wrong in assuming that we have no right or duty to defend a civilization, despite its imperfections, against worse alternatives. They are right in insisting that love is the ultimate law of life. But they have failed to realize to what degree the sinfulness of all men, even the best, makes justice between competing interests and conflicting wills a perennial necessity of history.

The perfectionists rightly recognize that it may be very noble for an individual to sacrifice his life or interests rather than participate in the claims and counterclaims of the struggle for justice (of which war may always be the *ultima ratio*). They are wrong in making no distinction between an individual act of self-abnegation and a political policy of submission to injustice, whereby lives and interests other than our own are defrauded or destroyed. They seek erroneously to build a political platform upon individual perfection. Medieval perfectionism, whatever its limitations, wisely avoided these errors. It excluded even the family from the possible consequences of an individual's absolute ethic, and it was profoundly aware of the impossibility of making its rigorous standards universal.

We believe that there are many Christians whose moral inclinations might persuade them to take the same view of current problems as our own, except for the fact that they are inhibited by religious presuppositions that they regard as more "purely" Christian than those represented by the consensus of the Church through all the ages. Therefore we will begin with an analysis of these religious presuppositions.

Christians are agreed that the God who is revealed in Christ is source and end of our existence and that therefore his character and will are the norm and standard of our conduct. It is only in recent decades, however, that it has been believed that the "gentleness" of Jesus was a sufficient and final revelation of the character of God, that this character was one of pure love and mercy, and that this revelation stood in contradiction to an alleged portrayal of a God of wrath in the Old Testament.

Both the Old and the New Testament take the wrath of God as well as the mercy of God seriously. The divine mercy, apprehended by Christian faith in the life and death of Christ, is not some simple kindness indifferent to good and evil. The whole point of the Christian doctrine of Atonement is that God cannot be merciful without fulfilling within himself, and on man's behalf, the requirements of divine justice. However difficult it may be to give a fully rational account of what Christ's atoning death upon the Cross means to Christian faith, this mystery, never fully comprehended by and yet not wholly incomprehensible to faith, speaks to us of a mercy that transcends but also satisfies the demands of justice.

The biblical answer to the problem of evil in human history is a radical answer, precisely because human evil is recognized as a much more stubborn fact than is realized in some modern versions of the Christian faith. These versions do not take the problem of justice in history seriously, because they have obscured what the Bible has to say about the relation of justice to mercy in the very heart of God. Every sensitive Christian must feel a sense of unworthiness when he is compelled by historic destiny to act as an instrument of God's justice. Recognition of the common guilt that makes him and his enemy kin must persuade him to imitate the mercy of God, even while he seeks to fulfill the demands of justice. But he will seek to elude such responsibilities only if he believes, as many modern Christians do, that he might, if he tried a little harder, achieve an individual or collective vantage point of guiltlessness from which to proceed against evil doers. There is no such vantage point.

Christians are agreed that Christ must be the norm of our human life as well as the revelation of the character of God. But many modern versions of Christianity have forgotten to what degree the perfect love of Christ was recognized both in the Bible and in the Christian ages as

3

finally transcending all historic possibilities. The same St. Paul who admonishes us to grow into the stature of Christ insists again and again that we are "saved by faith" and not "by works"; which is to say that our final peace is not the moral peace of having become what Christ defines as our true nature but is the religious peace of knowing that a divine mercy accepts our loyalty to Christ despite our continued betrayal of him.

It cannot be denied that these emphases are full of pitfalls for the faithful. On the one side there is always the possibility that we will not take Christ as our norm seriously enough, and that we will rest prematurely in the divine mercy. On the other hand an abstract perfectionism is tempted to obscure the most obvious facts about human nature and to fall into the fury of self-righteousness. The Protestant Reformation was in part a protest against what seemed to the Reformers an overly optimistic Catholic doctrine of human perfection through the infusion of divine grace. Yet modern Protestant interpretations of the same issue make the Catholic doctrine wise and prudent by comparison.

Once it is recognized that the stubbornness of human selfishness makes the achievement of justice in human society no easy matter, it ought to be possible to see that war is but a vivid revelation of certain perennial aspects of human history. Life is never related to life in terms of a perfect and loving conformity of will with will. Where there is sin and selfishness there must also be a struggle for justice; and this justice is always partially an achievement of our love for the other and partially a result of our yielding to his demands and pressures. The intermediate norm of justice is particularly important in the institutional and collective relationships of mankind. But even in individual and personal relations the ultimate level of sacrificial self-giving is not reached without an intermediate level of justice. On this level the first consideration is not that life should be related to life through the disinterested concern of each for the other, but that life should be prevented from exploiting, enslaving or taking advantage of other life. Sometimes this struggle takes very tragic forms.

It is important for Christians to remember that every structure of justice, as embodied in political and economic institutions, (a) contains elements of injustice that stand in contradiction to the law of love; (b) contains higher possibilities of justice that must be realized in terms of institutions and structures; and (c) that it must be supplemented by the graces of individual and personal generosity and mercy. Yet when the mind is not confused by utopian illusions it is not difficult to recognize genuine achievements of justice and to feel under obligation to defend them against the threats of tyranny and the negation of justice.

Love must be regarded as the final flower and fruit of justice. When it is substituted for justice it degenerates into sentimentality and may become the accomplice of tyranny.

4

Looking at the tragic contemporary scene within this frame of reference, we feel that American Christianity is all too prone to disavow its responsibilities for the preservation of our civilization against the perils of totalitarian aggression. We are well aware of the sins of all the nations, including our own, which have contributed to the chaos of our era. We know to what degree totalitarianism represents false answers to our own unsolved problems—political, economic, spiritual.

Yet we believe the task of defending the rich inheritance of our civilization to be an imperative one, however much we might desire that our social system were more worthy of defense. We believe that the possibility of correcting its faults and extending its gains may be annulled for centuries if this external peril is not resolutely faced. We do not find it particularly impressive to celebrate one's sensitive conscience by enlarging upon all the well-known evils of our western world and equating them with the evils of the totalitarian systems. It is just as important for Christians to be discriminating in their judgments, as for them to recognize the element of sin in all human endeavors. We think it dangerous to allow religious sensitivity to obscure the fact that Nazi tyranny intends to annihilate the Jewish race, to subject the nations of Europe to the dominion of a "master" race, to extirpate the Christian religion, to annul the liberties and legal standards that are the priceless heritage of ages of Christian and humanistic culture, to make truth the prostitute of political power, to seek world dominion through its satraps and allies, and generally to destroy the very fabric of our western civilization.

Our own national tardiness in becoming fully alive to this peril has been compounded of national selfishness and religious confusion. In recent months American opinion has begun to respond to the actualities of the situation and to sense the fateful destiny that unites us with all free peoples, whether momentarily overrun by the aggressor or still offering heroic resistance. How far our assistance is to be carried is a matter of policy and strategy. It could be a matter of principle only if it were conceded that an absolute line could be drawn in terms of Christian principle between "measures short of war" and war itself. But those who think such a line can be drawn have nevertheless opposed measures short of war. They rightly have pointed out that such measures cannot be guaranteed against the risk of total involvement.

The measures now being taken for the support of the democracies are a logical expression of the unique conditions of America's relation to the world. They do justice on the one hand to our responsibilities for a common civilization that transcends the hemispheres, and on the other hand to the fact that we are not as immediately imperiled as other nations. Whether our freedom from immediate peril will enable us to persevere in the reservations that we still maintain cannot be decided in the abstract. The exigencies of the future must determine the issue.

We cannot, of course, be certain that defeat of the Nazis will usher in a new order of international justice in Europe and the world. We do know what a Nazi victory would mean, and our first task must therefore be to prevent it. Yet it cannot be our only task, for the problem of organizing the technical civilization of the western world upon a new basis of economic and international justice, so that the anarchy and decay that have characterized our life in the past three decades will be arrested and our technical capacities will be made fruitful rather than suicidal, is one which must engage our best resources. We must give some thought and attention to this great issue even while we are forced to ward off a horrible alternative.

We believe that the Christian faith can and must make its own contribution to this issue. The task of building a new world, as well as the tragic duty of saving the present world from tyranny, will require resources of understanding and resolution which are inherent in the Christian faith. The profoundest insights of the Christian faith cannot be expressed by the simple counsel that men ought to be more loving, and that if they became so the problems of war and of international organization would solve themselves.

Yet there are times when hopes for the future, as well as contrition over past misdeeds, must be subordinated to the urgent, immediate task. In this instance, the immediate task is the defeat of Nazi tyranny. If this task does not engage us, both our repentance and our hope become luxuries in which we indulge while other men save us from an intolerable fate, or while our inaction betrays into disaster a cause to which we owe allegiance.

February 10, 1941

On the Devil and Politics

Denis de Rougemont

AT DESSERT, WE WERE IN AGREEMENT: what is most lacking in America is belief in the Devil. The table dispersed. It was at the club. While waiting for the elevator, I said to the Philosopher:

"That's the trouble: if I talked about the Devil, here, I'm the one that would be considered diabolical or, who knows, the Devil himself."

"Oughtn't you perhaps accept the risk?" he asked seriously.

The elevator door opened; we entered.

"That at last would be a new tragic situation: becoming the Devil himself in order to prove he exists! . . . After all, it may be that Nietzsche or Luther sometimes thought of it. 'I could wish that myself were accursed,' wrote St. Paul."

"I know a good story," replied the Philosopher. "One of the early Irish apostles who evangelized Switzerland explained to his peasant audience that the martyrs are our best interceders with God. The listeners believed him so sincerely that they killed him. And the best part of it is, it worked: they became Christians."

"We need these parables to remind us how dangerous it is to speak the truth generally, and the Christian truth in particular: I mean dangerous for the one who speaks it. Kierkegaard never stopped repeating this in all his works: if you want to be Christians, well and good, but know the price. For nineteen centuries that price has been fixed."

Drawing room. Coffee. There was fresh discussion of world events, as though the Devil did not exist. I told myself that I should write a book about him. Here are a few notes towards it.

The Devil's first trick, remarks André Gide, is to make us believe that he does not exist. This trick has never better succeeded than in the modern epoch. All America has fallen into the snare.

God says: "I am that I am." But the Devil, like Ulysses to the Cyclops, says: "I am Nobody. What should you be afraid of?"

Nevertheless, the Bible gives notice of the Devil's existence on every page. In the original text, it speaks much less of "evil" than of the "Evil One." It assigns the Devil a number of revealing names which ought help us to recognize him: the Accuser, the fallen Angel, the Prince of this world, the Father of lies, and finally—Legion. The latter furnishes one of the most valuable clues for our time. It means that the Devil assumes as many aspects as there are individuals in the world. It may also mean that the Devil is the mob, and that, being everybody or anybody, he necessarily appears to us to be nobody in particular.

Before achieving this result, the Devil has resorted to a homely device: for a few centuries, he had adopted a medieval appearance—the red-horned demon of the miracle plays—which made him out absolutely harmless and anachronistic. One might say that since the Reformation, since Luther hurled an inkstand straight at him, we have not known how to form a modern, contemporary picture of the Devil. Kierkegaard alone had perhaps recognized him with accuracy in the ink of the newspapers, when he noted that one cannot preach Christianity any longer in a world dominated by the daily press.

Yet the Devil's incognito became difficult to maintain in the course of the first half of our century, while glaring catastrophes shook the foundations of our faith in progress. And so the Devil resorted to a prudent alibi, meant to forestall any stirring of awareness in the democratic countries. From 1933 on, he made us believe that he was simply Hitler. That was his second trick.

Is Hitler the Antichrist? The question is not a simple one. For my part, I can only give it an answer that is at first sight enigmatic. Hitler is more diabolical than is imagined by those who believe him to be the Devil in person, or the Antichrist. (And there are many who believe this.)

I remember hearing Karl Barth say in Switzerland, a year ago: "This man whose name censorship causes me to forget is certainly not the Antichrist. For he has no power over our salvation. The true Antichrist will only reveal himself at the end of time, as our pitiless Accuser, and then we shall no longer have any other Intercessor but Christ himself. The man you are thinking of is still only a little gentleman, a first forerunner of the Antichrist. And the struggle that he is conducting against the Christian world is but a warning to prepare in earnest for the final Combat."

When we believe Hitler to be the Devil, we obviously do great honor to the Austrian ex-corporal, but what is more serious, we delude ourselves as to Satan's real stature. Let us not forget that Satan is Legion. The assassination of a dictator would by no means suffice to rid the present world of the evil that torments it.

In fact, the very thing that is diabolical about Hitler is the way in which he persuaded the Germans that all evil came from the Treaty of Versailles, or from the Jews, therefore from *others*. It is in such tactics that one recognizes Satan's handiwork among his delegates.

Today, the democrats who sincerely believe that Hitler incarnates all the evil of our time are the victims of an altogether similar tactic, this time promulgated by the Prince of this earth himself. "See, I am only Hitler!" he tells us. We see only Hitler, we find him terrible, we detest him, we weigh against him, with more or less determination, our ancient democratic virtues, and we no longer see our true demons. The trick is played, we are taken in, and it is humiliating to recall that not long ago this trick was considered just good enough for the primitives of Melanesia.

Everyone knows that the so-called primitives are in the habit of personifying or objectifying the evil forces which menace them. Whether it be a sorcerer or a profaner of the sacred, an animal, a cloud or a bit of colored wood, the cause of the evil from which these savages suffer is always external to themselves and must be combated and annihilated outside themselves.

On the other hand, Christianity has striven for centuries to make us understand that the Kingdom of God is in us, that evil, too, is in us, and that their battlefield is nowhere else than in our souls. Still, this education has largely failed, and we persist in our primitivism, holding the people opposed to us, or the force of events, responsible for our evils. If we are revolutionaries, we believe that by changing the disposition of the objects of this world—by displacing wealth, for example—we shall suppress the *causes* of our present evils. If we are good honest democrats, anxious or optimistic, we believe that by roasting a few dictators, profaners of the right, and sorcerers, we shall re-establish peace and prosperity. In this, we still have the complete magic mentality, and like choleric children, we beat the table we have run against. Or like Xerxes, we scourge the waters of the Hellespont—with great lashes of rhetoric upon the short waves.

We forget that in reality our adversaries do not differ essentially from us. Each man bears in his body and in his soul the microbes of all known diseases. Annihilating the external symptoms of the menace would by no means be sufficient to rid us of it. Those symptoms—Hitler, Stalin, the "wicked" in general—personify possibilities which exist in us too, latent temptations that might very well develop some day, under stress, or fatigue, or some temporary unbalance.

Let us try to avoid here a threatening misapprehension. The intention of these remarks is in no way to justify "the others" and to lump us all together, without distinction, as in 1939 the Oxford Group seemed to do in the pamphlet entitled: "We Are All Guilty." For what I mean is this: We are all guilty in the measure in which we *do not condemn* and *do not also recognize in ourselves* the mentality of the totalitarians, that is the active and personal presence of the Demon in our passions, in our need for sensation, in our fear of responsibilities, in our civic inertia, in our ignorance of our neighbor, in our rejection finally of any absolute that transcends and judges our "vital" (as they always are) interests.

Here is a very simple observation: nobody has ever pretended to act in bad faith. We are all, Hitler included, "men of good will." Yet look at what is happening, and who has brought it about. Is it the Devil? Yes, but with our hands and our thoughts. It is here that we should remember our democratic slogan: All men are equal!

There are degrees of evil. There are inequalities of responsibility. But we are all in evil, and we are all the accomplices of the most responsible in the world. And this much is certain: The true Christian would be a man with no other enemy to fear than the one he lodges in himself.

Not having known how to recognize what is truly diabolical about a Hitler—his manner of localizing all evil in the outsider so as to clear

9

himself—we fell into the same error as he. We turned him into an image of the Demon altogether external to our reality. And while we were regarding it, fascinated, the Demon returned by the back door to torment us in disguises that could not arouse our suspicions.

In the nineteenth century it was believed that automatic progress could replace providence, but when we see today what the blind faith has brought us to, we are forced to recognize that automatic progress was only the Devil's disguise. Not that all progress is diabolical in itself, obviously not. But if we abandon ourselves to progress, letting things go with the comfortable assurance that all will be well in the end, *then* progress becomes the most dangerous of soporifics, a veritable Demon's drug, and one of his new names.

In that age, apparently out of kindliness toward others, we believed in the fundamental goodness of man. But such a view can lead a person to believe in his own natural goodness, then to being blinded to the evil that he bears in himself, then to denying the active presence of the Demon, then finally to granting the Demon free scope to dupe him.

We believed that evil was *relative* in the world, that it sprang from an unsatisfactory distribution of wealth, from an ill digested education, from inadequate laws, or from pressures and injustices that might be eradicated by adroit measures. Yet, these superstitious beliefs had only one effect—to blind us to the reality of man, that is, to the reality of evil rooted in our essential freedom, in our primary data, "in the human nature in itself" (as Reinhold Niebuhr so forcefully has pointed out).

We were, and we remain, optimists out of principle—almost out of good manners, one might say—despite all contradictions from reality. This optimism is not the naive confidence of the child. It is a kind of lie. Specifically, it is a flight from reality, for in reality, we well know that there is evil, that there is the Devil's influence. But as this shocks us and alarms, we try to conjure away the evil by denying it, thus using the magic mentality. We think that whoever denounces evil as fundamental must himself be very wicked. We believe that by acknowledging evil, we create it in some way. We prefer not to dwell on it. We "repress," Freud would say. This flight and this lie, within the subconscious, leave us unable to understand what is happening in the world, and deliver us over to the simplest ruses of the Evil One.

Just as we say, in the presence of a miracle of good, "Too good to be true," we say in the presence of certain descriptions of evil, "Too frightful to be true!" Meanwhile, it is true, but that makes us uncomfortable, and irresistibly we dismiss it from our thoughts. For if it were truly true, it would be necessary to act, and if we set ourselves to act, we should very quickly see that this evil has roots in our lives too, and that, in a certain way, *we like it!* There is the great secret.

The Devil succeeded in making democrats believe that they did not like evil at all, that they in no way desired it, that they were good and others wicked, and that the whole thing was that simple! From that precise moment, democracy became the Devil's best instrument for duping our good intentions. The proof is that certain democrats are going to think I must be anti-democratic to speak thus, but I am simply speaking, here, as a European who has seen firsthand certain bizarre phenomena of democratic disintegration and of conversion to fascism.

The France of 1939 was on the whole democratic, and almost every Frenchman sincerely called himself anti-Nazi, and believed himself proof against this kind of temptation. He had his good conscience as a democrat. Hitler came, France capitulated, and today the "anti-fascist intellectuals" of Paris suddenly discover that at bottom Nazism is not so bad as all that, that, on the whole, they had always desired something passably resembling it, and that after all, "the Nazis are men like us, so let us work together."

That is the danger that American democracy is exposed to, as were the others. She too believed and still believes that the Nazis are animals of an altogether different race from Americans. She too risks discovering some day that "after all, they are men like us." And it is quite true that they are men like us, in the sense that their sin is also in us, secretly.

It seems to me that the clearest lesson which emerges from European events is this: The sentimental hatred of the evil that is in others may blind one to the evil that one bears in himself and to the gravity of evil in general. The overly facile condemnation of the wicked man on the opposite side may conceal and favor much inward complaisance toward that very wickedness. I suspect a profound ambivalence in certain democratic denunciations of Hitlerism, for in the violence of the tone and the obstinate simplism of the judgments, we betray our bad conscience, our secret anxiety, our unacknowledged temptation. In regard to anti-fascists who wish only to be *anti,* I cannot help thinking that sooner or later the *pro* which slumbers in a corner of their soul will suddenly awaken and overwhelm them. I have seen too many cases of this kind, individual and collective. I saw the population of the Saar throw itself into Hitler's arms in 1935. I saw a democratic Vienna transformed in twenty-four hours into a Vienna delirious with Hitlerian passion. I saw France, or let us say certain Frenchmen, discover inside a few weeks the "good points" of the totalitarian system. I believe that I know whereof I speak when I say to honest democrats: Look at the Devil that is among us! Stop believing that he can only resemble Hitler, or Stalin, or Senator Wheeler, for it is *you yourself* that he will always contrive to resemble the most. If you want to catch him, I am going to tell you where you will most surely find him—seated in your own armchair. It is in you alone that you will catch him in the very act. And then only will you be in a state to track him down in others. And then only will you be cured of your almost incredible naivete before the totalitarian danger and be able to escape hypnosis.

I sum up. We were lacking a modern picture of the Demon. We had therefore stopped believing in him. Then we imagined that the Devil was Hitler. And the Devil rejoiced. (Hitler too.) It would be more fruitful, more realistic, and finally more truthful, to try picturing the Devil to ourselves as having the features of a dynamic and optimistic playboy, lacking all thought. Or, if we are liberal intellectuals for example, as having the features of a liberal intellectual *who does not believe in the Devil.*

(Translated by Edward M. Maisel)

June 2, 1941

On Anti-Semitism

❧

Jacques Maritain

I HAVE ALREADY SPOKEN OF anti-Semitism many times. I never would have thought that I would have to do so in connection with anti-Semitic laws promulgated by a French government—which are a denial of the traditions and the spirit of my country. I am well aware that these decrees have been adopted under German pressure and through the machinations of Laval. I also know that the French people by and large are astounded at and disgusted with these laws. The fact remains, however, that the Vichy leaders have enforced anti-Semitic laws in a more and more strict and iniquitous fashion, depriving French Jews of every governmental and cultural position, imposing upon them all kinds of restrictions with regard to liberal and commercial professions, mercilessly striking many of them who were wounded for their country during the present war, and hypocritically trying to hide a bad conscience under a pseudonational pathos in which religious and racial considerations are

12

shamefully mixed. A small part of the bourgeoisie and the country gentry, poisoned by filthy newspapers, is letting itself be permeated by racist baseness. Anti-Semitic German films are shown in movie-theaters even in the unoccupied part of France, and we have been told that a Catholic periodical was suspended for one month for having boldly protested against such an action. Despite innumerable private testimonies of help and solidarity given—often at great risk—to persecuted Jews, despite innumerable touching signs of friendship and fidelity that dismissed Jewish professors received from their students, no public protest has been made by any educational body; and some new corporative institutions, among the liberal professions, are willingly admitting a kind of *numerus clausus.*

The psychic poisons are more active than the physical ones; it is unfortunately inevitable that, little by little, many souls should bow down. If the anti-Semitic regulations and propaganda are to endure for some years, we may imagine that many weak people will resign themselves to the worst. They will think that, after all, the concentration camps are more comfortable for their neighbors than the Jews say, and finally they will find themselves perfectly able to look at or contribute to the destruction of their friends, with the smile of a clear conscience (life must go on!). I have firm confidence in the natural virtues and the moral resistance of the common people of France. I know we must trust them; yet it is not only in thinking of the Jews, but in thinking of my country that I feel horrified by the anti-Semitic corruption of souls that is being furthered in France by a leadership that still dares speak of honor.

It is also for Christianity that I fear. Perhaps the danger is greater in countries that have not—not as yet—experienced Nazi terrorism. We have been told that in some countries of South America anti-Semitism is spreading among some sections of Catholic youth and Catholic intellectuals, despite the teachings of the Pope and the efforts of their own bishops. It is impossible to compromise with anti-Semitism; it carries in itself, as in a living germ, all the spiritual evil of Nazism. Anti-Semitism is the moral Fifth Column in the Christian conscience.

"Spiritually we are Semites," Pius XI said. "Anti-Semitism is unacceptable." I should like to emphasize in this paper the spiritual aspect of this question.

May I point out that the most impressive Christian formulas concerning the spiritual essence of anti-Semitism may be found in a book recently published by a Jewish writer who seems himself strangely unaware of their profoundly Christian meaning. I do not know whether Maurice Samuel shares even in Jewish piety; perhaps he is a God-seeking soul deprived of any definite dogmas, believing himself to be "freed" from any trust in divine revelation, of either the Old or the

New Covenant. The testimony that he brings appears all the more significant because prophetic intuitions are all the more striking when they pass through slumbering or stubborn prophets who perceive only in an obscure way what they convey to us.

"We shall never understand," Mr. Samuel says, "the maniacal, world-wide seizure of anti-Semitism unless we transpose the terms. It is of Christ that the Nazi-Fascists are afraid; it is in *his* omnipotence that they believe; it is *he* that they are determined madly to obliterate. But the names of Christ and Christianity are too overwhelming, and the habit of submission to them is too deeply ingrained after centuries and centuries of teaching. Therefore they must, I repeat, make their assault on those who were responsible for the birth and spread of Christianity. They must spit on the Jews as the 'Christ-killers' because they long to spit on the Jews as the Christ-givers."[1]

The simple fact of feeling no sympathy for the Jews or being more sensitive to their faults than to their virtues is not anti-Semitism. Anti-Semitism is fear, scorn and hatred of the Jewish race or people, and a desire to subject them to discriminative measures. There are many forms and degrees of anti-Semitism. Not to speak of the demented forms we are facing at present, it can take the form of a supercilious nationalist and aristocratic bias of pride and prejudice; or a plain desire to rid oneself of competitors; or a routine of vanity fair; or even an innocent verbal mania. In reality no one is innocent. In each one the seed is hidden, more or less inert or active, of that spiritual disease which today throughout the world is bursting out into a homicidal, myth-making phobia, and the secret soul of which is resentment against the Gospel: "Christophobia."

Léon Bloy said that the "veil" to which Saint Paul refers and which covers the eyes of Israel is now passing "from the Jews to the Christians." This statement, which is harsh on the Gentiles and on the Christian distorters of Christianity, helps us understand something of the extensive and violent persecution of which the Jews today are victims, and of the spiritual upheaval that has been going on for years among many of them, denoting deep inward changes, particularly in respect to the person of Christ.

The growing solicitude in Israel's heart for the Just Man crucified through the error of the high priests is a symptom of unquestionable importance. Today in America representative Jewish writers like Sholem Asch and Waldo Frank are trying to reintegrate the Gospel into the brotherhood of Israel. While not yet recognizing Jesus as the Messiah, they do recognize him as the most pure Jewish figure in human history. They themselves would be disturbed to be considered as leaning toward

1 Maurice Samuel, *The Great Hatred*, New York, 1940.

14

Christianity. Yet while remaining closer than ever to Judaism, they believe that the Gospel transcends the Old Testament and consider it a divine flower issuing from the stem of the Patriarchs and the Prophets. Never forgetful of the conflicts of history and of the harsh treatment received by their people, the authors of *Salvation* and of *The New Discovery of America* have long known and loved mediæval Christianity and Catholic spiritual life. They agree with Maurice Samuel that "Christophobia" is the spiritual essence of the demoniacal racism of our pagan world. Many other signs give evidence that Israel is beginning to open its eyes, whereas the eyes of many self-styled Christians are blinded, darkened by the exhalations of the old pagan blood suddenly, ferociously welling up once more among Gentiles.

"Jesus Christ is in agony until the end of the world," said Pascal. Christ suffers in every innocent man who is persecuted. His agony is heard in the cries of so many human beings humiliated and tortured, in the suffering of all those images and likenesses of God treated worse than beasts. He has taken all these things upon himself, he has suffered every wound. "Fear not, my child, I have already travelled that road. On each step of the abominable way I have left for you a drop of my blood and the print of my mercy."

But in the mystical body of the Church, the surplus humanity that Christ finds in each of the members of this his body is called upon, insofar as each is a part of the whole, to participate in the work of this body, which is the redemption continued throughout time. Through and in the passion of his mystical body, Christ continues actively to perform the task for which he came; he acts as the Savior and Redeemer of mankind.

Israel's passion is not a co-redemptive passion, achieving for the eternal salvation of souls what is lacking (as concerns application, not merits) in the Savior's sufferings. It is suffered for the goading on of the world's temporal life. In itself, it is the passion of a being caught up in the temporal destiny of the world, which both irritates the world and seeks to emancipate it, and on which the world avenges itself for the pangs of its history. This does not mean that Christ is absent from the passion of Israel. Could he forget his people, who are still loved because of their fathers and to whom have been made promises without repentance? Jesus Christ suffers in the passion of Israel. In striking Israel, the anti-Semites strike him, insult him and spit on him. To persecute the house of Israel is to persecute Christ, not in his mystical body as when the Church is persecuted, but in his fleshly lineage and in his forgetful people whom he ceaselessly loves and calls. In the passion of Israel, Christ suffers and acts as the shepherd of Zion and the Messiah of Israel, in order gradually to conform his people to him. If there are any in the world today—but where are they?—who give heed to the meaning of the great racist persecutions and who try to understand this meaning, they will see Israel as drawn along the road to Calvary, by reason of that very vocation which I have indicated, and because the slave merchants will not pardon Israel for the demands it and its Christ have implanted in the heart of the world's temporal life, demands that will ever cry "no" to the tyranny of force. Despite itself Israel is climbing Calvary, side by side with Christians—whose vocation concerns the kingdom of God more than the temporal history of the world; and these strange companions are at times surprised to find each other mounting the same path. As in Marc Chagall's beautiful painting, the poor Jews, without understanding it, are swept along in the great tempest of the Crucifixion, around Christ who is stretched

> *"Across the lost world . . .*
> *At the four corners of the horizon*
> *Fire and Flames*
> *Poor Jews from everywhere are walking*
> *No one claims them*
> *They have no place on the earth*
> *To rest—not a stone*
> *The wandering Jews. . . ."*[1]

The central fact, which has its deepest meaning for the philosophy of history and for human destiny—and which no one seems to take into account—is that *the passion of Israel today is taking on more and more distinctly the form of the Cross.*

Christ crucified extends his arms toward both Jews and Gentiles; he died, St. Paul says, in order to reconcile the two peoples, and to break down the dividing barrier of enmity between them. "For he is our peace, he that hath made both one, and hath broken down the dividing barrier of enmity. He hath brought to naught in his flesh the law of commandments framed in decrees, that in himself he might create of the two one new man, and make peace and reconcile both in one body to God through the cross, slaying by means thereof their enmity."[2]

If the Jewish people did not hear the call made to them by the dying Christ, yet do they remain ever summoned. If the Gentiles indeed heard the call, now racist paganism casts them away from it and from him who is our peace. Anti-Semitic hatred is a directly anti-Christic frenzy to make vain the blood of Jesus and to make void his death. Agony now is the way of achieving that reconciliation, that breaking down of the barrier of enmity—which the madness of men prevented

1 Raïssa Maritain, *Chagall* (Lettre de Nuit).
2 St. Paul, Ephesians 2:14-16.

16

love from accomplishing, and the frustration of which is the most refined torment in the sufferings of the Messiah—a universal agony in the likeness of that of the Savior, both the agony of the racked, abandoned Jews and of the racked, abandoned Christians who live by faith. More than ever, the mystical body of Christ needs the people of God. In the darkness of the present day, that moment seems invisibly to be in preparation, however remote it still may be, when their reintegration, as St. Thomas puts it, will "call back to life the Gentiles, that is to say the lukewarm faithful, when 'on account of the progress of iniquity, the charity of a great number shall have waxed cold' (Matthew 14:12)."[3]

October 6, 1941

The God of History

❧

Paul Tillich

*N*ow, *the Eternal cries, bring your case forward,*
     now, Jacob's King cries, state your proofs.
Let us hear what happened in the past, that we may
     ponder it,
Or show me what is yet to be, that we may watch it
     how it turns out;
Yes, let us hear what is coming, that we may be sure
     you are gods;
Do something or other that we may marvel at the
     sight!—
Why, you are things of naught, you can do nothing
     at all!

Here is one I have raised from the north,
     I have called him by the name from the east;

[3] St. Thomas Aquinas, *in ep. ad Romanos*, xi, lect. 2.

He shall trample rulers down like mortar,
    like a potter treading clay.
Now, we predicted this beforehand,
    Who foretold it that we might hail it true?
No one predicted it, no one announced it,
    Not a word ever fell from you.
As for your idols, I see no one, not a prophet in
    their midst,
    To answer my inquiries!
They are all an empty nothing, all they do is utterly
    inane, their metal images are futile, vanity.

—Isaiah 41 : 21-29, *Moffatt Trans.*

A DRAMATIC SCENE IS DESCRIBED BY the words of the prophet. Jahweh who is both judge and disputant calls the gods of the nations to a heavenly disputation while the peoples of the world listen. The point at issue is: Which god has proved to be the true God? The answer is he who is the God of history! And the decision is: Jahweh has proved to be the God of history therefore the god who is really God! Jahweh is the God of history, for he, through his prophets, has shown that he understands the meaning of history, that he knows the past and the future, the beginning and the end. And in having shown this, he has shown that he makes history; that it is he who has raised up Cyrus, the destroyer of the world powers, and the liberator of the remnants of the Jewish nation. The gods of that nation cannot answer *a word*. They did not know it, they did not predict it; they did not perform it. And so the disputation ends with the sentence that these gods are vanity, that their works are nothing, and their images are wind and illusion. Jahweh alone is God, for he is the God of history.

Seldom in history have men been as disturbed about history as we are today. We urgently want to have at least a *glimpse* of the future, *some* wisdom, *some* prophecy. Not merely a few thousand Jewish exiles, as those "by the rivers of Babylon" to whom our prophet speaks, but ten millions of exiles from practically all nations are trying fervently to penetrate into the darkness of their unknown future. Furthermore the great majority of men are longing for an illuminating and profound word about the future of mankind. But those who have the power to shape the future contradict each other in practically all fundamentals. Political leaders declare solemnly that it is almost impossible to carry the burden of their office in this time. Ministers at home and in the army are able to tell their people only in negative terms for what purpose they are sacrificing and dying. Those who must speak to the enemy (as I myself have done by radio for the hundredth time this week) realize that on the political plane they cannot say *one* word of real promise. Only the prophets of disaster who are without hope, reveal a complete certainty. But they are not the prophets of *God*.

Nor can we expect that the darkness about our history will soon be dispersed, either by another international conference or by the final victory, or by clever political strategy. Our darkness, uncertainty and helplessness about the future has profounder reasons. We cannot get an answer about the future because we ask those who cannot know the future. We ask the gods who are vanity and nought, the gods of the nations who are not the God of history. Everyone asks the god of *his* nation and tries to get an oracle from him through the mouth of his priests, the wise and mighty of the nation. We do get such oracles. Everyone, all over the world, is surfeited with oracles from the god of his nation, and from the gods of other nations. We compare them with each other and try to combine them for the most probable answer. But this process increases the darkness. These gods all speak of the future in terms of their nations; but even the greatest nation is a "drop in the bucket" before the God of history. No nation can say *"I* am the meaning, the purpose of history. *I* am he who knows the past, who shapes the future!" And *no* alliance of nations can say that. Even if all national gods were gathered together, they would still be subject to the judgment of Jahweh: "You are things of nought; you can do nothing at all!" Thus it is that we get many oracles about our future, but no prophecies. We have not yet turned to the source of prophecy, the God of history.

The way in which Jahweh revealed himself to Israel as the God who is the first and the last, the beginning and the end of history, was very painful. Only the complete national breakdown made the remnants of Israel ready to receive this revelation in its universal meaning. And whenever the Jewish nation made the revelation a reason for national pride and transformed Jahweh into the god of their nation, the national breakdown followed. Jahweh as a national god is condemned by Jahweh as the God of history. This is the mystery of Judaism to this very day.

There are two great figures in the teachings of this prophet. The first is Cyrus, the founder of the Persian empire, the greatest historical personage of his time, whom our prophet speaks of as the "shepherd" of God, as "the anointed" and as the man of God's counsel; the other is the "servant of Jahweh" (whoever he may be in flesh and blood), who symbolizes the saving power of innocent suffering and death. According to the prophetic teaching the glorious founder of an empire is ultimately the servant of the servant of Jahweh. He liberates the remnant of Israel from which the suffering servant arises.

Is not this conception the solution of the question of the meaning of history today? It is the only solution which I can see. There are two forces in our shattered world today. The one is the force of those who are similar to the suffering servant of God. We do not know where they are, as we do not know who prompted the servant-vision of the prophet. But we know that they exist, invisibly in *all* countries. We do not know what they will make of the future. But we know that their suffering will not be in vain. They are the hidden tools of the God of history; the aged and the infants, the women and the young men, the persecuted and imprisoned, all those who are innocently sacrificed for the future, to be *one* small stone in the building of the divine Kingdom, of which the *Perfect Servant* of God is the corner stone. And there is another force in our world, the force of those who are like unto Cyrus, the rulers of empires with all the greatness and all the shame of every empire (the rulers of America, Great Britain and Russia). They are the men of God's counsel, because they carry through his purposes in the service of the suffering servants of God. But they are as ignorant of God's counsel as Cyrus was. They do not know the future consequences of their policies. If we look to them in our attempt to know the future we will also remain ignorant. But if we look at the true servants and the true God whom they serve, the God of history, we will know! Cyrus is in the service of the servant of Jahweh. This is the solution of the riddle of history, including the history of our epoch.

June 1, 1944

The Death of the President

Reinhold Niebuhr

THE AMERICAN PRESIDENCY EMBODIES two levels of political authority and prestige which a constitutional monarchy separates. The president is both king and prime minister. He symbolizes the perpetual authority of government as such but also embodies the immediate will of the nation as it becomes crystallized in party politics. The American Presidency has become the greatest single center of political power in the modern world. The death of a president, particularly of a great president, is therefore a great emotional shock to the nation. And since Mr. Roosevelt's authority and prestige transcended the boundaries of his own nation and he had become a symbol to the world of our nation's growing maturity and sense of responsibility toward the community of nations, his death has brought grief, and also some dismay and apprehension, to all the nations allied with us.

Reinhold Niebuhr

Our sense of grief is naturally mingled with gratitude for the providential emergence of this man in our national life at just such a time as this. There were those who tolerated his foreign policy because they believed in his domestic policy, while others tolerated or opposed his domestic policy while they supported his foreign policy. But in a word, his greatness, surely, was derived from the fact that he understood the essential issue in both domestic and foreign affairs. He was the first of our political leaders who sought to bring the immense powers of government to bear upon the economic health of the nation and thus to break with the *laissez-faire* tradition, which had a stronger hold upon us than on any other modern industrial nation. While many feared, or pretended to fear, the accretion of political power which resulted from this policy, no one can deal honestly with the issues involved in this controversy if he does not recognize that the increase of political power in a modern industrial community is prompted and justified by the desire of the community to bring the economic power of a technical society under communal control. The idea that economic power is self-regulating belongs to the childhood of an industrial era and is refuted by all of its maturer experience. Roosevelt was no systematic political thinker, but he saw the main issue clearly and acted upon his convictions with as much consistency as the confused state of American public opinion would allow. Even his lack of consistency and his infinite capacity for improvisation had their virtuous sides, for it is a question whether a more consistent or doctrinaire exponent of his policy could have achieved as much national unity around his central purpose as he achieved. While it is much too early to assess his place in American history adequately, one may hazard the guess that future historians will regard his administration as a new level of maturity in domestic policy. Here the nation became aware of the depth of the problems of justice in an industrial society and of the necessity of dealing with them politically.

In the same manner his foreign policy represented a new level of maturity in our relations to the world. Just as fabulous wealth had made it possible for us to evade the profounder economic issues a little longer than other nations, so, also, our continental security tempted us to evade the problems of an unorganized world. Roosevelt came to power a year before Hitler did and by a curious historical irony the two careers run chronologically parallel even to the point where one may hope that the one will not outlast the other by more than a few months. Roosevelt was President of a nation which had recoiled from its previous effort in international affairs and which was almost psychopathic in its determination to stay out of the conflict which Hitler's movement made inevitable; yet he understood the nature of the international crisis from the beginning. On this issue, as well as in domestic policy, his political ingenuity matched the clarity of his vision. The clarity of his vision was fully revealed in his famous "quarantine speech" in which he warned the world of the consequences of allowing aggression to go unchecked. His political sagacity dictated a course which would not outrun the sentiments of a divided nation too far. A lesser statesman might have abandoned himself to a sense of futility. Yet Roosevelt was able to secure the passage of the Lend-Lease Act from a divided nation, a policy which made it possible for us to prevent the collapse of the anti-Nazi cause, though a part of the nation was almost hysterically committed to the proposition that we had no responsibilities for the defeat of Nazism. Surely the passage of this act will go down in history as one of the greatest of his political achievements.

As the war finally drew to a triumphant conclusion, Roosevelt, seeking to avoid Wilson's mistakes, developed an international policy which, though it may err on the side of making too many concessions to the pride and power of the great nations, does at least guarantee that America will not again withdraw from its responsibilities in the world community. Nor can the concessions be regarded as merely unwarranted expediency. They are derived from a shrewd understanding of the limits of the will of a nation in creating international authority above its own sovereignty. In both the conduct of the war and in the peace negotiations Roosevelt has, in other words, expressed a higher form of political maturity than this nation has previously achieved. If the measures of international accord now being taken should prove inadequate, as indeed they may, the fault will lie not so much in the judgment of a man as in the historic situation. More adequate measures would have little chance of acceptance, either by our own nation or by the other great powers.

One of the consolations in the loss of so great a leader is the knowledge that what was right and true in the course he charted may the more certainly become settled national policy, because death robs personal animus of its object and thereby removes a source of confusion to the conscience of the nation.

The sense of grief in the nation has been mingled not only with gratitude for the greatness of the lost leader but with a good deal of apprehension about the future. Is the new President, or any untried man, adequate to fill so great an office in so trying a period of national history? No one can answer that question. One can only hope and pray that the greatness of the office may, as it has sometimes done in the past, develop unknown resources in the man.

The American Presidency has undoubtedly become too powerful. It may be worth observing that this is not exactly the fault of Mr. Roosevelt as his critics have averred. Given the American constitutional system, which does not provide for a "responsible government" in the parliamentary sense of that phrase, only a strong President can save the nation from disaster in times of crisis. A weak President in times of depression and war, such as we have traversed in the past decades, would not have increased the powers of his office. But our system does not function in such a way as to make it possible for Congress as such to master a crisis. Without a strong President disaster might well overwhelm us. We are not fully conscious of this fact because by great good fortune we have had great presidents in critical times. The fact that this cannot always be so may well fill us with apprehension about the future, but it will not qualify our gratitude for past mercies, among which belongs the leadership of Franklin Delano Roosevelt during this fateful decade of our history.

March 30, 1945

Who Am I?

Dietrich Bonhöffer (1906-45)

This poem was written in the summer of 1944 in a prison cell at Berlin-Tegel. The translation is by I. B. Leishman.

Who am I? They often tell me
I stepped from my cell's confinement
Calmly, cheerfully, firmly,
Like a squire from his country-house.
Who am I? They often tell me
I used to speak to my warders
Freely and friendly and clearly,
As though it were mine to command.
Who am I? They also tell me
I bore the days of misfortune
Equally, smilingly, proudly,
Like one accustomed to win.

Am I then really all that which other men tell of?
Or am I only what I myself know of myself?
Restless and longing and sick, like a bird in a cage,
Struggling for breath, as though hands were
    compressing my throat,

23

Yearning for colors, for flowers, for the voices of birds,
Thirsting for words of kindness, for neighborliness,
Tossing in expectation of great events,
Powerlessly trembling for friends at an infinite distance,
Weary and empty at praying, at thinking, at making,
Faint, and ready to say farewell to it all?

Who am I? This or the other?
Am I one person today and tomorrow another?
Am I both at once? A hypocrite before others,
And before myself a contemptibly woebegone weakling?
Or is something within me still like a beaten army,
Fleeing in disorder from victory already achieved?
Who am I? They mock me, these lonely questions of mine.
Whoever I am, Thou knowest, O God, I am Thine!

March 4, 1946

Soberness in Victory

Reinhold Niebuhr

IT WAS MOST FORTUNATE THAT America received the news of the victory in Europe more quietly than a quarter century ago. The hysteria of the former occasion was absent for various reasons. We had had several weeks to anticipate the victory, while the Nazi power gradually collapsed. There was a difference of a day between the actual and the official knowledge of the surrender; and furthermore the war was not over.

These were the immediate causes of our comparative soberness. But there were even profounder reasons for sobriety in victory. Perhaps they also affected the public mood; and perhaps they prompted the rather large attendance at religious services on V-E day. These reasons are all comprehended in the magnitude of the drama in which we are involved. Everything which is happening is really too big and too complex for our comprehension. The war which has ended in victory was the costliest and most global conflict of human history. It has left even the wealthiest victor nations shaken in the very structure of their economic life; and it has reduced Europe to a physical and economic, as well as political, chaos. The price of victory has been very high.

The defeated enemy has been more completely destroyed than any nation in history, at least since the day when the Romans destroyed Carthage. That was partly because the nation was ruled by a tyranny which was able to hold a beaten nation in battle until almost the last ounce of life blood was drawn from it. The same tyranny has also been able to destroy every crystallization of new political life during its long and terrible reign, so that Germany is a political vacuum as well as an economic desert. It is still a question whether our obliteration bombing, which has reduced the whole of western and central Germany to a rubble heap, was necessary for victory, though no less an authority than Von Runstedt has affirmed that precision bombing was indispensable to our victory. If it was necessary for victory, we have another proof of the total character of total war.

The cost of this war has been so great for both victors and vanquished that many will undoubtedly arise to remind us of their predictions of its price and of their apprehensions about its consequences. We will have to remind them that some of their apprehensions were wrong. They had declared that we could not engage in this struggle without losing our democratic institutions. These have in fact survived the extraordinary exertions of the conflict very well. But it will be more important to call their attention to the fact that the war was an alternative to slavery. As the victorious armies liberated one concentration camp after another and unearthed the hideous cruelties which were practiced in them, they gave us some hint of what the dimensions of total slavery are like, from which we escaped by a total war.

However we measure the conflict, whether in terms of the evil we opposed, or the evils we had to commit in opposing it, or the destruction of the vanquished or the price of the victors, the dimensions of the drama in which we are involved are staggering. It is well that we should be shocked into sobriety by the magnitude of historical events and should be prompted to humanity and piety by a contemplation of the tasks which still confront us. All of them are really beyond our best wisdom.

The administration of a completely prostrate vanquished nation has suddenly become our responsibility. It is well that thoughts of vengeance will be qualified by the immediate tasks of preventing starvation among the vast population of destroyed cities. Whether this wealthy nation will have the grace to reduce its dietary standards for the sake of feeding a starving Europe will be one of the great moral and political issues of the coming months. We talked very simply and grandly, and sometimes very vindictively, of "eradicating" all the Nazis. We shall soon discover that even if we are more discriminating than we are inclined to be, there are more Nazis who deserve death than we can kill, or at least than we can kill without becoming infected with Nazism. Even the imprisonment of the most confirmed Nazi criminals is a staggering and in some respects an impossible task. Of course the prevention of future crime will depend primarily upon more positive measures, primarily upon our ability to elicit response from the healthy and sane elements in Germany. All these tasks are too great for human wisdom. They will not be done too well in any event because of their magnitude; but they will be done with a greater degree of wisdom if they are done with a measure of humility. If we had more awe before the tragic punishments which God has already visited upon a nation which took law into its own hands we would at least be saved the folly of spoiling the divine punishment by our own efforts to add and subtract. We might well remember that the greatest difficulty which a vanquished nation finds in turning from the "sorrow of this world" (despair) to the "sorrow of God" (repentance) is that the pride of the victor tends to obscure the divine punishment.

Let us therefore not seek to reduce the dimension of the history in which we are involved, so that it might be made more compatible with the limits of our powers. Let us recognize that we have faced the mystery of evil and of good, of tragedy and of victory, of divine judgment and mercy in more tremendous proportions than ever before in history. The humble consciousness of the inadequacy of our wisdom for the tasks which confront us may infuse our wisdom with grace and thus render it more adequate for the issues we must face.

May 28, 1945

About the Question of Guilt

Martin Niemöller

From a letter addressed to one of his critics, November, 1945.

YOU ARE CONCERNED WITH the question of guilt and about this I have much to say. First of all: I have never suggested that the German people as a whole are responsible for and guilty of the Nazi crimes, but again and again I have said that we have no right to throw all the guilt onto the shoulders of the bad Nazis and to pretend that we are innocent.

Again and again I have stressed: We are probably all murderers, thieves and sadists, but we have done little or nothing to stop the evil, and beyond all, we, that is the Church, have failed, for we knew the wrong and the right path, but we did not warn the people and allowed them to rush forward to their doom. I do not exclude myself from this guilt; on the contrary, I stress at every opportunity that I too have failed, for I too have been silent when I should have spoken!

It is just those who have done nothing and who have risked nothing and who have confessed nothing who now do not want to hear any guilt mentioned. However, I found among my co-prisoners much real repentance and know from my own bitter and spiritual experiences: *mea culpa, mea culpa, mea maxima culpa!* And this I know in view of the crimes which our fellow Germans have committed against the members of their own nation and those of other nations. First of all we have to be conscious of the question of guilt. If we do not face this, and if we do not turn away to confess to ourselves and to God that we took the wrong path out of our fear and our disbelief, then we shall remain banned from the society of men and no prophet will arise to bring us the comfort of the word of God into our darkness. And if we now begin to talk of the sins of the others, after we have filled the world with torture, blood and corpses, with ruins and desolation, then I can only reply: All this is only an ounce compared with the terrible weight with which we have burdened *our* conscience. I say this after having been in Berlin for twelve days; in Berlin where there is hardly a woman who has not been dishonored and where death stalks as nowhere in the world, except not so long ago in Poland and Czechoslovakia and in Western Russia! How did it happen that there were only forty-five Protestant clergy in Dachau as compared with 450 Roman Catholic priests? Probably you have never seen the inside of a gas chamber; probably you have never stood outside the crematorium in Dachau in which a quarter million human beings have been burned: to see this means losing one's senses.

No, the Church has not been victorious, she has betrayed her Lord and her Savior by saying again and again: I do not know this Man. She knew what was happening, but pretended that these victims did not concern her. How are we going to be able to hear the words of grace if we do not recognize our sin?

Everywhere I find people who justify themselves saying: I might have lost my life; perhaps I risked my position and occupation. There are still countless people today who ask: "Was it really as bad as the newspapers tell us?" and I always answer them: "No, it was not as bad, it was infinitely worse!" There are many excuses which people can find, but they all follow the strain: "Am I my brother's keeper?" You should have seen that self-satisfied clergy at Treysa! "We led the people along the right path; the Church has not failed, we taught the pure doctrine and did not wander into the maze of Arian Christianity."*

Please consider the matter in a new light. If one does this, one ceases to enquire about the sins of others. One becomes quite small and experiences the great revelation that the Son of God died to save men such as we. Then, a hidden abyss opens in front of us into which we throw ourselves—to fall into the arms of our Redeemer. But the self-satisfied who walk on the surface, who have ten times as much to eat as the poor people of Berlin and a hundred times as much as those thousands who wander along the roads in the East, who still close their eyes to the fact that the judgment has begun with the House of God, they will not experience this. The sweetest words of comfort will be lost, because when the truth appears, the earth opens itself to swallow up Korah and his company, who took it upon themselves to become priests without the call of God.

No, the Church has not been victorious, she has failed and is failing still because she assumes that the judgment that is passed around her applies to the world but not to herself. You must understand that this is my concern, which for the sake of the Church and for the sake of my people, I shall not abandon, that no one should lose the chance for forgiveness which still is being offered to us, perhaps for the last time in the history of our people. And yet the people talk of relief work and pacify their conscience when they have sprinkled another drop of water onto a hot stone; they talk of the only true doctrine of the Lutheran Church and of the necessity to hold oneself apart from the Calvinists, and other such blasphemies, and the knife of God is at their throat and they refuse to believe it. Look, I only preach of forgiveness and comfort, but comfort and forgiveness for the men who bend their head before God and his judgment, as the publican did in the parable, and as the Church should do it today. I know what joyful songs of praise the hungry and starving parishes in the East sing today; I have stood among them and my eyes have filled with tears, which does not happen easily. I want to return to these people who do not accuse anyone because they may suffer injustice, but to praise God that he has shown them his mercy in the midst of his judgment. No, we are not criminals, we have murdered no one, we have robbed no one, we have not lustfully and intentionally tortured; but also, we no longer think ourselves superior to those people who have done such things, because we know of

* Arius, who lived in the fourth century, taught that our Lord was not God himself, but created by God.

our own guilt, and, in the midst of this guilt, we know of the one great wonder, the mercy of God in giving us his only-begotten Son.

This seems a strange letter and I do not know whether it has at all convinced you. He who has seen and experienced what I have seen and experienced no longer approaches these things with cold reasoning, he ceases to compare and weigh the sins of men, but he also no longer asks how his enemies may react. That counts no longer, or it counts only in so far as these very enemies will also one day be suddenly terrified, and many are so already. If God will listen to our prayers, then the eyes, ears and hearts of these enemies will be opened to receive the one redeeming message which can vanquish all the ghastly machinations of men and the devil on this earth. The Lord protect you, and believe me: I love my people as much as anyone, just now in its guilt I love it with the love with which Christ has loved me, and I will not owe him this love for one day of my life. Therefore I speak as I do.

July 8, 1946

World Community and World Government

⌒◡⌒

Reinhold Niebuhr

ANOTHER PETITION HAS GONE TO the President, signed by a thousand distinguished people, asking our government to take the initiative in calling a constitutional convention for the creation of a world government. There were not many Christian leaders among the signatories to this petition, which gives one reason to hope that the Christian churches of America are beginning to realize that there is a difference between secular utopianism and the imperatives of the Christian gospel.

A Christian knows, or ought to know, that an adequate Christian political ethic is not established merely by conceiving the most ideal possible solution for a political problem. He must, in all humility, deal with the realities of human nature, as well as the ideal possibilities. He must know that the intransigeant elements in every historic situation are derived not merely from the sin of Russia or some other nation, or from the stupidity of statesmen, but from the difficulty which all of us find in conforming our actions to our highest ideals. It is very difficult to establish peaceful and just human communities, because the collective behavior of mankind is even more egoistic than individual behavior; our job is therefore to establish a tolerable community within the limits set by man's recalcitrance.

The problem of international relations in the present day is that we have minimal bases for an international community and we must extend them; but we cannot create a world government without more communal bases than we now possess. Our modern utopians are under the illusion that governments create community. The fact is that governments presuppose community and in turn perfect it, but they cannot create it. Communities are created by more organic processes than the fiat of a constitution. They rest upon mutual trust and other forces of cohesion. National communities possess various forces of cohesion such as a common language and culture, common traditions, and common concepts of law and morals. The international community lacks all these forms of cohesion. It has only a certain degree of mutual economic dependence, a certain measure of religious and moral sense of obligation transcending the national loyalty, and finally the fear of mutual destruction. This third element has been strengthened immeasurably by the prospects of atomic warfare and has encouraged the hope of some people that we might be able to scare each other into the acceptance of a universal sovereignty. But there is no record of nations coalescing because they feared each other, though some have arrived at a wider partnership because they feared a common foe.

Our immediate situation is that only minimal forms of mutual trust exist between the nations and that there is a particularly deep chasm between Russia and the West. There is no possibility of pure constitutional instruments bridging that chasm if quite a number of other, more provisional bridges are not thrown across it first. Even the proposed abolition of the veto provision in the present charter might do more harm than good. Lest we be tempted to think that only Russia stands in the way of the abolition of the veto we would do well to remember that the United Nations charter would never have passed the Senate if the veto provision had not been written into it.

What makes American proposals for ideal constitutional solutions particularly vexatious is that we present them to the world even while we prove in our day-to-day policies that we are only beginners in the lessons of international mutuality. We are for world government until it is decided that its headquarters are to be near our ancestral home. We are for world government, but we think the British loan agreement is too generous, proving thereby how little we understand the problems of a very wealthy nation's relation to an impoverished world.

We demand a complete abridgment of national sovereignty in one moment and in the next we are not certain that our economic power ought to be at least slightly abridged by various types of international accord. Failing to do our full part in establishing the minimal conditions for an international community, we tend to salve our uneasy conscience by presenting the world with an ideal constitutional solution for its problems. It is as if an errant husband, finding difficulty in working out the day-to-day conditions of happy marital life, beguiled his leisure by writing a book on The Ideal Marriage.

This kind of idealism will not do. It is not Christian idealism. Sentimentality never is. Let us strive to fulfill our obligations in the international community more imaginatively as they arise. Let us not forget the starving while we are feasting. We may then in time create the conditions for better constitutional solutions. The future is indeed perilous and it may be natural to try to find some absolute guarantee against another world war. But the peace of the international community is not secured by the logic of constitutional authority, even as no logic of law can maintain the peace of a national community, if more potent factors make for conflict. If we understand this we may give ourselves to our daily responsibilities with the greater devotion.

March 4, 1946

The American Situation

II

The Great Lie

⚬⚭⚬

Liston Pope

"In the size of the lie there is always contained a certain factor of credibility, since the great masses of a people . . . will more easily fall victims to a great lie than to a small one."—Adolf Hitler

WITHOUT HAVING BEEN exclusively privileged in this respect, citizens of the United States have long been subjected to public lying. Tall tales are a staple form of American humor, and absurd claims are characteristic of American advertising. Probably most people in this country have developed a sharp nose for the truth, as Hitler discovered at last. But the ability of the public to differentiate between truth and falsehood has seldom been so carelessly overlooked or cynically doubted as in two current propaganda campaigns.

Senator McCarthy of Wisconsin has made headlines for weeks with his charges that the State Department is "infested with Communists," variously reported by him to be fifty-seven, or two hundred and five, or eighty-one in number. He has changed his lists and his definitions repeatedly, cloaked himself in an E. Phillips Oppenheim penumbra of mysterious hints, made reckless and unsubstantiated accusations against a number of individuals, and carefully preserved his Congressional immunity from damage suits. He has produced virtually no evidence against the persons accused, demanding instead that confidential government files be opened to Congress for that purpose—though he had told the Senate at the outset, "I think I have a fairly good digest of the files." As this is written, he says that he is letting his entire case "stand or fall" on his charges against Owen Lattimore, whose connections with the Department of State have been practically nonexistent.

It is bootless to analyze Senator McCarthy's propaganda techniques; probably he has not done so himself. His devices are familiar ones, adequately described by experts on propaganda analysis and ably exploited by such practitioners as Adolf Hitler and Josef Stalin. The astonishing thing is that the Senator should continue to receive a prominent senatorial forum and the headlines of responsible newspapers for hurling his epithets. The shocking thing is that a Senator of the United States should engage so irresponsibly in defamation of character and in charges calculated to wreck his nation's foreign policy, both as to its bipartisan nature at home and as to whatever confidence it enjoys abroad.

Senator McCarthy's mendacity has been better publicized but is no more flagrant than the fabrications contained in John T. Flynn's recent book, *The Road Ahead*. Innumerable copies of this book have been distributed gratis by the admirers of its thesis, and a considerable amount of suspicion and opposition has thereby been aroused toward some of Mr. Flynn's targets, including the Federal Council of Churches.

With that same Anglophobia that caused his views of international affairs to resemble those of the Communists and Fascists in 1940, Mr. Flynn regards socialism of the British stripe as being more dangerous to American institutions than even Russian communism is. He proceeds to lump together as "socialists" and "planners" a great many American individuals and organizations having only one thing in common—namely, a tendency to be somewhere to the left of *Pithecanthropus erectus*. He is able to devote an entire chapter to an "expose" of the "Kingdom of God" as preached by certain clergymen and by the Federal Council of Churches; by quoting out of context, imputing guilt by association (including alleged associations that have not existed), conveniently ignoring the pronouncements of the Federal Council that do not suit his purpose, and relying on Carl McIntyre, Mr. Flynn proves to his own satisfaction that the Federal Council is heavily influenced by a group of dangerous socialists.

The methods and purposes of Senator McCarthy and Mr. Flynn have much in common. For sheer audacity and magnitude of falsification, they surpass most recent competitors in America. What could be more absurd, on the face of it, than to insist that the Department of State, which is widely regarded as one of Russia's principal enemies, is actually influenced decisively by Communists? What could be more incredible than the warning that the doctrine of the Kingdom of God will bring ruin to America? Such charges upset all known canons of plausibility. They are so fantastic that they command attention—which is the chief necessity of the political propagandist.

There is a biblical word immediately relevant to Senator McCarthy and Mr. Flynn: "Thou shalt not bear false witness against thy neighbor." In certain religious circles which pride themselves on their "social realism," it has been fashionable in recent years to assume that politicians are necessarily liars, that rules of logic and of evidence are largely beside the point in judging political conduct, and that the application of absolute standards to such matters is both presumptuous and naive. As a corrective to sentimentality and sheer moralism, such disenchanted sophistication is of value.

But there are occasions when a lie is obviously and transparently a lie, even if its audacity is so great as almost to compel belief. There is such a thing as incredible human irresponsibility, and it threatens the foundations of politics as well as of morality, since politics is the art of public order as well as a method for the distribution of power.

Senator McCarthy and Mr. Flynn deserve to have the Ninth Commandment called to their attention, since they do not appear to have been impressed by it. If they continue to be unimpressed, they will certainly discover that the American public has a greater respect for honor and fair play and a higher capacity to detect the truth than the perpetrators of the Great Lie have ever been willing to suppose.

March 17, 1950

The Communist Threat: Past and Present

༺☙༻

John C. Bennett

THERE ARE REASONS FOR HOPING THAT the Republican victory may mean the eclipse of Senator McCarthy. He will no longer have a Democratic administration to attack. Moreover, General Eisenhower, who must loathe what we have come to call McCarthyism, may be able to exercise strong influence on those Republican Senators who are inclined to follow McCarthy's lead. David Lawrence has published a report of an interview with Senator McCarthy in which the Senator says that his methods of exposing communism in government will no longer be necessary.

However, there are reasons for fearing that this expectation about the future of McCarthyism may not be well founded. One is the fact that recent events have indicated that there is a very considerable body of opinion in this country that is controlled by the kind of fears on which McCarthyism thrives and which evidently does not disapprove of what McCarthy has been doing. Another reason is that some Republican leaders will be greatly tempted to use their control of government to look for evidence that will discredit their Democratic predecessors in order to insure themselves against a Democratic victory in the Congressional elections in 1954.

It is disconcerting to read in as conservative a journal as *Newsweek* that we can expect a whole series of partisan inquisitions. In its issue of November 17th it says that we must expect "the greatest series of investigations in recent American history. Congressional probers, to discredit Democrats, will dredge up scandals that have not yet come to light and unmask Red sympathizers who may be clinging to government jobs. The White House will help, supplying secret files that Truman withheld." Perhaps this is only a rumor. But the temptation to carry on such a program will be enormous, and there will be leaders in Congress who would find it most congenial. There is less danger that evidences of corruption will be used to injure people on a large scale than that charges of connection with communism will have that effect.

General Eisenhower can keep any such partisan inquisitions in check if he appoints a non-partisan body to sift all new evidence in order to save innocent people from reckless smearing. What is said in this editorial is not said to protect Democrats as Democrats, but to protect American citizens from grave injustice and to protect the nation from deeds that might do more than all the Communists in America to undermine our institutions and our national morale.

Any more investigations by Congressional committees or by administrative agencies should take into account the following considerations.

(1) Acts and associations often had a very different meaning in the 1930's from what they would have had in the 1950's. It is almost dangerous to say so given the present state of mind on the subject, but communism itself had a different moral meaning from what it has today. At that time, many people gave some support to Communist causes because they saw in communism the chief opponent of Fascism, which was the form of

totalitarianism about which most was known. In the 1930's, before the great purge in Russia, it was quite possible for many honest and intelligent and loyal Americans to convince themselves that there was still hope that Russian communism would be redeemed. The 1930's were the period of the depression when it was natural for many of its victims and for many other sensitive observers to lose confidence in our own economic institutions. In the 1930's there was no cold war and Russia did not have power enough to be the great menace to the world that she now is. It was possible in that decade to have a hopeful and friendly attitude toward Russia without choosing Russia against America. In any decade, society must be protected vigilantly against treason and subversion, but many of those who are today easily accused of some connection with communism were not in any sense disloyal. As for membership in Communist fronts, there were scores of organizations which seemed to express the aspirations of millions of loyal citizens who loved democracy and hated totalitarianism. Often they did not begin as Communist fronts and they were not known as Communist fronts until they had been in existence for years.

Today communism is unmasked. It is not likely to deceive many Americans. The Communist front technique is now generally understood. The revelation of what happens in Communist countries and the Communist threat to the countries that are now free are clear enough for all but a few Americans to see, and those few are so isolated today that they can get very few non-Communists to join them in any of the organizations which they set up.

(2) We must distinguish between decisions about policy made at another time and under quite different circumstances, and the judgments about those decisions made today by people who are wise after the event. It is also important to distinguish between disloyalty and all matters of judgment under such circumstances. Many decisions were made while Russia was our much needed ally in war. Many decisions were made in the first months after the war, when most Americans of both parties still hoped that it would be possible to find a *modus vivendi* with Russia. If Congress spends the next few years raking over all of these things again and judging them by the wisdom of hindsight, and trying to allocate blame on a partisan basis, it will make it harder for our country to solve the problems of the future. If Congressional committees follow the example of Senators McCarthy and Jenner and create the impression that if one questions a man's judgment, one must also question his loyalty, they will do unspeakable damage to our institutions. They will unjustly harm loyal citizens. But they will also make it more difficult to find statesmen in the future who are willing to take the necessary risks of decision making.

(3) The distinction must always be made between those who seek various ways of social change by democratic methods in a way that is entirely above board and those who may advocate some of the same changes, but who do so as a part of Stalinist strategy. It is plain that Senator McCarthy does not recognize this distinction. His two broadcasts during the campaign confused people who have an open or a secret sympathy with Russian or Stalinist aims and those social liberals or progressives who for years have proved that they are deeply opposed to communism, to its ideology, its imperialism, its subversive methods, its whole program for the world. McCarthy's attack on the anti-Communist Americans for Democratic Action was one example of this. Recently the McCarran Committee has been hounding one of our most useful representatives abroad on the ground that he was a Socialist fifteen or more years ago. This is supposed to indicate that a person is unreliable in relation to communism. But Socialists in America have been fiercely anti-Communist for three decades and this man has long since abandoned Socialism for a more conservative position. This distinction between anti-Communist progressivism of various kinds and a willingness to be used by the Stalinist conspiracy is crucial. No one who does not consistently emphasize it is fit to participate in any effort to defend this country against subversion.

There have been two periods in which it was easy for the Communists to persuade many Americans to follow policies that were useful to them and to give them moral support. Those two periods were the time of the great depression in the thirties, and the time of the alliance with Russia in the second World War. Most of the evidences of pro-Communist sympathies in influential circles in American life belong to one of those two periods. In both periods the major international threat was Fascism of various kinds. Today, when there is so much fear of communism for obvious external reasons, things that happened during those periods are exposed and the exposure feeds the panic about the Communist threat. The external threat is real but there has not been a time since the Russian Revolution when there was as little internal danger from communism as there is today—as little danger that any considerable number of Americans will be tempted by communism. Where there is actual espionage or subversion it needs to be dealt with by experts and this usually means by quiet methods. To play upon the American fear of communism by noisy denunciations, by exaggerations, and by unjust insinuations is to serve the cause of communism by making people all over the world cynical about American democracy and by diverting the American people from the only effective ways of counteracting Communist influence and power.

December 8, 1952

Wayne H. Cowan

Moral Re-Armament:
A Dangerous Ideology

Wayne H. Cowan

MUCH ATTENTION HAS BEEN GIVEN IN the nation's press of late to the right-wing John Birch Society, with its questionable tactics of fighting communism and its exploitation of a generalized fear of a changing world over which we have no control. Moral Re-Armament (MRA) is another organization—much older and more respected—that is also making a bid for the American mind these days.

In full-page advertisements addressed "To the American People," MRA has warned in bold-face headlines: "The hour is late. Here is the answer. For God's sake, wake up!" Offering itself and its traditional Four Absolutes—Absolute Honesty, Absolute Purity, Absolute Unselfishness and Absolute Love—as "the answer" to godless communism abroad and godless materialism at home, MRA describes itself as "the moral ideology that rearms the living and thinking of men everywhere."

This emphasis on an ideology that will save the world from communism marks a shift from its earlier concern with changing individual lives. Prior to World War II, MRA's founder, Dr. Frank N. D. Buchman, was quoted as saying: "But think what it would mean to the world if Hitler surrendered to the control of God. Or Mussolini. Or any dictator. Through such a man God could control a nation overnight and solve every bewildering problem." Such statements apparently paid off precisely as they should have, for MRA was virtually discredited by 1940.

With communism on the rise again in the postwar world, MRA has found a new place for itself, and if you believe their claims, the choice before all peoples is "MRA or communism." Here are a few of their commendations: "But for MRA, Japan would be under Communist control today," ex-Prime Minister Kishi; "Through MRA we have seen the way to save our country from communism and set her on a new road," Jean Bolikango, Congolese Minister of Information and National Defense; "MRA is the ideology of freedom. It is the ideology Africa needs today," President Tubman of Liberia; "If we had had MRA, we would never have lost the mainland. Only with MRA can we recapture the mainland from communism," General Ho Ying-chin, wartime premier and commander-in-chief of the Chinese armies.

39

These are extravagant testimonies, and they come from high places. We have a right to wonder, however, if this is really an adequate understanding of the choices before the nations of the world today. Let us take a look at one specific area covered by these claims.

MRA is presently touring the country with *The Tiger,* "A drama of the Tokyo riots written and acted by the men who took part and have since found the answer." In its cast are four students who, we are told, were "leaders of the revolutionary students' organization, Zengakuren," one of whom says he stood at the door of James Hagerty's limousine when it was mobbed by student demonstrators at Haneda Airport last June. According to MRA ads, *The Tiger* has played to packed houses in New York, Washington and Detroit.

We attended the American premiere performance of the drama at Carnegie Hall. It is not easy to go to such a performance with an unprejudiced mind, especially after reading the ads in *The New York Times* that quoted Mr. Kishi's statement, "But for MRA, Japan would be Communist today." Perhaps it would be truer to say: "But for Mr. Kishi and his high-handed tactics in forcing the Security Treaty through the Diet, there would have been no riots at all."

Mr. Kishi's comment, however, was rather typical of the unreality of the whole evening. Not once during *The Tiger* was the Security Treaty even mentioned—the impression left by the play was that the riots were anti-American and pro-Peking. In fact, the program says it very clearly: "In an exchange of letters between Stalin and Mao Tse-tung in 1953, it was decided that Japan would be taken over in 1960. What happened in Tokyo last June was a bid to achieve this goal." If this statement is true—and judging from the best available information, it is not—then it was a real break for the Communists that the Security Treaty just happened to be in the process of being negotiated at this time.

This warped rewriting of history must not be allowed to stand, however. Not the least of the problems raised by these distortions is the fact that this picture of the riots plays right into the already troublesome American misunderstanding of events in Tokyo last year. In the eyes of the average American the choice before Japan was between the U.S. and communism, but to view the matter in this fashion is to seriously oversimplify and distort the real situation.

Our new Ambassador to Japan, Edwin O. Reischauer, wrote recently that many of the Japanese who participated in the riots or watched them on TV would agree with those Americans who believed that Japan stood at a point of historic decision. But, says he, "The diverging roads lead, not to Communist or democratic camps [to say nothing of MRA], but to somewhat vaguer goals labeled 'peace' and 'war' or 'democracy' and 'fascism.'" In his article, entitled "The Broken Dialogue with Japan" (*Foreign Affairs,* Oct. 1960), Reischauer calls this contrast in the images of the situation held by Americans and Japanese "the most alarming feature of the recent crisis."

We cannot help but wonder about many of the other claims made for MRA—that Cameroun gained its independence through the ideology of MRA, that the February 1960 victory over the Communists in Kerala, India, was "MRA-inspired," etc. (there seems to be nó end to it!)—whether they, too, don't strain Absolute Honesty.

The organization's change of emphasis from the Forties has actually been rather slight and of little significance. Over twenty years ago Reinhold Niebuhr wrote that he found it difficult to restrain a feeling of contempt for this "dangerous childishness" when "it runs to Geneva, the seat of the League of Nations, or to Prince Starhemberger, Hitler, or to any other seat of power, always with the idea that it is on the verge of saving the world by bringing the people who control the world under God-control." Today all we need to do in order to recognize how little has changed is to substitute the names of the places where the *status quo* is now in danger and add MRA's new role as the answer to communism.

"Selfishness, perversion and division within" is the naïve explanation of how communism takes over. Any awareness of the social dynamics and the historical vicissitudes of civilization is more than purely coincidental. MRA's failure to recognize the deep social and economic roots of German totalitarianism is merely repeated now in relation to every place in which communism is growing. Communism, according to this way of thinking, becomes the punishment inflicted upon those who do not practice Absolute Love and Unselfishness.

History does not validate the claims of such undaunted individualism. Offering a strictly individual redemption, MRA attempts to conform to an ideal world rather than the world of reality. Implicit in this formula is a lack of awareness that society also plays a causative role in the ills of the world. There is here the foolish assumption that by taking thought alone a person can improve himself—can add a cubit to his stature. Rational effort is the hallmark; the effect of such non-rational factors as emotions, prejudices, intuitions and loyalties is ignored.

Furthermore, persons in positions of responsibility and power are denied the luxury of living by such absolutes as the MRA ideology dictates. There is no comprehension that statesmen and politicians must always weigh claims against equally valid counter-claims in areas where there are seldom clear choices between the good guys and the bad. All this makes at least one fact stand out: these simple formulas, which distrust the political process and seek to evade the hard day-to-day decisions of politics in a world of power, are not only irrelevant but dangerous.

May 1, 1961

Manichaeism in American Politics

∾✧∾

William F. May

RICHARD HOFSTADTER HAS PUBLISHED a series of essays on the Radical Right entitled *The Paranoid Style in American Politics* (Knopf). He might just as well have called his book *The Manichaean Style in American Politics,* since the metaphysical and moral presuppositions of the Radical Right are Manichaean to the core.

The Manichaeans, of course, were dualists. They reduced all distinctions to the cosmic struggle between two rival powers: Good and Evil, Spirit and Matter, the Kingdom of Light and the Kingdom of Darkness. Hofstadter is not the first to note the element of dualism in American politics. Christian moralists have long bemoaned the tendency to reduce the complications of politics to the simple terms of a TV western, in which the forces of righteousness are pitted against satanic power.

In the Church this Manichaeism often expresses itself in the somewhat self-pitying struggle of "good church people" arrayed against the politicians. In the political Right Wing it generates—and anoints—a whole series of readiness committees, Minutemen and freedom evangelists pitted against the Communists, fellow-travelers and dupes in American education, press, church and government.

Although Christian moralists have recognized the analogy between the ancient Manichaeans and the Radical Right, for the most part they have left the analogy unexplored beyond references to a militant dualism. For this reason certain oddities in the behavior of the Radical Right have been only partly illumined. Why, for example, did Senator Joseph McCarthy hound and harry the relatively powerless domestic Communists and pay so little attention to the Kremlin and its power—if he were truly dedicated to a cosmic struggle against the Communist foe? Or again, why did the Goldwaterites in 1964 conduct a Presidential campaign so ineptly as to hand a massive victory to the liberal Democrats—if they were seriously opposed to "Socialistic" forces in the United States?

These oddities, of course, admit of certain ordinary political explanations. McCarthy in the Fifties saw enormous personal advantage in investigating domestic communism. Although he might not be able to touch the power of the Kremlin, he could be extremely effective in discrediting the power of "Socialistic" Washington. The Goldwaterites in the Sixties, on the other hand, were so absorbed in high revenge against the liberal wing of the Republican Party that they refused to undertake those reconciling actions essential to party unity and election victory.

But these explanations only beg for a further accounting of the obsessions that made such behavior seem plausible. McCarthy, after all, lost out eventually, and to Washington, not the Kremlin; and the Goldwaterites lost, not simply the election but control of the party. The behavior of the Right Wing has been altogether too contradictory for a solely political explanation of its strategies to give satisfaction. Perhaps a certain important feature of historic Manichaeism can shed some light on these peculiarities.

The Manichaean understanding of the three epochs into which cosmic history is divided is just as important for purposes of social analysis as their dualism. These stages were distinguished from one another entirely by the varying relations that obtained between the Kingdoms of Good and Evil.

(1) Originally the two kingdoms were separate from one another, but their separation was somewhat uneasy and unstable. The Kingdom of Darkness—out of envy, greed, resentment and the like—initiated acts of aggression against its rival.

(2) A consequent period of confusion and commingling occurred between the two forces. This confusion and commingling of Spirit and Matter, Light and Darkness, characterizes the created world that we know and its ongoing history. Since this epoch represents a net gain for satanic power, the created cosmos and its continuing life are not the work of the good God but rather a device of the devil to perpetuate his victories. Man, of course, is at the center of this confusion, inasmuch as he is an admixture of both spiritual and material powers.

(3) In the final, apocalyptic stage of history, a radical separation will occur once again. This stage will be distinguished from, and superior to, the first in that the forces of darkness will be shorn of their power of initiative and will retreat—wholly impotent and inert. The realm of Spirit prepares itself for this final stage of history by acts of purification in which it rigorously disengages itself from Matter. This disengagement entailed for the historic Manichaeans an ascetic ethic. It meant specifically the renunciation not only of sexual intercourse (as carnal) but also of its fruits in offspring. Children guaranteed to the devil the perpetuation of this present evil age.

Obviously the worst stage for the Manichaean is the second: the present era of confusion. The term "evil," in effect, has a double meaning. It refers primarily to Matter, Darkness and Flesh, but it also refers to the confusion of this Kingdom of Evil with its opposite. A clear-cut conflict between the two kingdoms is more tolerable than a state of affairs in which they overlap and blend.

Manichaean dualism and its consequent revulsion against the jum-

43

bling together of opposites is a metaphysics inhospitable not only to marriage but also to the Western sense of politics. Both marriage and politics presuppose the possibility of some kind of community or agreement between parties *distinct* from one another.

But the metaphysics of the Manichee does not allow for a fundamental distinction between beings or for a community between beings so distinct. There is either absolute identity (as Spirit without distinction is divinely good) or opposition (as Spirit and Flesh are anathema to one another) or confusion (as Spirit and Flesh overrun each other), but there is no community between entities in their distinction.

We have only to mention Christian metaphysics on the subject to sense the degree to which Manichaeism perforce is unfriendly not only to the ordinance of marriage but also to the development of political institutions. For the Christian there is a fundamental distinction in the Godhead between Father, Son and Holy Spirit and yet an indissoluble bond between them; there is a radical distinction between Creator and creature, Savior and sinner and yet a bond of covenant between them. Derivatively, there is a creaturely distinction between soul and body, and yet a unity; between man and woman, and yet the covenant of marriage is possible; between various human groups and communities, and yet certain kinds of agreements, bartering of interests and ties are possible between them.

The Manichaean, by contrast, wants metaphysical apartheid. The best state of affairs inevitably is that in which the Spirit, by virtue of its warfare with the Flesh, has won its final separation from the Flesh and its ties. (It would be interesting to know whether the Manichaean—and his successors—opposes commingling because he finds something evil or whether he finds something evil because it forces him into commingling. The relations may be reciprocal and reversible.)

Put in this way, it is quite obvious why a metaphysical abhorrence of marriage betrays itself in the very language that the Manichaean uses to describe the second stage of history: Spirit is "trapped" in the Flesh, or again, Spirit and Flesh "commingle" with one another. Both metaphors have overtones that are familiar to this day in the language of those revolted by sex and marriage, for whom marriage is a "trap" and the sexual act is a repugnantly intimate and messy commingling.

Just as surely as he opposes marriage, the Manichaean must abhor the realm of politics. From the vantage point of his simplicities and purities, politics is the realm of the imprecise and the confused, the impure and the compromised.

Perhaps this revulsion against commingling throws some light on the question of why Senator McCarthy and his followers were so obsessed with the domestic Communist while disinterested in practical measures against international communism. I do not think the explanation lies in the direction of the late Elmer Davis' interpretation, an analysis that Hofstadter cites and criticizes. Davis argued that the Radical Right compensated for its sense of insecurity before an international foe by attacking its more helpless domestic counterpart. W. H. Auden characterized this type of persecution rather succinctly when he observed:

> *Shameless insecurity*
> *Prays for a boot to lick*
> *And many a sore bottom*
> *Finds a sorer one to kick.*

Hofstadter revises Davis' theory. He does not believe that the general insecurity of the nation before international communism accounts for the emergence of the Radical Right as much as the more special insecurities (over status) felt by those who are marginal within American life. Rootless and without status, certain folk (especially certain ethnic groups) flock to the superpatriots, who will confirm their identity as Americans at the expense of the Socialist, Communist, New Dealer and fellow-traveler.

The theories of insecurity, however, fail to explain the passionate moral outrage that energized the McCarthy and Goldwater movements. (Hofstadter in a sense revises his own theory in favor of this moral factor when, in a later essay, he credits "fundamentalist Christianity" more than ethnic and status factors for the fervor of the Goldwater movement.) This moral outrage, like all Manichaean vehemence, is doubly compounded. Communism itself is evil, but even more evil is its confusion with our national life. A clearly defined enemy in the Kremlin is not half so upsetting as the obscenity of the Communist or Communist dupe in our midst. This is the intolerable confusion of which our national life must be purified, even to the neglect of measures taken to protect the nation against an admitted foe.

An abhorrence of commingling produces not only an obsessive and ritualistic persecution of the "traitor" but also a certain incapacity for the ordinary agreements, compromises and alignments that characterize political life. McCarthy, toward the end of his career, and the Goldwaterites after him proved themselves to be remarkably apolitical. (The indifference of the Right Wing to the development of a foreign policy in any political sense of the term is perfectly consistent with its incapacity for political agreements on the domestic scene.)

Hofstadter has persuasively detailed all this in his account of the unbending and rigid—indeed frigid and infertile—Presidential campaign of 1964. Goldwater's advisers were unwilling, from his nomination onward, to negotiate in any form or fashion with the progressive wing of the Republican Party; they did not treat the selection of a Vice Presidential candidate as a marriage of convenience dictated by the political needs of the campaign; they refused to move to the center for strategic purposes to recover the independent voter (it is difficult for a dualist to take a "neutral" with enough seriousness to yield to him on many issues); they were insensitive to the full impact of Goldwater's speeches upon groups beyond the assembly of believers in his audience; for prudential reasons, they kept Goldwater from mingling with the press, but they also saw to it that the poor, the crowds, the slums and the ghettos were assiduously avoided. (See Robert J. Donovan, *The Future of the Republican Party*, p. 55, quoted by Hofstadter.)

All these stratagems were pursued relentlessly to their dismal conclusion in a massive election-day defeat and the consequent cascade of liberal social legislation that poured out of the 89th Congress. Meanwhile, the movement itself remained pure, unadulterated, uncompromised and unconfused—and to this degree undefeated!

The use of language from the sexual sphere is not altogether forced. Being consistent, Goldwater's campaign reached one of its climaxes with his address in the Mormon Tabernacle. There he talked about the safety of our women in the modern city—a legitimate issue, to be sure, but not one that he proposed to solve by action other than the moral example set by the occupant of the White House. Obviously he chose the issue not because he had political solutions for the problem of violence in the city, but because sexual violence offered symbolic statement for everything profoundly feared in the way of commingling by the movement and its followers.

Perhaps this general account of the passional presuppositions of the Right Wing also throws light on why the arguments and rhetoric of racial Manichaeans inevitably take on a sexual cast. Though the liberal may be talking about housing, education and job opportunities, the racist inevitably climaxes the argument with the sex question, "Would you want your daughter to marry one?" And if this question is not terrifying enough, the racist continues with dark prophecies concerning the mongrelization of the white race. The liberal is baffled by this apocalyptic leap from politics to sex, but for the Manichaean it only brings these broader social questions to their repellent but intrinsic consummation.

Hofstadter is careful to point out that the Radical Right is not truly conservative. While seeking to dominate our more conservative political party, it is actually pseudo-conservative. It seeks to root out and not to conserve, to purify and not to nurture, to deny rather than to preserve much of the American heritage.

However, the corresponding question is never raised as to whether this movement in its spiritual content might not, with equal justification, be called pseudo-Christian rather than Christian. Instead Hofstadter uses the terms "paranoid style," "fundamentalist Christianity," "Christian apocalypticism" and "Manichaean dualism" somewhat interchangeably.

At best, he takes only marginal note of the existence of a Protestantism and Roman Catholicism distinguishable from this religious phenomenon. Undoubtedly there is some warrant for this identification. Manichaeism has intruded itself into certain reaches of Christianity. But no one sophisticated in the Christian tradition from Augustine onward can deny the difference between this faith and Manichaeism, no matter what Manichaeans in later ages may choose to call themselves.

This question as to whether the two can be distinguished from one another is more than a matter of academic objectivity or of Christian patriotism. For the secularist concerned with the health of the political order it has certain practical consequences for his attitude toward Christianity.

If the Christian faith and dualism are, in fact, inseparable, then the secularist would have good grounds for fearing the influence of the faith on American culture. Specifically he would fear its presence and influence in the sphere of education, and through education its impact upon political life. Conversely, he would hope for an increasingly "secularized" education as a means of purging American life of a dualism whose influence is deleterious.

Hofstadter is not without leanings in this direction. Puzzling over the fact that Birchites have usually attained more formal education than their fellow Americans, he raises the question as to whether they were educated in the great cosmopolitan colleges and universities or in denominational colleges. The hint is that a more secular and cosmopolitan education might help to rescue Americans from the influence of this pernicious movement.

In the absence of all the facts, one might offer a quite different conjecture. The John Birch Society and other radical movements from the Right (and Left) are notoriously strong precisely in those regions in which education is dominated by the modern state university. For the most part, until recently, theological studies have been absent from the curricula of such institutions. Consequently in many states the choice offered to college students is between religious fundamentalism (which is admittedly Manichaean) and religious illiteracy. To this degree it has been correspondingly difficult for clerical leadership to develop a theologically sophisticated laity, a laity that would find it more difficult to confuse the Christian faith with a primitive Manichaeism.

Obviously it would be foolish to exaggerate the political consequences of educational oversights. Nevertheless, there is a certain poetic justice in the predicament of the secular professor who opposes vehemently the teaching of religion at state institutions but confronts in his state an unholy alliance between the Right and a fundamentalistic Christianity. In a sense, he gets what he deserves.

While Hofstadter may be faulted for his failure to distinguish carefully the two religious traditions, he can only be admired for the objectivity, imagination and compassion with which he enters into the passional life of the Radical Right. He does not assume that there is no objective warrant for some of its fears or that a conspiratorial interpretation of events is invariably wrong; he enters compassionately into the insecurities and aversions that help to produce its mania. In this regard, Hofstadter offers an admirable model for the Church's own mode of relating to such movements. Even though the Church opts for action aligned with the political liberal or the revolutionary Left, it cannot afford to do so (even when it must do so decisively) in such a way as to produce from its side a sterile impasse. It will do little good if the Church only matches the paranoia from the Right with a paranoia from the Left. (No one can read certain Leftist journals without recognizing that a paranoid element can develop in its literature as well. See Staughton Lynd, "Waiting for Righty: The Lessons of the Oswald Case," *Studies on the Left,* Vol. 4, No. 2, Spring 1964, pp. 135-141.)

It will also avail little if the Church simply looks down upon the Right (and the Left) from the smug vantage point of a liberal establishment. If its contribution to the political sphere is to be health-giving instead of self-satisfying, the Church will have to do more than seize upon the inadequate formulations, inconsistencies and omissions in the argument of the Radical Right for the sake of winning a debate. The Church will need to understand Manichaeans in their passional life better than they understand themselves.

But to do this, the Church may have to divest itself of some of its diagnostic assumptions about the modern world. Increasingly theologians have assumed that the modern age is secular and secular without remainder. This is a diagnostic error of major proportions for which the presence of Manichaeism in the Right Wing is only secondary evidence. No adequate exposition of the passional elements in this movement will be forthcoming if the Church does not recognize that the Radical Right (and much else in modern life) cannot be understood in secular terms alone. The movement actually reeks of religion.

It should be a cause for some gratitude then that Richard Hofstadter, a secular historian, has painstakingly reminded the Church of this fact.

May 2, 1966

John C. Bennett

A Protestant Looks at
American Catholicism

❧

John C. Bennett

THE ATTITUDES OF AMERICANS TOWARD CHURCH-STATE relations depend in considerable measure on their attitude toward Roman Catholicism. The chief concern that lies back of the convictions of non-Catholics is the concern for religious liberty, and the chief threat to religious liberty is seen in the tremendous growth of Roman Catholicism as a cultural and political power in the United States.

There are two deep problems connected with Catholicism that must be emphasized at the outset of any discussion. One is the *dogmatic intolerance* that is itself a part of the Roman Catholic faith. This dogmatic intolerance need not lead to *civil intolerance,* but there is a tendency for it to do so just as was the case when it characterized the major Protestant bodies. This dogmatic intolerance becomes all the more difficult for non-Catholics when it is associated not only with distinctly religious dogma, but also with elements of natural law that are not accepted as divinely sanctioned moral demands by most non-Catholics. This is true of birth control and of some matters of medical ethics. It is true even of gambling under limited conditions, though this has to do not with a moral demand but with a moral permission! One symptom of the dogmatic intolerance that is most objectionable to non-Catholics is the strict Catholic regulation concerning the religion of the children of mixed marriages.

The other basic problem is the real tension between an authoritarian, centralized hierarchical church and the spirit of an open, pluralistic, democratic society. There is abundant evidence that Catholics in this country do sincerely believe in democracy and practice this belief, but I do not see how they themselves can deny that their polity poses a problem for democracy that is not posed by churches which make their decisions in regard to public policy by processes of open discussion in which both clergy and laymen share. The polity of the Episcopal Church does give bishops meeting separately a veto over many things, but it also gives the laity voting separately in the dioceses a veto over the choice of bishops. I mention this as an example of one of the more hierarchical forms of polity outside the Roman Catholic Church.

The Roman polity is itself a matter of faith, and therefore religious liberty includes the liberty to preserve that type of polity. And if it is

49

said that the papacy creates a problem of peculiar difficulty because it is from the point of view of the nation a "foreign power," the answer that Protestants should be able to accept is that the Church as Church is supranational and the religious liberty of all Christians includes their right to have relationships, suitable to their polity, with the universal Church.

American Protestants are troubled over far more than these abstract problems created by the Catholic faith and ecclesiastical structure. They resent much that is done by the Catholic Church in America and they fear greatly what may yet be done. The books by Paul Blanshard, especially his *American Freedom and Catholic Power* (Beacon Press, 1949), marshal many facts that both Catholics and Protestants should take seriously. It is unfortunate that Mr. Blanshard has presented his material in such a way as to confuse criticism of many particular applications of Catholic teaching with what seems to be an attack on the freedom of a church to have its own authoritarian structure as a matter of faith. Also, he writes not from a Protestant but from a secularist point of view, and thus sees no inherent problem in the relation of religion to public education. He is quite satisfied with the complete separation of school and religion. There is a tendency to exaggerate the monolithic character of world-wide Catholicism under papal direction, and Mr. Blanshard's projection upon the future of the indefinite threat of Catholic power to American democracy does not, it seems to me, do justice to the four considerations I will emphasize later. The book is the work of a very energetic and well-informed prosecutor and should be used as such.

The general thesis of this article is that, while many of these resentments and fears are justified, it is a mistake to project them in indefinitely extended form upon the future and to allow all of our thinking about Catholicism and most of our thinking about church-state relations to be controlled by them in that extended form. After outlining the grounds for some justified resentments and fears in this article, I will deal with other facts about Catholic life that should play a larger part than they do in Protestant attitudes toward Catholicism.

The Catholic Church is not a majority church in the country at large and, since immigration has been greatly limited, its rate of growth has not been quite as rapid as the rate of growth of the Protestant churches. But its strength is distributed so as to give it great majorities in some cities, and enormous political power and cultural influence in many states. It is extremely difficult for Protestants and other non-Catholics to live with Catholicism as the religion of a large local majority. It has likewise been difficult in the past for Catholics to live with Protestantism as the religion of a large local majority.

The centralized organization and the absolute claims of the Church enhance the difficulty, but Protestants must not forget that any small minority feels pressure that arouses resentments and fears under these circumstances. Part of the problem is a universal human tendency that does not depend on a particular ecclesiastical situation. However, it is the threat of a local majority that leads non-Catholics to emphasize the protections of religious liberty in the Federal Constitution. Catholics also have had occasion to appeal to these same protections, but today their chief desire is to establish a somewhat flexible interpretation of the First Amendment.

Non-Catholics have grounds for resenting the tendency of Catholics to use their power to impose Catholic ideas of natural law. They see it in the birth control legislation in Massachusetts and Connecticut; they see it elsewhere in the Catholic pressure to remove welfare agencies that have birth control clinics from local community chests; they see it in the Catholic objection to divorce laws that are much more flexible than the law of the Church; they see it in the attempts to have non-Catholic hospitals adopt the Catholic ideas of medical ethics in the field of obstetrics.

Non-Catholics have grounds for resenting and fearing the tendency of Catholics, when they have the power, to seek control of the public school system so as to bend it to Catholic purposes. Parochial schools could operate as safety valves for the public schools, but this is often not the case. When Catholics dominate the public school boards, they sometimes discriminate against non-Catholic teachers. In extreme cases that have been much publicized, they have operated public schools as though they were parochial schools. Perhaps more serious in the long run is the tendency of Catholics in some places to oppose needed bond issues or appropriations for the public schools. This is not a surprising reaction to the double burden of education costs that they themselves bear, but it is very bad for education.

Non-Catholics have grounds for resenting and fearing Catholic boycotts of communications media, including the publishers of books, and boycotts of local merchants who have some connection with a policy that they oppose. Fear of Catholic boycott often operates as a reason for self-censorship. Newspapers are influenced by this fear, and it is very difficult to get news published that may be unfavorable to the Catholic Church.

No one can criticize the Catholic Church or any other church for seeking to discipline the theater-going or the reading of its own constituency. Boycotting that consists only of this self-discipline within the Church may be unfortunate in some of its effects, but it is not open to objection in principle. It is the punitive boycott directed against all that a particular agency may do that interferes with the freedom of non-Catholics.

The desire of many Catholics to have the United States send a diplomatic representative to the Vatican has become a symbol to most Protestants of the many things that they resent in the use of Catholic power. This issue is confused because it is obvious that in the world at large the representation of a nation at the Vatican is not interpreted as a sign that the nation involved shows favoritism to the Catholic Church. Otherwise there would not be representatives from many non-Christian countries, from Britain, which has a state church that is not the Catholic Church, nor from France, which is secularist and anti-clerical in its politics.

But it is only fair to recognize the fact that the very size of the Catholic Church in this country and the absence of any state church, the existence of which would prove that the Catholic Church is not the favored church, makes American Protestants feel that diplomatic representation at the Vatican is a great concession to one American church in contrast to others. American Protestants emphasize the fact that the Pope is the head of one American church rather than the fact that the Vatican is the center of a diplomatic service which, as a unique institution of the old world, cannot be grasped by the American logic governing church-state relations.

Though I do not believe that this issue is as important as most Protestant leaders have made it, I have come to see that the meaning of representation at the Vatican to American non-Catholics in view of the actual religious situation in this country is natural, and the fact that this meaning exists here is more important than the fact that it does not exist in Britain or in Japan, for there are objective reasons for the difference. Because of them I believe that diplomatic representation of the American government at the Vatican will inevitably be interpreted as unfair to non-Catholics in this country.

Having summarized the grounds for Protestant fears and resentments in the face of the growth of Catholic power, I would now like to call attention to four characteristics of Catholicism that are often neglected in American Protestant discussions of this subject.

The first of these characteristics is Roman Catholicism's great variations from culture to culture and from country to country. The vision of many Protestants of a monolithic Catholic Church, built somewhat on the lines of the Stalinist empire and controlled from the Vatican, is very wide of the mark. Historically it has proved itself capable of adjustment to the greatest variety of cultural conditions instead of being one kind of religious ethos exported from Rome.

The difference between French Catholicism and Spanish Catholicism almost belongs to the study of comparative religion. Catholicism in Western Europe is utterly different from Catholicism in Latin America. In Germany, France, Holland, Belgium, Switzerland and England we see what Catholicism can be when it is religiously and culturally mature and when it has learned to live with strong Protestant and secularist competition. There is remarkable intellectual ferment in the Catholic Church in those countries. Catholic thinkers take considerable theological freedom and they are especially free in their thinking about political issues. There is a long standing effort to overcome the political and economic conservatism that has been the great handicap of the Church in reaching the working classes.

There is very much more discussion between Protestant and Catholic thinkers on a theological level in Europe than there is in this country. One interesting phenomenon is the fresh study of Luther and the Reformation by Catholic scholars that has shattered the old Catholic stereotypes. American Catholicism differs from Western European Catholicism in that it has no rich cultural background. It has a strong feeling of cultural inferiority to American Protestantism as well as to European Catholicism. Intellectual ferment is exactly what it lacks. The reasons for this are obvious, as American Catholicism represents the tides of immigration that brought to this country millions of Europeans who had had few opportunities in their own countries.

Protestants, as they view the development of Catholicism, have good reason to assume that as it becomes more mature culturally and theologically it will have more flexibility of mind and that there will be greater tolerance and breadth in dealing with non-Catholics and 'with the public issues that concern Protestants most.

I should add here that Catholicism needs not only the kind of maturing that takes time in a new country, but it needs to have two other things. One is the strong competition from non-Catholic sources—Protestant, Jewish, secularist. It has had one or more of these types of competition in every one of the Western European countries that I named. The worst thing that can happen to Catholicism is for it to have the religious monopoly to which it feels entitled because of its exclusive claims! Protestants, therefore, have a responsibility to confront Catholicism with a positive Protestant theology, and that is happening today in many countries because of the recent theological revival in Protestantism.

The other element that is very important in the environment for the development of Catholicism along the lines that I have suggested is the presence of a liberal, democratic political tradition. This has greatly modified Catholic political attitudes and it is most fortunate that, under the stimulus of democracy, Catholics can find the antecedents of democracy in their own tradition, especially in the great Jesuit political philosophers, such as Francisco Suarez, in the sixteenth and seventeenth centuries. They also discover antecedents of democracy in Thomas Aquinas.

This combination of continuous encounter with non-Catholics on a basis of political mutuality and the influence of liberal democratic ideas enables Catholics to avoid the *civil intolerance* that causes most anxiety among Protestants.

A second characteristic of Roman Catholicism is suggested by the fact that much of the Catholic aggressiveness that is most offensive to Protestants is sociologically conditioned. It is a result of the sheer energy that it has taken for Catholics to improve their position in a new country and in an alien culture, and it also reflects some social resentment for past disabilities on the part of people who have won social power.

We forget today the long and bitter history of nativist anti-Catholicism, but the memories of it do not die so easily among Catholics themselves.

Today, changes are coming so rapidly and the economic, social, and cultural opportunities for Americans of many ethnic backgrounds are so much alike that we can expect to see the particular sociological reasons for Catholic aggressiveness become less important.

Paul Blanshard recognizes that there is some truth in this consideration. After describing the role of the Irish in American Catholicism, he says:

> This Irish dominance explains many of the characteristics of American Catholicism. The Irish hierarchy, which rules the American Church, is a "becoming" class. It represents the Irish people struggling up in a hostile environment, using the Roman system of authoritative power to compensate for an inner sense of insecurity which still seems to survive from the days when Irish Catholics were a despised immigrant minority. Boston is aggressively Catholic largely because it is aggressively Irish, and it is aggressively Irish because its people have not quite overcome their sense of being strangers in a hostile land.[1]

One of the most convincing pieces of evidence in favor of this judgment concerning the social dynamics of American Catholicism is found in Kenneth Underwood's study in depth of Protestant-Catholic relations in one city that has had a large Catholic majority for some decades. Professor Underwood reports on the attitudes of both laymen and clergy from various parishes in Holyoke, Massachusetts. He finds that it is the parishes made up of recent immigrants who have not been much assimilated into American life where the most intolerant attitudes are found. It is in those parishes where the rigid ideas of the priests are most readily accepted by laymen. He says:

> The upper income, well educated Catholic laymen are much less receptive to clerical guidance as to the practical social implications

---

[1] *American Freedom and Catholic Power* (Beacon Press, 1958), p. 38.

of moral and religious laws of the church than are the lower income, more poorly educated Catholics. The former tend also to be much more appreciative of the role of the Protestant churches in supplementing or correcting Catholic action.[2]

A third fact about Catholicism that needs to be understood by Protestants is that the Catholic Church is divided from top to bottom, in this country and abroad, on matters of principle in regard to religious liberty. There is a traditional main-line position that favors the confessional Catholic state as the ideal type of relationship between church and state. This view would limit the rights of religious minorities in a nation that has a very large Catholic majority. These limitations would have to do with public propagation of the non-Catholic faith rather than with freedom of worship or freedom of teaching inside the Protestant Church. Under such circumstances there would be a union of state and church and the state as state would profess the Catholic faith.

This position is sometimes called the "thesis," and the adjustments of the Church to religiously pluralistic nations, including the acceptance by American Catholics of the American constitutional separation of church and state, involve a second-best position called the "hypothesis." Father John A. Ryan, a noted Catholic liberal on all economic issues, is responsible for a famous statement on this subject. He states the traditional thesis and then tries to soften it for Americans by saying:

> While all of this is very true in logic and in theory the event of its practical realization in any state or country is so remote in time and in probability that no practical man will let it disturb his equanimity or affect his attitude toward those who differ from him in religious faith.[3]

So long as Protestants, especially those who live in cities that already have large Catholic majorities, realize that there are authoritative statements of the so-called Catholic thesis of the confessional state as representing the ideal possibility, they will not be greatly comforted by Father Ryan's assurances. It is simply not enough for a church that operates in the light of very clear dogmatic principles to make concessions on the issue of religious liberty for non-Catholics on a pragmatic basis alone if its dogmatic principles still point to a confessional Catholic state in which, as the ideal, the religious liberties of minorities are severely restricted.

2 *Protestant and Catholic* (Beacon Press, 1957), p. 94.

3 J. Ryan and F. Boland, *Catholic Principles of Politics* (Macmillan, 1940), p. 320.

It is important to realize that a very able and earnest attempt is being made by Catholic scholars in this country, with much support from Catholics in Western Europe, to change the principles as well as the practice of the Church in this matter. This attempt is associated chiefly with the work of Father John Courtney Murray, but it is gaining a good deal of support elsewhere too. A careful statement of his position is found chiefly in his many articles in the Jesuit quarterly *Theological Studies*. (See especially March, 1953; June, 1953, December, 1953; March, 1954. Also, "Governmental Repression of Heresy" reprinted from the Proceedings of the Catholic Theological Society of America.)

Here I shall attempt to summarize his main conclusions, but it should be recognized that these are abstracted from very complicated historical expositions and come in large part from Father Murray's analysis of the encyclicals of Pope Leo XIII in order to show what is permanent and what is historically conditioned in those encyclicals. With apologies to Father Murray for oversimplification of the kind that is alien to his own mind, I shall attempt to give the substance of his position in the following propositions:

The idea of a confessional Catholic state belongs to an earlier period in European history and it has become an irrelevancy under contemporary conditions.

Anglo-Saxon democracy is fundamentally different from the democracy of the French Revolution which was totalitarian in tendency. The state in this country is, by its very nature, limited, and in principle the Church does not need to defend itself against such a state as it did with the nineteenth century revolutionary states that formed the immediate background of Leo's political thinking.

There is no anti-clerical or anti-religious motivation behind the American constitutional provision for church-state relations, and the Church need not defend herself against this doctrine as such.

The Church in America has, as a matter of fact, enjoyed greater freedom and scope for its witness and activities than it has in the Catholic states of the traditional type.

It is important to emphasize the rights of the state in its own sphere, the freedom of the Church from state control, and the influence of Catholic citizens upon the state.

It is impossible to separate religious freedom from civil freedom, and there can be no democracy if the freedom of the citizen is curtailed in religious matters, for such curtailing can often take place as a means of silencing political dissent.

Error does not have the same rights as truth, but persons in error, consciences in error, do have rights that should be respected by the Church and state. The Church should not demand that the state as the secular arm enforce the Church's own decisions in regard to heresy.

It does more harm than good to the Church for the state to use its power against non-Catholics.

I think that all of these propositions fit together into a self-consistent social philosophy. They are presented by Father Murray as a substitute for the traditional Catholic thesis concerning the confessional state. They have made considerable headway among both clergy and laity in this country. They correspond to views that are held in Europe and have support in the Vatican itself.

In December, 1953, after this point of view was strongly rebuked by Cardinal Ottaviani in Rome in an address defending the Spanish conception of a confessional Catholic state as the ideal, Pope Pius XII somewhat ambiguously made room for Murray's position in a speech to a convention of Catholic jurists. The fact that he did this in the midst of a trans-Atlantic controversy within the Church has encouraged American Catholics who hold this view to believe that the Pope was sympathetic to it. That is the most that can be said.

American Protestants should realize, therefore, that the Roman Church is not a vast international machine designed to overturn their liberties, if this were to become politically possible, and that they have many allies in the Catholic Church who share their belief in religious liberty on principle.

The fourth fact about the Catholic Church is that there are many points of disagreement on social policy among Catholics; there is no one Catholic line on most public issues. There is agreement on birth control as a moral issue, but even here there is no agreement as to what the state should do about it. Catholics generally do not today advocate strict laws on the subject except in the two states in which those laws are already in force. On economic issues, there is a broad Catholic pattern based upon the organization of producers' groups, but this is far from obligatory and it gives rise to endless differences so far as application is concerned.

Catholics differ as to whether a war with modern weapons can be just. There is a deep difference between Catholics in various nations on forms of government. Catholic doctrine makes room for governments based upon popular sovereignty but does not prescribe this universally. Even on communism there are great differences in temper between European and much American Catholicism.

It is an understatement to say that the Catholic hierarchy did not act helpfully on the issue of McCarthyism, but that was because they were deeply divided. There is no doubt that McCarthy had a strong hold on large groups of Catholics, especially Irish Catholics, but it is also true that some of the most eloquent opposition to McCarthy came from Catholic sources, notably such journals as *The Commonweal* and

America. American Protestants need not fear that Catholics will usually throw their great weight as a religious community in the same political direction. This will tend to be even less a danger as Catholics move further away from the status of an immigrant bloc. In general we can say that natural law does not guarantee agreement on concrete issues, but we can also say that natural law plus prudence equals flexibility.

I have outlined briefly four aspects of Catholicism of which American Protestants should take account. Though they give no assurance as to the direction that Catholicism may take in the next generation, they may release us from exaggerated fears based on past experience in this country alone. Protestants should put more rather than less emphasis upon positive elements of Protestant faith and doctrine. They should join Catholics in rejecting superficial forms of religious harmony so often urged in the interests of national unity. But they can live with their Catholic neighbors in the hope that greater mutual understanding and the sharing of moral and political purposes may become possible.

August 4 and September 15, 1958

Federal Aid to Education: A Call to Action

❧

The Editorial Board

THE CURRENT SCHOOL YEAR HAS brought new worries and growing despair to thousands of U.S. families. The seething discontent with public education—not everywhere, but among vast groups of our people—becomes more evident each autumn as the schools reopen. Americans have always seen public education as a doorway to opportunity for their children. Today that hope and confidence are gone for many citizens. The contemporary problem has two major aspects.

In city after city across this land the schools are not meeting the needs of the people. They see their children pushed around, put on half-schedules in crowded buildings, bored with inadequate instruction. Teachers, often working heroically in difficult situations, know all too well the inadequacies of the schools where they struggle.

In a time when technological progress destroys some job opportunities and opens new ones for the educated, dropouts have increased in frightening numbers, and the victims doom themselves to future years of futility. Especially in the inner city, where slums and racial tensions make life oppressive, the schools are too dull and feeble to challenge the interest of students. From New York, Chicago, Detroit, Washington, Houston and many other cities come reports of desperation over the plight of education.

The need for financial aid is stupendous. Money alone will not do the job, but nothing else will work without it. And the money is simply not available in city budgets from the usual sources of revenue.

The proud American tradition of local support for schools has a strong appeal to anyone with roots in our cultural history. But today local support simply is not enough. The cities carry an immense educational burden. They must:

> improve student-teacher ratios, enlist teachers with special training, find more space and better buildings, develop new programs that will equip children to live in a world where traditional skills are fast becoming obsolete;
>
> overcome the legacy of generations of racial injustice by desegregating schools and creating educational communities with enough harmony to function effectively in the midst of tense neighborhoods;
>
> motivate children who see no chance to break out of the ghetto-traps where they live;
>
> teach students from homes where the English language is not used.

All of this must be accomplished within a political system that often returns to the cities an unfair share of the taxes their residents pay. One of America's favorite legends is being reversed: once it was Wall Street that presumably milked the countryside of wealth; now legislators draw heavy taxes out of cities and take little account of the special requirements of urban education.

The need is critical, and no practical solution is in sight without federal aid. In Congress there is a better chance than in the many state legislatures to designate money for the cities.

But federal legislation is bogged down almost hopelessly. The Administration, embroiled in the more spectacular problems of international policy, taxation and civil rights, has given education a low priority. The people who elect Congress are generally apathetic; those who might be most concerned have fled the problem by moving to suburbs or by sending their children to private schools.

Some citizens are genuinely worried about the danger that the nation's schools would be controlled from Washington if aid came from the federal treasury. These concerns must be taken seriously and procedures developed to prevent improper federal interference. However, we think this approach is quite practical since the Federal Government has already poured vast sums into higher education with less political manipulation than one frequently finds in state legislatures and local school boards.

Ultimately, however, legislation favoring federal aid founders on the religious issue.

The perennial discussion about public funds for church-sponsored parochial schools has unquestionably entered a new phase. If anyone doubts that this is the fact, let him look at the evidence.

Walter Lippmann urges that we break "the religious knot" and find a way to extend financial aid to parochial schools "without getting involved in the question of the teaching of religion." Robert Hutchins takes the stand that "children in schools supported by religious denominations should not be excluded because of their faith from the benefits of a national program of education."

The New Republic, breaking with the dogmatisms of conventional liberals, advocates tax aid for parochial schools provided they accept standards of education set forth by public agencies. Wilber G. Katz, a distinguished teacher of law, argues on the constitutional issue: "Religious schools may not be singled out for preferential aid, but they need not be excluded from a program of general aid."

These separate proposals may not make a totally convincing case, but they surely demonstrate that the movement to help pupils in private as well as public schools cannot be dismissed as a sectarian power play aimed at raiding the public treasury. The issue as set forth in these statements is not help to churches but help to education. Their concern is the welfare of American society and particularly of children—some in private schools and some in public schools starved financially because of religious controversy.

The customary responses of the "professional Protestants" are not very helpful. Often they sound like a broken record stuck in the eighteenth century. Even in the National Council of Churches, a source of fresh thinking on many subjects, the comments on this issue frequently seem to express a conditioned reflex rather than a thoughtful response to a major social problem.

Surely any realistic thinking by Christians must start from an awareness that the stars in their courses do not prescribe any one set of arrangements for education. Human societies have found various ways of dividing responsibility among family, church, state, press and other cultural agencies. Such diversity is all to the good.

Our society long ago decided to exercise major public responsibility for education through government; thus most formal education has come through government-sponsored schools. The benefits of this policy are so great as to need no argument. But we have made exceptions—notably the G.I. Bill, which subsidized students, letting them take their education in any certified school. Such a plan was surely better than requiring veterans to attend state universities if they wanted financial help. The same logic might endorse a comparable plan for elementary and secondary education.

We say it *might* or it *might not*. We reject any argument that pretends to establish an absolute principle denying that government funds should ever find their way into nongovernmental educational channels. Likewise we deny any absolute claim of religious groups to subsidies, direct or indirect, from public funds. Rather we urge that the whole issue be decided not on ideological grounds but as a policy question requiring the constant reexamination of facts and the effort to achieve political wisdom.

In this context there are serious arguments against direct financial aid to parochial schools, especially at the present time. In many regions of the country part of the public would leap at any possibility of tax aid to set up racially segregated private schools in competition with public integrated schools. Sound legislation could of course prevent any absolute segregation, but manipulators might still tap the public treasury to support various forms of token integration.

Furthermore, tax help to private schools might easily speed the flight of middle-class children from public schools and aid the proliferation of parochial schools of all sorts. In this time of severe trials for public education, our society must beware of any measure that would weaken the support for the public schools or let them deteriorate further.

In so perplexing a situation we are not ready to pull "the answer" out of a hat. What we urge is experimentation, openness to new ideas, willingness to reason and discuss. One possibility, which is not the whole answer but which is workable in some situations, is "shared time," which allows children to study some subjects in public schools and others in parochial schools. Other possibilities will emerge as partisans cease to stand on dogmas that cannot be compromised and begin to search for policies on which men of good will may negotiate. In such negotiations we see no absolute incompatibility between some element of public support for private schools and democracy or Protestant faith. In forthcoming issues, as in the past ("Stalemate Over Aid to Education," April 1 issue), we will endeavor to set forth affirmative proposals for breaking the present deadlock.

Certainly the American society, exercising the ingenuity and human concern that have marked its history, can work out solutions to this impasse. Many of our children enjoy good education in fine schools, public and private. Others endure insufferable education. In the name of justice and of public welfare, this discrimination must cease.

Today the top item on the American domestic agenda is civil rights. Close behind it—in fact part of any comprehensive solution to the issues of civil rights—must come a massive effort to improve education. We urge our political leaders, even while working on civil rights legislation, to begin moving on education. Above all, we urge Protestants, Catholics, Jews and secularists to pay less attention to rigid traditions and vested interests and more attention to the needs of our children and youth.

October 28, 1963

A Roman Catholic for President?

John C. Bennett

THE ISSUE RAISED BY THE POSSIBILITY of a Roman Catholic candidate for the Presidency is the most significant immediate problem that grows out of the confrontation of Roman Catholicism with other religious communities in the United States. There are a great many Protestants of influence who are inclined to say that they would never vote for a Roman Catholic for President. Many of them refuse to say this with finality, but there is a strong trend in this direction. Our guess is that it may be stronger among the clergy and among official Protestant spokesmen than among the laity.

Aside from crude forms of prejudice and a reluctance to accept the fact that this is no longer a Protestant country, there are two considerations behind this position that have some substance. The first is that the traditional teaching of the Catholic Church is at variance with American conceptions of religious liberty and of church-state relations. There is a fear that a Catholic President might be used by a politically powerful Catholic Church to give that church the preferred position to which, according to its tradition, it believes itself entitled.

The other consideration is that there are a few specific issues on which there is a Catholic position, and, short of any basic change in our institutions, the nation's legislation and policy might be deflected by a

Catholic President toward these known positions of his church. One example that is not often mentioned is the intransigent view of the problems of the cold war that was expressed in the American Catholic Bishops' statement late in 1959. (We would not vote for any man, Protestant or Catholic, who takes such a view.)

On matters of this kind most Catholics are more likely to be affected by the position taken by the authorities of their church than would a Protestant. Even though they may not agree with the bishops, it would be embarrassing to oppose them publicly. Catholic bishops do their debating privately; American Catholicism on the hierarchical level, therefore, gives the impression of a united front that no Protestant churches are able to give.

We want to direct three comments to those who take a negative view concerning a possible Roman Catholic President:

(1) If the American people should make it clear that a Catholic could never be elected President, this would be an affront to 39,500,000 of our fellow citizens, and it would suggest that full participation in American political life is denied to them as Catholics. This would be true even though Catholics are governors, senators, congressmen and Supreme Court justices. We believe that this situation would wound our common life and damage our institutions more grievously than it would be possible for a Catholic President to do even if he chose to. We are shocked that so many Protestants seem unwilling to give any weight to this.

(2) We are justified in ascertaining what view of church-state relations and of the basis of religious liberty a particular Catholic candidate holds. We may learn this without grilling him, for his record of public service and its implications would be an open book.

There are two main views of religious liberty that are held among Catholics. The traditional view regards as normative the idea of a Catholic state with the church in a privileged position and with at least a curtailment of the liberties of non-Catholics. This view is an inheritance from an earlier period of history, and many Catholic theologians and ecclesiastical leaders now reject it. They believe in religious liberty for non-Catholics on principle and not merely as a matter of pragmatic adjustment to the American situation.

This more liberal view is not limited to this country; it is held widely in Western Europe. It is one view held in Vatican circles. Those who hold this view believe that Pius XII was at least open to it, and they are even more sure that this is true of his generous-minded successor.

In emphasizing the importance of ascertaining the Catholic candidate's views on these matters, we are supporting a contention of Bishop James Pike in his *Life* article (Dec. 21, 1959). We are sorry that he seemed to suggest that American Catholics were arrayed against Catholics elsewhere and against the Pope.

The Roman Catholic world is divided from top to bottom on the question of the basis of religious liberty, whether it is to be accepted only pragmatically·in a pluralistic country or whether it should be defended on Christian principle, even in situations in which the church has the power, through its influence on the electorate, to impose its will on the state.

The American laity are emphatically on the side of the more liberal interpretation. It is quite certain that any Catholic layman who reaches the point where he can be considered a likely candidate for President will be sufficiently influenced by the democratic ethos to represent that position. This was true of Alfred E. Smith as it is true of Senator Kennedy. But anyone who is troubled about this matter is justified in asking where a Catholic candidate stands on this question.

We believe that it is quite possible that a Catholic in the Presidency who is himself liberal on this matter and who is sophisticated enough to know what is happening in the church might be better able to deal with Catholic pressures than a Protestant. He would be in a better position to measure them and to appeal from one part of the church to another.

(3) So far as the specific issues on which there is a known Catholic position are concerned, there are very few that come to the desk of the President. More of them are dealt with by mayors and governors, and the Republic has survived many Catholic mayors and governors. And on many issues within the purview of the President, the Catholic community is divided—even, for example, on the appointment of an ambassador to the Vatican. (It was a Baptist who made the latest appointment to the Vatican.) Furthermore, a President is subjected to so many pressures and counterpressures that he is less vulnerable to any one form of pressure than most other public servants.

There is the vexing problem of birth control. As a domestic problem it belongs chiefly to the states, and it is fortunate that many Catholics, while they do not reject their church's position on birth control in terms of morals and theology, do not believe there should be a civil law that imposes the Catholic moral teaching upon non-Catholics. As one element in a program of foreign aid, this may belong to the President's province. (We may say in passing that President Eisenhower has gone as far as the Catholic authorities in rejecting its inclusion in governmental programs.)

Among the various alternatives open to a Catholic President, Father John R. Connery, S.J., suggests in *America* (Dec. 12, 1959) that the President could allow a foreign aid bill, of which he basically approved but which included financial provision for a birth control program, to become law by ignoring it for ten days. This procedure presupposes that there would be in his mind a conflict between his religiously directed conscience on a specific point and his broader judgment as to what was good policy.

There is general agreement that this country should not urge on another country a birth control program but that it should cooperate with a country that desires it. The birth control feature of a broader program of economic development could be paid for by the government of the aided country while the United States Government would support the program as a whole. This merely suggests a possibility that might enable a Catholic President to handle this issue constructively.

However, it must be noted that the issue of birth control must be weighed along with all the other issues that are at stake in an election. Even if a Catholic candidate were to take a line here that we might regret, this would not necessarily outweigh all the other considerations of which we need to take account. Furthermore, we do not know what line a Catholic President would take in a complicated situation, for Catholic moral theology gives a high place to the virtue of prudence.

We should like to add to these considerations a more positive note: a Catholic President who is well instructed in the moral teachings of his church would have certain assets. (It is chiefly in the areas of sex and medicine that the Protestant finds elements of an intolerable legalism in Catholic moral teaching.) If he is of an essentially liberal spirit he may absorb the best in the real humanism of Catholic thought.

A Catholic President might have a better perspective on the issue of social justice than many Protestants. He might be guided by the ethical inhibitions present in Catholic views of the just war so as to resist the temptation to make military necessity paramount in all matters of national strategy. He might have a wiser and more seasoned understanding of the claims of the person in relation to the community than many a one-sided Protestant individualist.

We are not now speaking of any particular Catholic candidate, and there are elements in Catholic moral doctrine that we reject. When these are interpreted by the narrower type of ecclesiastic, we often find them repellent. But Catholic teaching has its better and more humane side, and it is the repository of much wisdom that could stand a Catholic President in good stead.

March 7, 1960

The Old Question:
Politics and Religion

೧⊘ഔ

Roger L. Shinn

"I feel strongly that it is wrong to mix political opinions with personal Christianity."

"Am I wrong in thinking that Jesus never took a political stand?"

". . . The church's responsibility is to preach the Gospel of Jesus Christ and to induce people to . . . lead Christian lives."

THESE THREE STATEMENTS FROM ONE week's mail raise once again an old, old question. It seems strange that such statements should need an answer in the year in which Rolf Hochhuth's stinging play, *The Deputy,* has made painfully clear the moral failure of churches in Germany that neglected political issues and concentrated on spiritual and institutional questions.

Actually, almost all Christians believe that their faith relates to politics at some points. Some see the issue in communism, some in devotional exercises in public schools, some in concern over pornography, some in issues of social justice. Although many people accused pre-Civil War churches of "interfering" in politics when they opposed slavery, today we wonder how any churches were able to avoid the issue. Future Christians will probably wonder why the churches of our time did not do more about the ethical problems that are the stuff of politics.

Let us admit that Christians and churches can make dangerous mistakes in the political arena. Churches have used pressure to gain special privileges; hierarchies have dictated to church members. Christians have made foolish ethical judgments because they lacked technical competence in economics and politics. They have introduced religious prejudice into electoral campaigns and have so tied themselves to political factions as to neglect their ministry to men of diverse views. Sometimes churches have written into public law their specific moral standards.

When so many mistakes are possible, the temptation is strong to divorce "personal Christianity" from "political opinions." Yet because politics deals constantly with human welfare and ethical issues, the Christian Church cannot neglect it.

The most celebrated economist of our time, John Maynard Keynes, once wrote to the Archbishop of Canterbury that economics had its origin, at least partially, in ethics. He continued, "There are practically no issues of policy as distinct from technique which do not involve ethical considerations. If this is emphasized, the right of the Church to interfere in what is essentially a branch of ethics becomes even more obvious." The same statement can be applied with equal force to politics.

To evade major issues of social ethics is cowardice. Surely any reading of the Old Testament makes that point clear. The New Testament puts less emphasis on direct political judgments, both because of its eschatological setting and because Jesus and his disciples were not even citizens of the political empire in which they lived. Nevertheless the New Testament indicates that Jesus took his stand against one political group, the Zealots, and did not hesitate to call King Herod "that fox." His followers, when they are voting citizens, deny his lordship if they neglect to serve him in politics.

66

There are good reasons for Christian restraint in political judgments. Politics involves questions of fact, of probability, and assessment of leaders on which men of ethical sensitivity often differ. In a world of sinners, purity is rarely set against corruption in the way campaign oratory makes it appear. Furthermore, the loyalty of faith must always live in some tension with the tentative opinions and bargaining methods that politics appropriately cultivates. These factors should keep the Church from becoming a community of the politically like-minded.

Christians should readily recognize that they may be mistaken in political judgments. This is no excuse for evasion: the fact of fallibility does not reduce men to silence in theology, ethics or politics. But there is need for three kinds of restraint. (1) Churches should be more cautious than individuals or groups of Christians in taking political stands. (2) Christians, especially churches, should be more ready to make pronouncements on issues than on candidates—always recognizing that times come when issues and men are inseparable. (3) Christian judgments should never stem solely from the clergy but should involve lay specialists with skill in public affairs.

After all this is said, the Christian must always remember that the cardinal article of his faith is that the Holy God has entered fully into the life of mankind. The Church cannot claim holiness by escaping the common life.

November 2, 1964

We Oppose Senator Goldwater!

The Editorial Board

Christianity and Crisis, throughout its almost 25 years, has lived by the belief that Christian faith calls men to involvement in the social issues of their time. We have held that theological and moral commitments have political consequences, that politics is full of religious and ethical meaning. This journal was founded as a response to the threat of Hitlerism, and ever since we have taken stands on public issues.

But we have never allied ourselves with any political party. We have sought to appeal to the intelligence and conscience of persons with varying political loyalties. We have praised and blamed men and policies in various parties.

We have specifically criticized the idea of a "Christian" political party for three reasons: (1) we think no party has a right to claim the Christian banner; (2) we recognize that Christians can differ in political judgments; (3) we deem it healthy for Christians to work in parties alongside men of other faiths.

Nothing in 1964 has changed our basic convictions. We expect to continue acting on them. But these convictions never ruled out the possibility that occasions might arise when men and issues would become so identified that "A Christian Journal of Opinion" might have to take sides on candidates for public office. This is such an occasion.

The difference this time is the forces crystallized around the candidacy of Senator Barry Goldwater. We have no desire to argue that Mr. Goldwater is an evil man. For people who like to personify the devilish forces in history, he is an inappropriate stand-in for Satan. He is a man of personal charm and disarming amiability. It is hard for Americans to get angry at a ham radio operator with a handsome smile, who rides horseback, has a house full of electrical gadgets, and crusades for law and public decency.

We point simply to the objective, unarguable conflict between his record and the judgments of the Christian churches on most of the major issues of social ethics in our time. We have in mind neither some imaginary consensus of church members nor the stands of the agencies specifically organized for social action. We mean the sizable body of ethical convictions that have been endorsed, after long processes of study and debate, by the major American denominations, by the National Council of Churches and by the World Council of Churches. Although Roman Catholicism and Judaism work through somewhat different processes, we can make the same assertion about their most authoritative teachings on social ethics.

As a lover of moralism, Mr. Goldwater may be surprised to know this—as will many church members who are won by his simplifications, his praise of virtue, his denunciation of crime and evil. But the evidence is incontrovertible.

The clash comes at four major points:

(1) Senator Goldwater and many of his supporters repeatedly describe the international situation as a kind of holy war. They see the United States as the defender of true faith, fighting for its life against "godless communism." Such identification of national destiny with a religious cause is not a uniquely Goldwater confusion. *Christianity and Crisis* has had reason to decry it on many occasions.

In the Goldwater movement, however, the religion of national destiny goes to an extreme that is new in recent American history. It provides the motivation for the Senator's repeated insistence on "victory" and on "winning" when we are not at war and when, if we were, the war would be of such a kind that neither side could win, though both could be destroyed. The Senator seems deaf to those who plead for restraint in any contemplated recourse to atomic weapons. Why? Because "restraint" does not belong to the vocabulary of religious enthusiasts.

Since the Senator sees himself as the leader of a crusade, he attracts the support of countless persons who, impatient with the slow procedures of diplomacy, seek to relieve their frustrations by heralding a messianic figure who will lead them to victory. The danger thus created for the entire human community is great. We have never believed, nor do we now, that a religious zeal that endangers mankind is a proper point of departure for making policy decisions.

(2) Mr. Goldwater has *never* voted in the Senate for a foreign aid appropriation. He has voted against ratification of the nuclear test ban treaty. He has shown a cavalier delight in brandishing nuclear weapons. His insensitivity to the political meaning of military decisions is evident in his claim that, as President, he would solve the problem of Southeast Asia by telling the military officials: "Fellows, we made the decision to win, now it's your problem." Our objection to all these stands comes not from pacifism, which we have consistently criticized, but from a belief that America must *both* maintain strong military power *and* exercise that power with moral and judicious restraint. We exalt wisdom over "winning."

(3) Senator Goldwater voted against cloture in the Senate debate on civil rights, then against the Civil Rights Act of 1964. On no legislative act in a quarter of a century have the churches mobilized so decisively as on this one; Mr. Goldwater opposed their efforts entirely. Although it is obvious that he is not a segregationist, he does cultivate their votes. As pollster Samuel Lubell has said, without the white backlash Mr. Goldwater would not stand a chance in this campaign. As we oppose the backlash, we oppose the man who counts on it to win.

(4) The Senator from Arizona is committed to a social and economic individualism that was always fallacious and that has become peculiarly inept in our age. He has opposed most of the legislation that has helped to improve health, education, housing, relief of poverty, opportunity for the oppressed. He has made a long series of incredible and insensitive statements about the poor, the graduated income tax and the efforts of government to improve the general welfare. At a time when 70 per cent of our people lead urban lives he shows no evidence of understanding the problems of the modern metropolis.

Senator Goldwater won the nomination by cultivating a hard core of enthusiasts who liked his radical conservatism. Now he knows that he must win the undecided votes of more moderate people. Since the meeting with President Eisenhower and other Republican leaders at Hershey, Pa., he has shown that he sees the profit in reversing his tactic and offering more echo, less choice. He has already begun to project the image of moderation during the campaign. But at this late date he cannot hide his long record or do much to modify it. We are convinced that a vote for Mr. Goldwater is a vote for irresponsibility, recklessness and reaction.

We not only oppose Mr. Goldwater, we favor President Johnson.

October 5, 1964

From Supporter of War in 1941 to Critic in 1966

John C. Bennett

SOME OF OUR READERS MAY wonder how it is possible that a journal founded in 1941 to support the war against Hitler and to combat pacifism in the churches can now be highly critical of the American Government's policy of belligerence in Vietnam, often finding itself making common cause with today's pacifists. The point of this editorial is suggested by Paul Ramsey, who writes: "Even Reinhold Niebuhr signs petitions and editorials as if Reinhold Niebuhr had never existed."

Christianity and Crisis has not come to share the religious and ethical assumptions of Christian pacifism; we still recognize the necessity for the military ingredient in national power and the moral obligation to use power at times to check power. Yet we believe that the circumstances under which military power is being used in Vietnam are sufficiently different from those under which it was used to defeat Hitler to lead to quite different political and moral judgments concerning the issues raised by this war.

This is not to say that we are now advocating immediate withdrawal from Vietnam. Rather it means that we are on the side of those

70

who keep pressing for the reduction of the violence, for a negotiated end to the fighting and for a political settlement that will not depend upon the defeat of the other side. We have welcomed the President's emphasis on negotiations and his appeal to the United Nations, but these are accompanied by statements and policies that threaten to nullify them, especially in the context of commitments made to the Saigon government. We deplore the resumption of the bombing of North Vietnam.

We see at least four differences between 1966 and 1941:

What is at stake in the case of communism is different from what was at stake in the case of national socialism. Stalinism had many of the worst features of Hitlerism, but it proved to be a passing phase of Soviet communism. It showed itself more open-ended than we had supposed, capable of varying degrees of humanization if not democratization. It is not monolithic, nor is it permanent slavery; and, in its later phases, cooperative as well as competitive coexistence becomes politically and morally possible. We doubt if such coexistence would have become possible with Nazism.

The threat of communism is not primarily a military threat, as was Nazism. We have supported the policy of developing military strength to deter Soviet communism from taking a military short cut, but even in so doing we realized that developing the political and social health of the nations of Western Europe was more important. Communists readily use force but they have not chosen to rely on massive military attacks on other nations. They prefer to exploit revolutionary situations and situations of disorder with a limited use of military force. In this respect they are quite different from the Nazis. This fact alone, as we have pointed out with regularity, means that the repeated use of the Munich analogy in the context of today's debates about Vietnam is misleading.

The Munich analogy is misleading also because of the differences between what was defended in Europe and what can be defended in Asia. Against Hitler we could help defend nations with real or potential political strength and a will to be independent. Against Stalin the same was true. Also, the nations of Western Europe had already achieved some of the results promised by a Communist revolution: modernization and a high degree of social justice.

In Asia there are greater limits to what we can do with our military power to help countries to maintain their independence of communism. This does not mean that we have no responsibility to help nations remain free. But we need to be realistic about what we as a predominantly white country can do to counteract communism in Asia, especially when nations that are threatened need stable governments and revolutionary changes that we may not be able to help them achieve.

Whether our responsibility extends to the creation of a nation in South Vietnam that can only be kept independent by American power is at least an open question. It is different from the question of whether we should have supported the freedom of Western Europe by war against Hitler or by the presence of force that could be used against Stalin.

It should also be said that our decisions today, unlike those of the Forties, must take account of the danger of nuclear war. How this factor is to be weighed in relation to the others may be debatable, but one of the reasons for opposing escalation in Vietnam and pressing for a negotiated end of violence (whether we call it "peace" or not) is that we can never be sure this conflict will not lead to a nuclear war. At present our Government is intent on avoiding the bombing of North Vietnam cities and the Chinese nuclear installations; but if the war should continue for years, we might not be able to hold the line against such brutal and provocative acts.

We hope we are still "Christian realists" and that we are as "realistic" in emphasizing the limited relevance of American military power today as we were in calling for its use to defeat Hitler in 1941. Those who speak with most conviction in favor of our Vietnam policy seem to me to be blind to many intangible factors in the Asian situation that could cause military successes to lead to political and moral defeats.

February 21, 1966

How Free Can a Free Society Be?

Roger L. Shinn

IN AMERICA TODAY a number of citizens, how many we do not know, are caught in a tragic moral dilemma. They are those young men subject to military draft who are conscientious objectors (CO's) to the war we are now fighting.

The selective service law provides consideration for those unwilling to bear arms in all wars; it has no place for those who reject a specific war. We want to call attention to the moral problem of the society that includes dissenters from public policy.

To do so requires consideration of the ethical dilemmas inherent in social life. Every society makes demands that some people resent. Compliance with public policy is one of the costs of living in a society—the only kind of living that most men find tolerable or possible.

One test of a morally sensitive people is its concern for the integrity of dissenters. A free society guarantees specified liberties—notably freedom of speech and due process of law—to its minorities.

Freedom finds its severest strains in time of war. The nation mobilizes its resources and drafts men for military service. In modern America, selective service is regarded as the fairest way of distributing burdens and dangers. At the same time we have taken account of the CO. The law provides the possibility of noncombatant assignments or alternative service, involving an element of compulsion comparable to that for men who fight but with regard for the moral sensitivity of pacifists. Some CO's have fulfilled their responsibilities with a high courage and fidelity.

As national policies go, ours shows a rather high degree of imagination. The Government protects the rights of those who protest against it. Such action is possible only on the basis of a strong belief in freedom and respect for persons. Few societies have gone this far. Perhaps we would not go so far if our wars were closer to home. Yet this policy represents a minimal concession to conscience—a precious, though often unappreciated, asset in any nation.

But what can we say to those men whose protest against the war in Vietnam—which President Johnson has clearly labeled *war*—is as much a matter of conscience as the stand of any CO to all wars? Some who might conscientiously have fought against Nazism cannot so fight the Vietcong.

It is understandable why the state has never found a way to take account of this "selective CO," whether in uniform or about to be drafted. If we are going to have armies at all, the assignment of men becomes a matter of military efficiency. When a division is ordered overseas, it is pretty late to ask which men are willing to go. By entering military service, the soldier subjects himself to authority.

Yet the person cannot surrender his conscience to the state. The Christian, in particular, will always remember the apostolic protest, "We must obey God rather than men." And all who believe in the dignity of the person must be reluctant to compel anyone to act against deep conviction.

Certainly there is nothing inherently unreasonable in the view that some wars are justifiable and others are not. Nobody can believe that all parties in all wars have defensible positions. Men of conscience thus are responsible for making some ethical distinctions about specific acts of war. The Nürnberg trials rested on the assumption that individuals should— in some cases—refuse to obey orders. Yet no government actually allows this right, presumably because all governments think *their* orders are morally valid.

In the last analysis, there is no solution to the conflict between society and the dissenting individual. Each inevitably insists on its own demands. But before the last analysis there are many possibilities of adjustment. We have made one for the CO and we are a better society because of it. The next step is to take account of the selective objector.

We can expect disagreement. Soldiers and relatives of soldiers fighting what has often been called a "dirty war" will not feel kindly toward those who refuse to fight there. But the scope of the problem will be modest. The mobilization of national morale in any time of combat makes it hard to object to military service, and only the man of considerable courage is likely to do so. If many object then the society must ask searchingly whether its policies are justified.

The implementation of such a proposal is not easy. It will require more subtle application of present procedures to distinguish conscientious objectors from men who simply want exemption from painful duties, and it will require further thought about alternative forms of service.

With all these difficulties any government would prefer to avoid the whole issue. But it is by facing such issues that we discover how free a free society can be.

November 1, 1965

We Protest the National Policy in Vietnam

❧

The Editorial Board

The hardest strokes of heaven fall in history upon those who imagine that they can control things in a sovereign manner, as though they were kings of the earth, playing Providence not only for themselves but for the far future—reaching out into the future with the wrong kind of farsightedness, and gambling on a lot of risky calculations in which there must never be a single mistake.

Herbert Butterfield, *Christianity and History*

The Editorial Board

THE UNITED STATES INVOLVEMENT IN Southeast Asia has become a case study in Herbert Butterfield's thesis. In the last decade *Christianity and Crisis* has frequently appealed for a change in American policies in Asia. Now we must register our emphatic protest against the policies and acts that are leading to increasingly portentous war.

Nobody planned this war. Neither brute malice nor innocent miscalculation brought it about. It is the result of a series of fateful decisions in which human fallibility, accentuated by moral insensitivity and pretension, turned a brush-fire war into a major conflict. In the process, the nature of the initial United States commitments has changed beyond recognition.

Beneath all the immediate perplexities is the deep confusion in our Government's aims. Sometimes the stated policy is to prevent any gains for communism. At other times it is to give the people of Vietnam their free choice of a government—and that, everybody knows, may be a Communist government. Talk of unconditional readiness to negotiate is mixed with adamant unwillingness to concede anything. These contradictions may not be confusing the enemy, but they are certainly confusing the American public and our allies.

We would like to assume the best, although much that the Administration does makes this difficult. Let us acknowledge that Washington has engaged in a dramatic peace offensive that has drawn scornful rebuffs. Let us grant that the national leaders have told the world and particularly the United Nations that we want a solution based on the Geneva accords of 1954, a solution that will offer self-determination to the people of Vietnam. Let us point out that we see slender clues of willingness to modify the refusals, previously adamant, to give the Viet Cong a place in negotiations.

Even if this best possible case is made, the United States still finds itself engaged in a war that is destructive to the people whom we claim to be helping, to the peace of the world, and to our best interests.

The burning of villages, the killing and maiming of civilians, area bombing, and the use of napalm and chemical destruction of crops inflict immediate human suffering that makes incredible the official promises of pacification and remote benefits. Repeatedly such tactics alienate and harm the very people we purport to save.

The United States is concentrating on one dubious battleground the brainpower and resources needed for meeting a world that bristles with unsolved problems. Constructive acts in Latin America, Africa and the Middle East get little attention because of the hypnotic preoccupation with East Asia.

Contrary to the evidence of history and the wisdom learned in Europe, our leaders still treat Asian communism as a single enemy. Instead of promoting diversity within it, their acts drive Ho Chi Minh to greater dependence on China (despite the traditional feelings of his people). Thus American policy creates the monolithic Communist unity that it fears.

The war in Asia aggravates irritations between the United States and the Soviet Union at a time when the two share more common purposes than in any period since World War II.

Our nation is becoming increasingly lonely in the world, losing or embarrassing European, African and Asian allies, and building a legacy of hatred and resentment for "neo-colonialism."

The Government is neglecting or deferring its attacks upon urgent needs of American society, needs that the President has heretofore met with impressive resourcefulness.

By continuing to isolate China from the world of nations, United States policy reinforces the Chinese paranoia and isolation that a wiser policy would seek to overcome. A look at a map of American bases near China makes obvious some reasons for Chinese fear and distrust.

Our society is letting the specific struggle in Vietnam blind us to the nature of world revolution, which calls for far greater understanding and appreciation that we have yet shown.

Thus we find the American nation deeply committed to a self-defeating course of action. Every intensification of the war makes the ultimate resolution more difficult.

We do not pretend that there are ideal solutions. Rather than look for painless ways out, we need to compare various possibilities with the present grim realities. For example:

We are told that American prestige is at stake and that we cannot settle for anything less than victory. We answer that our country has shown in Korea that a strong people can afford to value peace above victory. We believe that a stubborn vanity, provoking continued hostility, is more damaging to prestige than is a wisdom that seeks peace.

We are told that only our military power can protect our allies from vengeance at the hands of their enemies. We do not deny that all factions in Vietnam have a capacity for vengeance. Any settlement should make all possible provision for the protection of people. But we also know that our present policies inflict great cruelties on our friends as well as our enemies.

We are told that any concession will start dominoes falling throughout Asia. We do not accept this simplistic theory, especially when, as in Vietnam, the United States must both create and support the domino. (At the same time, we endorse efforts to strengthen viable governments and economies that afford alternatives to communism.) But we readily grant that a settlement in Vietnam will have consequences elsewhere. These must be compared with the evident effects of the present perilous course.

Our Government has sufficient political, military and diplomatic ingenuity to work through these very real difficulties. What is lacking so far is the willingness to look at realities and the moral imagination to seek better methods than the present contradictory mixture of peaceful rhetoric and stubborn policy. If the President and the Secretary of State find the will and insight, they can devise the precise maneuvers that hold most hope.

Such maneuvers must show "a decent respect to the opinions of mankind"—to use a phrase from a more glorious time in our national history. They must involve a greater concern for the well-being of people than for ideological abstractions. They must include some sense of proportion in relating means to ends.

The shape of such a settlement may include a convening of the Geneva powers under the persuasion of the United Nations. More likely will be a series of steps of de-escalation, disengagement, multilateral diplomatic efforts and economic reconstruction. Alternatives can be found to the present bitter impasse, but only if policy-makers will give up the dogmatic illusions that lead to a fixation on rigid ends regardless of the costs.

Scripture warns that "where there is no vision the people perish." The failure of vision in our time is a blindness to realities no less than to ideals. The threat of this moment is a preoccupation with the enemy that destroys our society's power to understand itself or its foes. In such a time the greatest service to the society comes from those voices—in church, politics and press—that risk the displeasure of the powers that be in order to challenge dogmatisms that imperil ourselves and our world. To these voices we again add our own.

March 7, 1966

77

Witness to a New World

III

Christianity and the Status Quo

❧

Herbert Butterfield

AFTER WORLD WAR I there emerged a form of international "idealism" which was gravely weakened by legalistic and pharisaical heresies. It involved a system which was very convenient for the French and the British: It outlawed any attack by external powers on existing empires; it vetoed even international action on issues which such empires might regard as internal; and at the same time it rendered illegitimate for all the future any attempt on the part of a new power to build up similar empires on parallel methods. The resort to violence was condemned without regard to the provocation that might have been given, but protection was assured for imperial systems which were held together only by the latent operation of force. This form of internationalism was bound to function in fact, therefore, as a gigantic machine for the freezing of the *status quo*. An enemy might say of the system that the most unscrupulous experimenter in *Realpolitik* could not have devised a cleverer way of maintaining an empire which lacked the material force for its defense in a competitive world. With their bags full of plunder, France and Britain declared: "There shall be no more competition; there shall be no more stealing now."

The supporters of this type of internationalism were more virtuous than would appear from this account of the system—an account rather from the point of view of those who were not interested in its maintenance. Such supporters were not so clearly conscious of the end which the system served, though they were aware that they were parties to forms of imperialism which could only survive under a regime of stabilization and peace. They were virtuous in a way, for in politics there is some virtue in a power that marries its private interests to a universal cause, an international good. But they were unimaginatively pharisaical, because their internationalism coincided with their vested interests and, therefore, it was comparatively easy for them to be virtuous and to act as lovers of peace. The real test of the virtue of Britain and France was bound to come when they found themselves in a position analogous to that of the Hapsburgs in 1914—when, as declining empires, they would be faced with the decision whether they would consent to go under without making a last desperate fight.

Under the legalistic kind of internationalism described above, it is not possible to prevent issues and problems from developing to the point of desperation. Nor is it possible to prevent occasions from arising which will provide plausible opportunities for violent action on the part of a state or a people that feels itself the victim of injustice. The kind of internationalism which implies the legalistic defense of the *status quo* is, in fact, more calculated to provoke a sudden act of violence than the system of diplomatic relations which existed before 1914 and which allowed for a greater degree of "give-and-take." In the latter case men do learn that it may be necessary to concede something in order to release the tension; they do not simply dig themselves in, relying on the whole international order to halt any attempt to change the *status quo*.

In the hands of men who evaded the real moral issues and who were narrower in their comprehension than so many of the statesmen of the nineteenth century, it is a question whether the established form in internationalism produced a single new idea of any significance between 1919 and 1939. It is a question, in fact, whether before 1914 there did not exist diplomatic methods for meeting crises which were lost or rendered inapplicable owing to legalistic prejudices in the after-period. Let it never be suggested in any case that between 1919 and 1939 a regime was established in Europe which made it more difficult for aggressors and dictators to arise—more difficult for men to resort to the politics of the *coup d'etat* or to take the world by surprise—than in the preceding generations.

The Franco-British adventure in the Suez has taken the mask away from the internationalism which seeks to "police" the *status quo*. But the leaders of the Suez enterprise have perhaps been too uncharitably condemned, for they merely brought the older system to its climax (which happens also to be its *reductio ad absurdum*)—they merely carried a stage further the kind of policy they had been pursuing all their lives. Precisely because it was one of the points of weakness in the older system, "colonialism" has become a primary issue, and three large sections of the globe—the Communists, the United States and the Afro-Asian bloc—have made their separate and varying attacks upon that order of things. And the fact that Britain feels that she has conceded much already, and that she has performed many acts of generosity, is no answer to those who insist that she had no right to what she possessed, no right to the things which she was pretending to give away. Colonies do not present the only issue, however, and Nasser's own attack has been extended against very indirect forms of "colonialism"; nor is it clear that he would allow himself to be humoured or bribed into becoming a satellite of the West, which after all is not so very different a matter. The point is that we are all in the position of Metternich—and Time is bound to be against us—if, in the face of the new forces that have emerged in the world, we merely seek to hold the fort, to dam the flood, to cling to the existing *status quo*.

There are some who believe that time and custom, prescriptive right and continuity of possession are good grounds for retaining territory or economic privileges or various forms of property. The war of 1914—in its effects on the Hapsburg Empire or on Germany's overseas possessions, for example—shook the very basis of such "legitimist" doctrine; and in a wider sense France and Britain should have the credit for the democratic ideas and the nationalist teaching which are working to their detriment at the present day.

We are still faced with the question: how can we have an international order that will not simply freeze the *status quo* by its legalistic insistence on the sanctity of the existing order? Even in the eighteenth century it was recognized that the internal development (perhaps the economic development) of one state or another might change the distribution of power in the world and change even the distribution of rights, so that treaties would need revision. Today the existence of an international order depends on our discovery of some method (other than war or revolution or similar acts of violence) for the changing of the *status quo*.

The Communists are bound to have the strategic advantage if they are promoting change, with the wind at their back, while the Western powers are desperately struggling merely to keep the barriers firm. Since public opinion, or world opinion, or the opinion of governments in general has become a powerful factor in the situation, and since the West must depend very much on capturing the opinion and the sympathy of what might be called the uncommitted powers, our future is going to depend on the kind of internationalism which does not attempt to freeze the existing situation in a legalistic manner but takes the lead in predicting and preparing the necessary changes in the *status quo*.

On this view England and France were at fault in that, years ago, they did not foresee how precarious was their situation in the Suez. They ought to have placed the Canal on an international basis so clear and unobjectionable that Nasser would have had neither the motive nor the opportunity for behaving as he did in 1956.

One of the dangers presented by the Afro-Asian peoples—and indeed by all countries which are newly awakened—is that of excessive nationalism. Yet excessive nationalism is just one of those things which expand through any effort to repress them; it is quickened by any suggestion of "colonialism" and stimulated even by the memory of such a thing, and it resents paternalist treatment. There is poor hope for the world if the newly arisen peoples share the infatuations and make the mistakes which characterized the European states at the period when they were at the same stage of development—the same stage of political consciousness.

Yet while the Afro-Asian peoples are still in a sense unachieved— still not formidable as autonomous and well-constituted powers—there is always a danger that if the Western nations withdraw their interest from them, a vacuum will be formed, a vacuum which Soviet Russia will infallibly try to fill. If "colonialism" exists it provokes resentment; if it exists merely in economic forms that seem more appropriate to our age, it is still going to lead to difficulties, and danger is going to arise if the Western nations imagine that all problems can be solved by the power of money. It would be to our interests if the Arab nations were thoroughly modern states, completely independent and autonomous. In fact, their genuine transformation and development are things that cannot happen as quickly as we want them to happen. If they were free, strong, independent modern states, or if they formed a powerful autonomous bloc, the great Russian mass is so very much on the top of them and the danger of the Communist kind of "colonialism" is so real, that nothing could prevent their being on our side in the event of a conflict with communism. Nothing could prevent their being on our side except the suspicion that we retained designs of direct or indirect "colonialism," or the memory of humiliations suffered in the past.

The genius of Britain, discovered both in the internal relations of the home country and in the various parts of its actual Empire, is a curiously flexible method for the changing of the *status quo*—a method which prevented crises from reaching the desperation point, ensured the gradual development of liberty, and provided a model of the kind of change which is just in time to anticipate the resort to violence. It has never been easy to secure the extension of the same technique to the realm of international affairs; and in some respects it is possible that the traditional diplomatic methods (or a continuation of the development they were undergoing already) were more capable of the required flexibility than the legalistic methods which tended to characterize the more recent types of internationalism. This would seem to be one of the things which the world requires at the present day. And a Christianity that disengages itself from the defense of the *status quo* is well fitted to carry on the required conflict—the fundamental moral conflict of our time—the conflict against legalistic and pharisaical notions of righteousness.

June 10, 1957

The Theology of Missions

೧೨‿◡‿೨

Paul Tillich

EVERY ACTIVITY OF THE CHURCH must be derived from the foundation of the Church itself. It must be an activity which follows *necessarily* from the very nature of the Church. Not accidental, but necessary, functions of the Church are the subject of theological consideration.

The theological problem of missions belongs to two groups of theological problems: first, to those which deal with the doctrine of the Church, and secondly, to those which deal with the Christian interpretation of history. The following discussion is not that of an expert. I am not a specialist in missions, but a systematic theologian who is trying to bring the great reality of missions into the framework of a Christian interpretation of history and a Christian doctrine of the Church.

For the Christian interpretation of history the meaning of history is the Kingdom of God.

There are three main riddles of history. History runs toward a goal which is never actualized in history. History runs in one direction, and this direction is irreversible. Historical time moves ahead toward something new, namely, toward the Kingdom of God. The Kingdom of God is the answer to the question, "Toward what does history run?" The answer is, "Toward the realization of the Kingdom of God, through and above history."

History is disrupted into innumerable large and small, comparatively independent historical movements, in different sections of the world, in different periods of time. The question is: If we say "the history," do we not presuppose a unity of history? But this unity is never actual. There are always divergent tendencies. There is always human freedom, which has the power and the possibility of disrupting any preliminary unity of history. Nevertheless, this unity is always intended, and the Kingdom of God is a symbol for the unity of history in and above history.

In history there is always a struggle going on between the forces which try to drive toward fulfillment in the Kingdom of God and its unity and the forces which try to disrupt this unity and prevent history from moving toward the Kingdom of God; or, in a religious-mythological language, there are always conflicts going on in history between divine and demonic forces.

From this it follows that in history there is a continuous mixture of good and evil, in every group, in every agency which carries the historical process, in every period, in every historical actualization. History has a tragic ambiguity; but the Kingdom of God is the symbol for an *un*ambiguous situation, a purification of history, something in which the demonic is conquered, the fulfillment is reached, and the ambiguous is thrown out. In this threefold sense, as fulfillment, unification, and purification of history, the Kingdom of God is the answer to the riddles of history.

Of course, the Kingdom of God seen in this light is not a *stage* of history. It is not a utopia which is somewhere and nowhere. There is no such stage, even in the farthest future of history, because history is always a battlefield of divine and demonic forces. However, history is running *toward* the Kingdom of God. Fulfillment transcends history, but it is fulfilled through history.

The second statement about the Christian interpretation of history is that the historical representative of the Kingdom of God, insofar as it fights in history, is the Christian Church. The Christian Church, the embodiment of the New Being in a community, represents the Kingdom of God in history. The Church itself is not the Kingdom of God, but it is its agent, its anticipation, its fragmentary realization. It is fighting in history; and since it represents the Kingdom of God it can be distorted, but it can never be conquered.

The third statement about the Christian interpretation of history is that the moment in which the meaning of history becomes fully manifest is to be called the center of history, and that this center is the New Being in Jesus as the Christ. In this center the contradictions of historical existence are overcome, in "beginning and power." (This is the meaning of "principle.")

The fourth statement about the Christian interpretation of history is that history is divided by the center of history into two main sections, the period before the center and the period after the center. However, this is true in a different way for different people and different nations. Many people, even today, are still living *before* the event of Jesus as the Christ; others, those who have accepted Jesus as the Christ, are living *after* the center of history. The period before the manifestation of the center of history either in history universally, or in particular individuals, nations and groups, can be called the period in which the bearer of the Kingdom of God in history is latent. It is the period of latency of the Church, the period in which the coming of the Church is prepared in all nations. This is true of paganism, of Judaism, and of humanism. In all three groups and forms of human existence, the Church is not yet manifest, but it is latently present, and it prepares for the coming of the center of history. Then, after the center of history has come and after it has been received by pagans, Jews, and humanists, there is a Christian church in its manifest state, in a state which is no longer preparation, but reception, namely reception of the New Being in Jesus as the Christ.

From this fundamental statement issues directly the meaning of missions. Missions is that activity by the Church by which it works for the transformation of its own latency into its own manifestation all over the world. This is a statement with many implications.

The first consequences are critical consequences, namely, critical against misinterpretations of the meaning of missions. One should not understand missions in a lower sense than this just mentioned. First of all, one should not misunderstand missions as an attempt to save from eternal damnation as many individuals as possible from among the nations of the world. Such an interpretation of the meaning of missions presupposes a separation of individual from individual, a separation of the individual from the social group to which he belongs, and it presupposes an idea of predestination which actually excludes most human beings from eternal salvation and gives hope for salvation only to the few—comparatively few, even if it is millions—who are actually reached by the message of Jesus as the Christ. Such an idea is unworthy of the glory and of the love of God and must be rejected in the name of the true relationship of God to his world.

An attempt to interpret the meaning of missions was made by nineteenth-century liberal theology, namely, the idea that missions is a

85

cross-fertilization of cultures—of the Christian cultures with the Asiatic cultures, first of all. With the primitive cultures it is not so much a cross-fertilization as a transformation into higher cultures. But missions is not a *cultural* function; it is rather the function of the Church to spread all over the world. It is one of the functions of extension of the Church, of its growth; and it is (as growth is generally) an element of a living being without which he finally must die. This is quite different from the idea of cross-fertilization. Cross-fertilization can only claim that the limited values of one culture should be completed by the limited values of another culture. But culture is not the problem of the interpretation of history. Cultures come and go, and the question of the meaning of history transcends any culture and any cultural cross-fertilization. Therefore, since missions is supposed to contribute to the *answer* to the question of the meaning of history, the suggested answer "cross-fertilization" is utterly inadequate.

Moreover, missions is not an attempt to unite the different religions. If this were the function of missions, a uniting point, a uniting center, would have to exist. Then, however, *this* uniting center would be the center of history, and the Christ would have been "decentralized." He would no longer be the center; but the center would be that which is above him and also above Buddha, Mohammed and Confucius. The Christian Church would then be *one* religious group among others, but it would not be the agency of the Kingdom of God, as we have described it and as it always felt itself to be.

The Christ, according to Christian conviction, is *the* center of history and, therefore, the uniting point in which all religions can be united after they have been subjected to the criticism of the power of the New Being, which is in the Christ. Therefore, we must say: missions is neither the attempt to save individual souls, nor an attempt at cultural cross-fertilization, nor an attempt to unite the world religions. Missions is rather the attempt to transform the latent Church, which is present in the world religions, in paganism, Judaism and humanism, into something new, namely, the New Reality in Jesus as the Christ. Transformation is the meaning of missions. Therefore, the mission is a function which belongs to the Church itself; and it is an element, a basic element, in the life of the Church itself.

The transformation of which I spoke is the transformation from the Church in its latency, in its hiddenness, under the forms of paganism, Judaism and humanism, into its manifestation. This refers not only to the nations and groups *outside* of the Christian nations but also to the Christian nations themselves. There must always be missions—or attempts to transform the preparatory state into the manifest state of the Church, not only outside the Christian orbit but also within the Christian orbit. This is because there is always paganism, Judaism and humanism in the midst of the Christian nations themselves.

86

The transformation of the state of latency into the state of actualization is a necessary function of the Church. It is a function which is always present and which has never been missing. There were periods, of course, in which there were no official institutions for missions. However, while institutions are historically changing, functions are unchangeable, as long as there is a Church, because functions belong to the essence of the Church itself. Even in periods in which the mission toward those outside the Christian orbit was very small, it was never completely lacking, because there were always contacts between Christians and non-Christians. Where there are contacts there is witness to Christianity, and where there is witness to Christianity there is implicitly missionary activity. In this sense we can say: the process of transformation is always going on; it is going on both within and outside the Christian nations and cultures. The claim of the Church that Jesus is the bringer of the New Reality for the universe is identical with the demand made upon the Church to spread itself all over the world. And that is what missions does.

Let us now consider this transformation and its theological meaning. There was a discussion, especially in the last period of liberal theology, about the absoluteness of Christianity. Is Christianity the absolute religion? Is Christ the center of history? Is he the bringer of the New Being? Or are the other religions of equal value and does each culture have its own proper religion? Christianity, according to these ideas, belongs to the Western world, and it should not interfere with the religious developments of the Eastern world. This, of course, would deny the claim that Jesus is the Christ, the bringer of the New Being. It would make this statement obsolete, because he who brings the New Being is not a relative figure but an absolute figure of an all-embracing character. The New Being is one, as being itself is one.

This universality of the Christian message, its universal claim, includes what has been called, with a not too happy term, the "absoluteness of Christianity." Let me call it its universality. Now, how can you prove, today, as a Christian, or as a theologian, that the Christian message is universal and valid for all cultures and religions, so that Christ must become what he potentially is, the center of history for *all* historical developments? How can you prove this? The answer obviously is: you cannot prove it at all in terms of a theoretical analysis, for the criteria used in order to prove that Christianity is universal are themselves taken from Christianity. Therefore, they do not prove anything except for those who are in the Christian circle. This means: there is no theoretical argument which can give the proof of the universality of Christianity and the claim that Jesus is the Christ. Only missions can provide that proof. Missionary work is that work in which the potential universality of Christianity becomes evident day by day, in which the universality is actualized with every new success of the missionary endeavor. The action of missions gives the *pragmatic* proof of the universality of Christianity. It is a *pragmatic* proof. It is the proof, as the Bible calls it, of power and Spirit. It is not a theoretical proof, which you can give sitting in your chair and looking at history; but, if you are in the historical situation in which missions are, then you offer a *continuous* proof, a proof which is never finished. The element of faith is always present, and faith is a risk. But a risk must be justified, and that is what missions does. It shows that Jesus as the Christ and the New Being in him has the power to conquer the world. In conquering the world, missions is the continuous pragmatic test of the universality of the Christ, of the truth of the Christian assertion that Jesus is the Christ.

In the same way, missions bears witness on behalf of the Church as the agency of the conquering Kingdom of God. This also cannot be proved in abstract theoretical concepts. Only missions can prove that the Church is the agent through which the Kingdom of God continuously actualizes itself in history. Missionaries come to a country in which the Church is still in latency. In this situation the manifest Church opens up what is potentially given in the different religions and cultures outside Christianity. In some way and on some level, every human being is longing for a new reality in contrast to the distorted reality in which he is living. People are not *outside* of God; they are *grasped* by God, on the level in which they *can* be grasped—in their experience of the Divine, in the realm of holiness in which they are living, in which they are educated, in which they have performed acts of faith and adoration and prayer and cult, even if the symbols in which the Holy was expressed seem to us extremely primitive and idolatrous. It was distorted religion, but it was not non-religion. It was the reality of the Divine, preparing in paganism for the coming of the manifest Church, and through the manifest Church the coming of the Kingdom of God. This alone makes missions possible. One might call this preparation, which we find in all nations, the "Old Testament" for these nations. But I hesitate to do so, because the term "Old Testament" is used, ordinarily and rightly, for a very special preparation, namely for the preparation of the coming of Christ as the center of history through the elected nation.

This leads me to the second consideration: the Church is latent also in the elected nation, i.e., in Judaism. It is prepared in it, so that it can become manifest in it, but it is not yet manifest in it in the full sense of the word. It drives toward manifestation; and certainly the community of the Jewish nation and the community of the synagogue into which Jesus was born are preparatory stages for the coming of the center of history, the Church and the Kingdom of God. But they remain preparatory. They anticipate, in prophetism; and they actualize, fragmentarily and with many distortions, in legalism. However, they are not the manifest Church; they are still the latent Church. If Christianity comes to them, they might or might not accept the transformation out of latency into manifestation. We know that what in some forms of paganism is comparatively easy is in Judaism almost impossible. Paul had this experience. He writes, in Romans 9-11 (one of the great and rare pieces of an interpretation of history in the New Testament) about the question of missions toward the Jews. He believed that this mission to the Jews would not succeed until the pagans would have become members of the manifest Church. One of the great problems of missions toward the Jews today is that we often have the feeling that it is by historical providence that the Jews have an everlasting function in history. "Ever" means as long as there is still history, and, therefore, paganism. The function of Judaism would be to criticize, in the power of the prophetic spirit, those tendencies in Christianity which drive toward paganism and idolatry. Judaism always stood against them as a witness and as a critic, and perhaps it is the meaning of historical providence that this shall remain so, as long as there is history. Individual Jews always will come to Christianity; but the question whether Christianity should try to convert Judaism as a whole is at least an open question, and a question about which many Biblical theologians of today are extremely skeptical. I leave that question open. I, myself, in the light of my many contacts and friendships with Jews, am inclined to take the position that one should be open to the Jews who come to us wanting to become Christians. Yet we should not try to convert them but should subject ourselves as Christians to the criticism of their prophetic tradition.

The third group in which we have the latent Church is humanism. I think not only of Greek, Roman and Asiatic humanism but also of humanism with the Christian nations. There are many people who are critical of Church, Christianity and religion generally. Many times this criticism comes from the latent Church, is directed against the manifest Church, and is often effected through the power of principles which belong to, and should be effective in, the manifest Church itself. Nevertheless, in spite of the important function of the latent Church, it is, as the word "latent" indicates, never the last stage. That which is latent must become manifest, and there is often a hidden desire on the part of people who belong to the latent Church to become members of the manifest Church. This can happen, however, only if the manifest Church accepts the criticism which comes from the latent Church.

These foregoing remarks show that missions is by no means one-sided. There is also missions to the Christians by those non-Christians to whom Christian missions are addressed. What Christian missions have to offer is not Christianity—certainly not American, German, or British Christianity—but the message of Jesus as the Christ, of the New Being. It is the message about Jesus as the center of history which, day by day, is confirmed by missions. It is *not,* however, Christianity as an historical reality that is this center of history. Not cross-fertilization of American culture with Asiatic cultures is the goal of missions, but the mediation of a reality which is the criterion for *all* human history. It stands critically not only against paganism, Judaism, and humanism wherever it may be, but it also stands critical against Christianity, outside and inside the Christian nations. All mankind stands under the judgment of the New Being in Christ.

This leads me to the last point, namely to the praise of what missions has done in creating churches in sections of the world which are outside the Western cultural orbit and which are able, and will be able, to undercut the unconscious arrogance of much Christian missionary work. I speak of the unconscious arrogance which assumes that Christianity, as it has developed in the Western world, is the reality of the New Being in Christ. It is only *one* of its expressions, a preliminary one, a transitory one, as Greek Christianity was, and Roman Christianity was, and Medieval Christianity was. It is not the end. These new Christian churches provide another and one of the greatest and most important proofs for Jesus being the center of history. They demonstrate that his message and the New Being in him were able to overcome not only the resistance of those outside Christianity but also the unconscious and almost unavoidable arrogance of those churches which carried out the missionary work. The fact that there are new churches, in another cultural orbit, developing their independence and resisting the identification of the Kingdom of God with any special form of Christianity, is perhaps the greatest triumph of the Christian missions.

March 4, 1955

Christian Ethics and International Affairs

꧁ ꧂

John C. Bennett

THREE ELEMENTS OF THE CHRISTIAN message should continually illuminate the mind of Christians as they deal with the problems of world politics.

(1) Each nation is under the judgment, providence and mercy of

God. This is a corrective for the most common temptation of any nation —to make itself absolute. But the mere affirmation of an ultimate deity may have little effect, because it is easy for the nation to assume that such a deity is on its side, especially when the adversaries are avowed atheists.

To see the nation under God as revealed in Christ, however, gives a different perspective. God is no vague Almighty who can be made over in the image of one's nation. God as he comes to us in Christ can be seen to be the Father and Lord of all communities of men, who has no favorites among the nations, who cares about justice, about the freedom of men to develop their capacities and to be true to their consciences.

Christians who affirm the transcendence of God above every human group and earthly power must also affirm their faith in the divine involvement in the history of mankind. The Incarnation is the central demonstration of this involvement. Christian understanding of God's transcendence raises questions about the extent of the claims of every historical community or movement or ideal, but these questions are given clearer focus by the fact that they are asked in the light of the revelation of God's solidarity with all men in Christ. The fact that the Church exists in every country points to the revelation that comes to each from beyond its history and culture, and it is another way of expressing God's transcendence of the nation.

(2) The commandment of love for the neighbor, for all neighbors. Christians are expected to reflect in their lives God's love for all mankind. This seems obvious, but it cannot be left unsaid or taken for granted. Love, in terms that are relevant to international politics, means caring for the welfare and the dignity of all—those at a great distance, those on the other side of every boundary, those whose interests may conflict with our national interests, those who are enemies or opponents. It must be translated in terms of empathy, humaneness, a sense of justice, the development of mutual relations between peoples.

Love should inspire Christians as they form or support policies, though of itself it does not determine policy. It should, however, set limits to policy. In this context love should set up a moral obstacle to any policy that assumes readiness to destroy the populations of other countries.

(3) The understanding of man that is implicit in Christian teaching about man's creation in the image of God and the depth and universality of sin. Granting differences between traditions, there is still much that can be said by those who have learned to criticize the one-sided historical optimism of liberal Christianity.

The revival of Protestant theology and the events of our time have encouraged a view of man that respects human dignity but takes a sober view of historical developments. Panaceas and utopias are no longer credible. We now know we live with permanent problems that are the result of man's finiteness and sin. The Christian warning is just as much against cynicism or a fatalistic pessimism as it is against confidence in over-all rational solutions of international problems.

At least two implications for foreign policy may be deduced from these convictions. Both have been illumined by the thought of Reinhold Niebuhr. One is the recognition that schemes of world government are no short-cut to the solution of the problem of international anarchy. For three reasons: First, world community of the sort necessary to sustain an effective world government cannot be created by a constitutional fiat. (One of the strong points of the United Nations is that it is based upon a recognition of the given situation. This situation need not be static, and the moment the nuclear powers reach agreement on arms control or disarmament the UN can assume new functions that might be the functions of an incipient world government.) Second, no legal changes can of themselves change the location of the substantial forms of power, whether military, economic or demographic. Third, the road toward world government must not be taken under the illusion that concentration of power at the center would in itself be an ulti-mate solution, for it might raise new problems of a tyranny on a world scale or of a world-wide civil war to capture the centralized organs of power.

The second implication is a critical attitude toward pacifism as a self-sufficient political party. Pacifism as personal witness or even some-times as the witness of a Church may serve as a corrective. But pacifism as a political party does not take account of the limits of what a govern-ment can do; nor does it take account of the need to find ways of checking power by power if the world is to preserve freedom of choice for nations.

What has come out of all of these considerations is often called Christian political realism, a position that recognizes the limits of ration-ality, the fact of finiteness and sin, and the reality of power that cannot be wished away but which must be checked and used. I have regarded my-self as a Christian political realist. However, this realism has often gained too much momentum of its own and has not been kept under a sufficient degree of Christian criticism.

The original proclamation of this approach was against the back-ground of a too moralistic or idealistic form of Christian social ethics. It emphasized the necessity of choosing between evils, and there was a genuine emancipation in the idea of taking responsibility for the lesser evil and living under the mercy of God. But years of living with this realism during a period in which most of the voices of moral criticism have been silent have too often made it little more than a rationalization of whatever has seemed necessary for Western strategy. What began as a corrective now stands in need of correction.

What are the implications of these theological and ethical convic-tions for the pressing problems of American foreign policy? I shall deal briefly with three areas: (1) The role of nationalism in the emerging nations; (2) The present conflict of ideologies; and (3) The dilemma of nuclear deterrence.

(1) Nationalism has a bad name in Christian circles in the West. It is associated with the familiar chauvinisms, the absolutizing of national sovereignty, the overripe nationalism of National Socialism and Fascism, the grandiose pose of General de Gaulle and American isolationism or self-righteousness. Nationalism in any of these forms must be criticized as a kind of idolatry.

But nationalism in the emerging nations has a constructive role—so long as it avoids idolatry and is open to accommodation and cooperation with neighboring states. The temptation to chauvinism is always present even in the new countries. However, nationalism may often be the means of overcoming tribal conflicts, providing the incentive for loyal and responsible citizenship, and causing people to sacrifice narrow interests for the welfare of the larger national community.

One of the most important meanings of nationalism is that it inspires movements for independence that may lead to significant forms of human freedom. One must walk warily here in view of the danger of the balkanization of a continent.

No Christian answer can be given to the question of which political units are viable or whether one kind of federation or another should become the political unit. These are all relative matters; each case must be discussed on its merits. Yet nationalism can be a great good when it inspires a particular national community to win freedom from external control for the development of its own national life.

Christians must preserve some detachment from the fierce passions of nationalism, but they should not reject the goal of independence that enlists these passions. They need not reject in principle all revolutionary violence, but they should seek to neutralize the hatred and vindictiveness that often accompany it. This is no easy task.

If the most extreme nationalists have the dynamism that is creating the new political community and Christians must choose between supporting their policies or detaching themselves from the forces that are realizing the aspirations of the nation, their dilemma is grave indeed. Both individuals and churches face this predicament. They must live with it and, without separating themselves from their people, find answers that may not satisfy the absolute partisan who claims that he is the only true nationalist.

(2) The relationship between Christian faith and ethics and the ideological conflict of East and West. There is no question that communism, as a total system of life and thought, and Christianity are in radical opposition. Rationalized political terror is the chief symptom of the evil in the Communist absolutism we reject. While much terror exists or is

perpetrated in non-Communist nations today, it seldom becomes a system supported by an interpretation of history.

The struggle will continue within nations and across national boundaries between Christian faith and Communist faith. The religious aspect of the struggle must be carried on by Christians through their witness to the truth as they see it and by deeds of love.

I am concerned here especially with communism as an international force, and I want to address myself to the relationship of the churches to the Cold War as an ideological conflict. I have said on many occasions— usually I am scolded for saying it by American Rightists—that we should avoid identifying the conflict between Christianity and communism with the international conflict. One reason for this has become increasingly clear in recent months. The clash between Christianity and communism is a reality within the Communist nations, and nothing can handicap churches in those nations more than for them to appear to be allies of the West in the international struggle.

A few years ago it may have been plausible to dismiss this consideration on the ground that the leaders of the churches in the Communist countries, especially the Orthodox and Protestant leaders, were collaborators with their governments. Now I am convinced that, however much some of these leaders may be criticized on particular counts, their churches have in important instances preserved independent Christian vitality, and they remain the major organized force bearing witness to the ultimate criticisms of what intends to be a Marxist culture.

The role of these churches is not to serve the policy of the United States but to keep alive in their own societies a deep challenge to the official ideas of God, man and history. In the Soviet Union and in some of the Eastern European countries the Communist ideology is losing much of its power for post-revolutionary generations. We have reason to hope that the Christian churches in those countries, while they may have no direct political influence, will help many people to rediscover God and the true humanity of man.

Another reason for emphasizing the distinction between the international conflict and the religious conflict is that we need to avoid the hardening of differences between nations. Such hardening usually results when the passions of religion and of politics are united. Today we have new opportunities for constructive relationships with Communist countries, and we should be able to deal with them as human communities not fully controlled by any ideology.

One hopeful development in this area is the gradual change that has taken place in the Roman Catholic Church. That Church had seemed to be engaged in a holy war against communism as an ally of the West in its political conflict, but now it seems to have accepted the reality of coexistence. No diatribes against communism were issued by Vatican II. There are many indications that the Roman Church will no longer be a spiritual arm of the West in the Cold War. (The World Council of Churches has sought to avoid that role.)

It is significant that, while McCarthyism was in large measure a Roman Catholic phenomenon, today Catholic authorities seek to discourage Rightist movements. Unfortunately these movements now seem to be a Protestant phenomenon, though it is a sign of the health of Protestantism that its national institutions are under attack by these Rightists.

When we speak of ideologies I must note a development that has become very dangerous to our national sanity and to the peace of the world. It is a type of anti-communism distinguished by the following characteristics: it has no understanding of the causes of communism and emphasizes only self-defeating methods of opposing it; its starting point is a type of economic individualism that cannot tell the difference between the modest institutions of the welfare state in this country and the first stages of communism; and it closes minds to the changes that have taken place in the Communist world. This wild confusion is present in the minds of a small but financially powerful minority, though a much larger part of the population has a tendency to hold rigid ideas about the kinds of economic institutions in other nations with which we should cooperate.

Another problem is our obsession with fears of Communist military attack. A frontal military attack that would destroy the world the Russians hope to change makes no sense from the Communist point of view. These obsessive fears have crowded out all awareness of the degree to which our own immense military superiority is regarded as a threat by the Soviet Union. We have no empathy for the Soviet Union as a human community, and herein, too, lies a great danger to peace.

In discussing this American ideology it is important to emphasize how little the assumptions that govern our policies are publicly debated. People are afraid of being considered soft on communism if they raise serious questions about national attitudes and policies in the Cold War.

An important difference exists between our ideological blinders and those characteristic of the Communist world. Here they are not primarily the creation of the American Government. Indeed, those most responsible for our governmental policy seem to be struggling for freedom to maneuver against the limitations imposed on them by our popular ideology. In the Communist world, blinders are in large part the result of government education, propaganda and censorship.

Our churches, as members of the universal Christian community, may make their major contribution to better international relations by helping the American people to think with greater freedom about the world in which they live. They should tear off all Christian wrappings from the individualistic American ideology. In the context of the Church, Americans should be helped to adjust to the fact that many nations with which we must cooperate are in revolutionary situations, and their governments are certain to be Leftist by our standards. Americans should be helped to see the world as it appears to the Communist nations and to take more seriously the changes that have taken place, especially in the Soviet Union, Poland, and even Hungary. On the political level the most important change in the Communist world is the split between Russia and China, but perhaps on the cultural level the fact of Poland has greater significance.

(3) The dilemma of nuclear deterrence. The dilemma is easily stated: The non-Communist world needs nuclear power to deter Communist nuclear power (to prevent nuclear blackmail and pressure in the interests of Communist expansion); but if we ever use our nuclear weapons, they are likely to destroy all that they defend as deterrents. The dilemma has another dimension: If the deterrent is to be credible, we must not give the impression that under no circumstances would the weapons ever be used.

We can no longer take comfort in the belief that the deterrent will certainly deter and that there will therefore be no need to use the weapons. The chief danger of nuclear war is that it might develop by escalation from a limited military operation.

Not being a pacifist, I cannot suggest an absolute solution of this problem. I can only present considerations that, if taken seriously, might result in the reduction of the number of occasions that could lead to war and in keeping down the degree of violence if war should come. This is not very satisfactory, but there is a vast difference between those who emphasize restraint and those who keep pressing for more provocative and reckless action.

Two aspects of nuclear war need to be emphasized. The first is that nuclear war would not only result in hundreds of millions of casualties and in the material destruction of nations; it would also probably destroy the institutions of freedom and the moral, cultural and political conditions on which our values depend. If we do not realize this, we are likely to say too easily, "Let us accept the casualties for the sake of freedom." But what if freedom is also a casualty?

Secondly I want to emphasize the moral necessity of shifting the emphasis from the fear of being destroyed to awareness of the moral meaning of our being destroyers. Talk about destroying the population centers of other countries springs from a combination of fatalism and callousness. There is much emphasis on a counterforce strategy in the Government, but many people are skeptical as to whether it would be possible to adhere to this. The tendency of both sides to stress invulnerable retaliatory forces undermines this more limited strategy.

Against this background I want to raise several questions.

How can we justify the assumption that we should, at a given point in a military conflict, initiate the use of nuclear weapons in order to avoid a conventional defeat? The possession of nuclear weapons that are kept to deter their use by the other side has some justification, but the moment we accept the actual possibility of our using them to initiate the nuclear stage of a war, we are taking upon ourselves an unexamined moral responsibility. We find ourselves thinking in strategic not moral terms, and we are not very realistic about the consequences of such a choice for the people we might be defending.

When will we cease threatening the use of ultimate violence every time there is a crisis involving Russia? We pride ourselves on being less ruthless than the Communists, but actually our threats seem to presuppose that *any* violent action is permitted, no matter how destructive, if it serves our political purposes. How is this different in principle from the Communist assumption that anything is justified if it serves the revolution?

When will we take seriously our moral responsibility for the effects of our actions upon the hundreds of millions of people who have no part in the decisions and who do not even share our view of the issues at stake? A demonic pretentiousness has developed that needs to be examined. There may have been and there may still be justification for our taking upon ourselves this responsibility in some cases, but there is a danger that it may become an unexamined habit. The same thing can be said of the decision to engage in nuclear tests that have consequences not foreseen by the scientists who plan them and affect distant nations that have no part in the decisions.

When will we begin to evaluate the world conflict in the light of the changes in the Communist world? This means, for one thing, reconsideration of the military threat to us in view of the fact that Mr. Khrushchev has a better understanding of the meaning of nuclear war than either the Chinese or some American Senators. This does not erase the need for a deterrent, but it may affect the degree of power that is needed. It may also help us to keep in view the risks of an unlimited nuclear arms race as compared with the risks involved in disarmament. Perhaps the most important practical point is the need to assure the Administration of support if it does secure agreements on nuclear tests and the reduction of arms. The danger is that such an agreement might not be upheld by the Senate.

Another consideration growing out of the changes in the Communist world is that new alternatives are available. The assumptions underlying our country's attitudes and strategies were based upon the realities of Stalinism. We feared that if we let down our guard we would be inviting the extension of Stalinist terror from country to country. While we still need to preserve deterrent power in the non-Communist world, there can be a gradual change in the feelings on both sides concerning what is at stake in the Cold War.

Such a change may well go with a shift in emphasis from all-out nuclear deterrence to reliance on limited military methods and with a shift away from preoccupation with the military to a search for political and economic alternatives to communism. These shifts have already taken place to some extent, but as "our side" ceases to feel surrounded by a monolithic "slave world" the public may be ready to accept much greater changes in policy.

Though it is difficult to measure the effect on public opinion of the present dependence of our economy on defense spending, this is one factor of great importance in supporting the psychology of the cold war. I do not mean that we are confronted by a capitalistic plot to preserve the arms race. Rather, we face the combination of many local pressures to keep the factories open for the sake of employment. Such pressures can only be met by a national plan not now in sight.

I have moved here from the theological and ethical convictions that should guide the mind of the Church to many concrete issues about which there is no uniquely Christian guide.

I have concentrated on issues that require changes in assumptions. These issues call for wisdom on the part of policy-makers, but my chief concern is to counteract pressures upon the Government by vociferous elements in the public.

The churches at this point have a great responsibility not to advocate over-all idealistic solutions but to emphasize the distinctively Christian message that is relevant to these issues, to help their members to see the world without the characteristic American ideological blinders, to challenge many of the prevailing assumptions about the cold war and nuclear armaments, and to encourage the debate on public questions about which most people prefer to be silent. In this way our churches can be, more clearly than they are at present, part of the world-wide Christian community that never allows us to forget the humanity of those beyond the barriers that limit our understanding.

August 5, 1963

The Danger of Disillusionment with Africa

Robert C. Good

WE ARE IN DANGER OF BECOMING disillusioned with Africa. Like the proper ladies of a recent cartoon, we thought we were attending a lecture on "African violets" and discovered to our dismay that the topic was really "African violence." If we are upset by our disappointed hopes, we will be tempted to wash our hands of Africa. This will be Africa's great loss, and our own.

Paradoxically, our trouble arises partly from our fine anti-colonial and liberal traditions. It was not very long ago that we placed unquestioning faith in those touchstones of the new age, self-determination and collective security. Self-determination would liquidate one of the chronic causes of war—the unfulfilled demand for independence on the part of subjugated nationalities. Collective security would assure stability for a self-determined world in which all would guarantee the right of each to its own dependence.

We no longer suffer the illusions of liberal international political theory. But we are only beginning to realize that, far from a solution to the problems of disorder and far from the guarantor of amicable relations, the era of independence-for-everyone simply reshapes the frame within which the persistent problems of politics must be viewed.

Not understanding this, we may become, as Charles Burton Marshall has suggested, the victims of our own "revolution of rising expectations" concerning our relations with the new African states. For deep down we hoped, and half expected, that once the hue and cry of the colonial revolt was past, we would be able to associate ourselves with democratic, Western-oriented African governments seeking their orderly development in relative concord with one another—an association free from the rigors of the cold war (for, after all, "there are no Communists in Africa") and free, too, from the constant embarrassment of compromise between colonial and anti-colonial interests that has characterized our Afro-Asian policy.

Regrettably, none of these expectations bears much relationship to reality. Our first responsibility, then, is to apprehend what is real—neither ignoring it nor excusing it, but understanding it. For disillusionment is the consequence of misunderstood facts and misplaced hopes. African actualities may be set forth in five propositions.

(1) Most of the new African states will not be democratic, as we understand democracy; in general they will be one-party states.

The trend in Africa is clearly toward regimes that either forbid an organized opposition or fetter the opposition sufficiently to make it politically meaningless. Sekou Touré of Guinea expresses this trend in its most radical form when he says: "The Government and the [National] Assembly are for nothing except to apply the decisions of the party."

Democracy is based upon meaningful restraints on the exercise of power. But the problem in many of the new African states is not to restrain power, but to accumulate sufficient power to make the government's writ effective across the land. Democracy presupposes countervailing power sufficient to bring the government to account in its management of the public's business. But in many African states, social and economic resources are too thin to provide for the construction of more than one pinnacle of power—that of the party and the government it controls.

It is loyalty to the ruling party that gives access to influence and wealth, quite unattainable in equal measure outside the party. In Senegal, a major oil company selected twenty-seven of its brightest employees for executive training. Two years later all but two were in the Government.

Democracy demands a sense of the commonweal so compelling that the ruling elite and those who compete for leadership see themselves and each other as trustees of some larger interest than that of class or section. But the "opposition," such as it is, tends in many African states to express not national but tribal or sectional loyalties and interests. It is, therefore, condemned as unpatriotic or even subversive.

In short, autocracy in Africa is a response to the problem of building a nation. None of these states is founded on a deep, historical consciousness of nationhood; to the contrary, almost all are artificial creations of the colonial era, and the personal loyalties of most individuals extend no farther than the tribe. Their countries have been recognized as independent national states abroad; leaders now must create viable national societies at home. To overcome parochialism, great stress is placed on the omnipresent legitimacy of the national party and on the person of the national leader.

(2) Independent Africa will not evolve with orderly progress but, from time to time, will conjure up grave disorders and injustice.

It is strange how naive we are concerning the political dynamics of the new states. We are tempted to think that chaos in the Congo is a terrible mistake. That centralism in Guinea is the regrettable result of Communist subversion. That Nasserism is the unfortunate vainglory of one man.

The naïveté with which we approach the political realities of the new states is the consequence of the sublimated character of our own political processes. In developed Western countries, political competition is muffled by a long history, by long-established institutions, and by the gradual emergence of a large area of consensus concerning the rules of the game, the basic values underlying the political process, and procedures for arbitrating our most serious political cleavages.

Within the new states these sources of cohesion—history, institutions and agreement concerning the rules of the game—are minimal. Such as they are, they have begun to emerge only very recently under the tutelage of colonial rule, or still more recently in rebellion against colonial rule. Political power has been achieved first; the procedures and institutions necessary to make power compatible with justice and with the requirements of orderly change are still to be developed.

All this is only to say that the situation in many African states—the chaos of the Congo, the kidnapping of a government in Kivu Province, the extremes of strong-man rule and of what Mr. Nehru calls the "grave fissiparous tendencies" of the new states—are not the exception to the rule nor the aberration; often they *are* the rule, the reality. We ought not be quite so dismayed that this is the case.

More than eighty years after the Union was founded, the United States endured one of history's bloodiest wars in order to maintain an integrated political society. For all of its ancient institutions, its long history and its ardent nationalism, France continues to suffer from "grave fissiparous tendencies." And the most cursory review of political developments in Latin America over the past century ought to teach that the development of satisfactory political life is surrounded by vast difficulties.

Developing relations between the new African states do not augur well for stability either. We think of Africa too simply if we think only of Africa "aspiring to be free." For most African leaders, what counts is how freedom will be used to reconstruct Africa. To this end, there are about as many plans as there are leaders. Increasingly, Africa's turbulence will arise, not from the struggle against a declining foreign order, but from the clash of competing African conceptions of Africa's future.

We had a vivid example of this clash a few weeks ago. Early in January, five African neutralist states met in Casablanca. They gave strong support to Lumumba, proclaimed their distrust of de Gaulle's policy in Algeria and denounced Mauritania as a French "puppet state." Three of the five, meeting later in the capital of Guinea, condemned "all regroupings of African states based on the languages of colonial states."

Only a few days before, however, just such a grouping had convened in Brazzaville. There the leaders of twelve French-speaking African states acknowledged the legitimacy of the Kasavubu government, indicated their confidence in de Gaulle's Algerian policy and agreed to press for Mauritanian membership in the UN.

(3) Most of the new African governments will not be Western-oriented; they will be neutralist—some with a pro-East slant.

There are exceptions to the neutralist mood of emergent Africa. But they are giving ground rapidly. Not long ago it was expected that Nigeria would be tied closely to the West. It is now clear that Nigeria will tolerate no strings to its independence. The statesmen of former French Africa who praised French liberality at the UN last fall were speaking with deep sincerity. But the fact that each of these states opted for independence from France indicates the swiftness of the tidal flow in

Africa and the pull it exerts, through the young radicals in each regime, on those in control.

The rising tide is that of Africanism—not French Africanism, nor British, nor least of all "Western"—but a fixation on the future as Africa's future and a reconstruction of the past as Africa's past.

Just as important, there is, one suspects, an unexpressed conviction among many African leaders that Africa can be held erect as an independent area only if it can skillfully balance the pressures of both East and West. We may deplore the opportunities in this situation for international blackmail. But these opportunities are built-in; we had better get used to them.

From the point of view of these relatively impotent countries, however, this is not blackmail. It is the equally ancient but more honorable art of maintaining political equilibrium. If you are almost totally independent on the outside world for your expertise, your capital, your education (the list is endless), you had better diversify your dependence sufficiently so that there will always be an "alternative" should the influence of one side or the other become too imposing.

For some leftist governments, like that of Ghana, "positive neutralism" sometimes is interpreted as a rather silly, not to say dangerous, mathematical balance between East and West. If three thousand Ghanaian students attend Western universities, Kwame Nkrumah observed the other day, we must send three thousand to the East.

But the trend is not limited to radical governments. In Morocco, the left-wing government of Abdullah Ibrahim was ousted by royal fiat last spring and the conservative Crown Prince Moulay Hassan was invested with governmental authority. Yet, paradoxically, conservative Morocco has continued to move to the left in foreign policy, partly to contain its dissident radical opposition, but also to pursue the first requirement for independence—neutralism based on an attempt to balance the preponderant dependence on France by expanding trade, aid and diplomatic ties with the East.

(4) The collapse of colonialism in Africa will not release us from embarrassing political choices; it will only change the form of these choices.

We have often assumed that our chronic embarrassment, standing as we have between the colonialism of Europe and the anti-colonialism of Afro-Asia, will disappear as the colonial system is dismantled. Once Europe is out of Africa, we thought, we will be able to support African aspirations without having to worry about our relations with our allies. We will have a *real* African policy, uncompromised by "colonial thinking." But history seldom comes wrapped in such neat parcels.

Conflicts of interest between the former metropole and its former colonies do not conveniently terminate with independence. There are cases in which they get worse. And frequently we are confronted with the agony of choice. When Tunisia's Bourguiba, over French protests, asked for small arms from Britain and the United States, we could not please both France and Tunisia. We chose the latter. When the issue of Mauritania's admission to the UN split France and Morocco, we could not satisfy both. We chose quite correctly to back Mauritania, thereby supporting France and slighting Morocco.

Nor with independence do the legitimate interests of our European allies automatically terminate in their former colonies. Belgium, for example, has very real interests in Moise Tshombe's Katanga, as does France in President Ahidjo's Cameroun Republic. In contemporary African politics, both are controversial governments. Our policies respecting them must weigh with care the conflicting views of a variety of states with which we wish to maintain good relations. Again, the end of colonialism brings no escape from politics, the very essence of which is choice in situations where one confronts incompatible demands.

Incompatible demands are arising also from political issues indigenous to Africa. Whenever possible, we should refrain from taking sides in Africa's struggle to define its own destiny. But occasions will arise when we shall not be able to remain aloof. We shall have to take sides. That time is now upon us in the Congo.

(5) In Africa we face not an escape from the rigors of the cold war, but competition on a new front.

Despite African protests to the contrary, the cold war is in Africa and cannot now be exorcised from Africa. East and West are competing vigorously for the friendship of the continent.

In this competition, the West enjoys some obvious advantages. Most African governments are receiving important aid from the West: Expatriate civil servants for their bureaucracies, education for their cadres, loans and technical assistance for their development programs, training and weapons for their armies.

But there are serious disadvantages for the West and we might as well be fully aware of them. First, Africa has won, or is in the act of winning, emancipation from Western, not Soviet, imperial rule. Western imperialism is a part of Africa's experience; Soviet imperialism is only a part of an hypothesis. Moreover, the Communist bloc has been an ally in the task of dismantling colonialism in Africa. Second, the Communists offer models for development and political integration that appear to be much more relevant to African needs than the opulent and libertarian societies of the West. The example of disciplined, austere, bootstrap-lifting Red China is more and more frequently invoked by many African leaders. Third, Africans want to give tangible evidence that they are in fact independent; there is a natural inclination to do so by opposing positions taken by those Western powers to whom they were so long subservient.

Finally, there is a natural concurrence of interests between the more "radical" African regimes and the Communist bloc. Neither endorses the *status quo;* both seek to disrupt existing relationships between Africa and Europe. The radical African regimes—Ghana, Guinea and Mali, for example—want to reduce Europe's influence in Africa to a minimum and, as quickly as possible, to transform existing political units into a true pan-African state. The Communists naturally support any move designed to undo Europe's position and enthusiastically support the centralist, socialist, pan-Africanist objectives of the radical regimes.

Similarly, there is a natural concurrence of interests between the more "conservative" regimes and the West; both want to maintain the stability of the present system. This is particularly true of France, which is closely identified with the more conservative regimes of its former colonies. Thus, intra-African disputes, as in the case of the Congo, are likely to polarize into "radical" and "conservative" positions, with Communist bloc and Western involvement an ever-present danger.

In a continent as vast and volatile as Africa, any generalization will be challenged, and exceptions are almost as easy to produce as the "rules" themselves. Thus the outlook for democratic institutions is much brighter in federated Nigeria than in unitary Ghana. The road to pan-African cooperation may not be nearly as rough in East Africa (Kenya, Tanganyika and Uganda) as in West Africa. Prospects for stability in Guinea and Ghana are vastly greater than in the Congo.

Yet the generalizations reviewed above represent trends that will be ignored only at the risk of serious disillusionment. They should, above all, instruct us to be sober in defining our expectations for Africa. But under no circumstances should they prompt defeatism. We may not like the trend toward autocracy in many new African states, but we ought to be realistic enough to understand that, excessive though it will be in many cases, state centralism is a response to the very real problem of developing the requisites of order and progress in fragmented, traditional societies.

We may be offended at the gauche and sometimes irresponsible neutralism of the new Africa. But, removed from the periphery of the Communist bloc, Africa does not present the same security problems as most areas in the Middle East, South and Southeast Asia. A neutralist Africa is not inimical to our interests.

We may be alarmed, and properly so, at the leverage the Communist bloc is developing on many of the more radical African states. But African radicals, with only a very few exceptions, are not Communists.

Even those who call themselves Marxists see their future not in terms of a Communist order, but in terms of an African order.

We will be required time and again to weigh our obligations to Europe against our obligations to Africa, and our interests in one bloc of African states against our interests in an opposing bloc. Whenever possible we must avoid intervention in purely African struggles, leaving to Africans the responsibility of putting their own house in order.

Using the UN and other channels, we must work to prevent the partition of the continent into rival spheres of the great powers. But Soviet adventurism combined with the reckless ambitions or the revolutionary fervor (the two are hard to distinguish) of some African states may create situations in which we are required to intervene. When such occasions arise, it is fatuous to suppose we will be able to support all factions all the time.

Independent Africa is irrevocably entering the international political arena. It cannot remain isolated from the forces that agitate the world, nor can we from the forces that agitate Africa.

Still, it is not a contradiction to insist that our guiding principle must be to maintain access to all of Africa. It would be tragically premature if we were to write off this or that state, particularly during this period when more and more Africans are reacting emotionally to colonialism and to the West, and are determined to experiment with a variety of political, economic and social forms. In extreme cases, "access" may mean nothing more than a holding operation against a future when relations may be improved. But I am inclined to think that, given the potentialities of our aid programs and the possibilities inherent in imaginative diplomacy, the opportunities everywhere in Africa are much broader.

March 20, 1961

The Chinese Revolution in Historical Perspective

꒰ஐ꒱

Edward B. Jolliffe, Q. C.

LET US BEGIN BY RECOGNIZING THE OBVIOUS. The Chinese Revolution was and is a revolution in the full sense of the word and not merely a change of government such as every country experiences from time to time. It was much more than the establishment of discipline and stability after a long period of disruption and division. This revolution had the quality of all the great revolutions in history; that is, it was made possible by the decline and collapse of an ancient social order, which was finally brought to an end, through war and civil war, by a single-minded group that was not only hostile to the old but determined to create a new order.

A second and equally obvious generalization is this: It is extraordinarily difficult for even the most rational man to regard a revolution in historical perspective—unless it happened more than a century ago. We can look back on the British Revolution of the seventeenth century and the American and French Revolutions of the eighteenth century with calm detachment, almost with indifference. Yet all of them overturned what had been assumed to be eternal verities. They all took heresies and transmuted them into orthodoxy—and all had a part in shaping the modern world. Many of their slogans and doctrines are part of the Western heritage; we give them lip service at least and tend to accept them without question.

The trouble with the Chinese Revolution is that we are all its contemporaries. And contemporaries have difficulty looking at it objectively or in perspective, whether they be victors or victims, participants or observers, in China or abroad. The cost of revolutions comes high, not only in human life but in the human passions they arouse. And, as in war, among the first casualties are the truth and rationality.

We have all noticed two extreme attitudes. One is the extremist who takes the romanticized or idealistic view that revolutionary change is glorious and desirable in itself, the dynamic force in the painful upward progress of mankind, the best if not the only way of achieving necessary social change. The other extremist believes that every revolutionary movement is purely destructive and evil in itself, and must be suppressed or contained, that even a social and political volcano should be capped, if it is at all possible to do so.

To regard revolution *per se* as either good or evil is an error. Certainly the deliberate violence, the calculated cultivation of hatred, the massive injustice—the high price of revolution (or counter-revolution)—are repugnant to civilized men. They cannot be reconciled with the Christian ethic. But there are times and places when the *only* alternatives may seem equally repugnant, equally irreconcilable and so unacceptable to so many people that revolution has become inevitable.

It was inevitable in China. When did it begin there? Not in our day, but during or just after the lifetime of Robert Morrison, with the arrival in China of our traders, diplomats, gunboats—and our missionaries. In 1949 it came to full term. It has not reached maturity, as the Russian Revolution has, and it will *not* be mature for some years to come.

In a truly revolutionary situation men may be faced with an unacceptable *status quo* and an unacceptable remedy. The revolutionary, the

Edward B. Jolliffe, Q. C.

counter-revolutionary, the unprincipled opportunist and the pure pacifist know exactly what to do. But for some men there is a *moral* problem, not easily solved, and it can be a severe trial of conscience. This has been true of many Chinese churchmen in recent years.

Let us now consider certain features of the Chinese Revolution that concern all of us. In the perspective of history they are not unique; in some degree we find them in all great revolutions.

The first is that, for better or for worse, the Chinese Communist Party has wrought great changes in China. They are not superficial or merely political. They go very deep and have destroyed much of what seemed indestructible and unchangeable. This is not to say that they have discarded all that was Chinese; on the contrary, they have adopted or adapted most skillfully parts of their ancient heritage, including even a few Confucian concepts under different names.

As revolutionists they always took full advantage of the old doctrine that the unworthy ruler may forfeit the mandate of Heaven, which is a potentially revolutionary doctrine and a far cry from the misguided faith of King Charles I in the divine right of kings. They have created a new way of life for about one-quarter of the world's population; and, for those born since 1949, they are creating a new man. The transformation is more intensive and certainly more speedy than that of any previous revolution.

The second feature is that the People's Republic has been ruthless to its enemies, the supporters and beneficiaries of the old regime. We need only recall what was done, or permitted to be done, to the rural landlords. The Chinese Communists, however, have behaved with much more intelligence and restraint than the Russians did forty years ago. They did *not* liquidate the businessmen and traders; instead, a tremendous effort has been made to enlist their cooperation and to recondition or re-educate them to give useful service in a new society, as many of them are doing.

Earlier revolutionaries were not particularly kind to their enemies either. King Charles I was beheaded by the British, of all people. Louis XVI of France and thousands of others were guillotined. Revolutionists who come to power by killing find it hard to stop, and the threat of counter-revolution can always be used to justify anything. Even in America, the loyalists were cruelly persecuted, and many of them were driven to endure the horrors of exile.

The third significant feature of the Chinese Revolution is what some people would term totalitarianism. But that word has acquired special significance, making it almost a proper name. A more appropriate word might be universalitarianism, which will perhaps eventually be shortened to Maoism: The system of thought that claims to provide an answer for every human situation, public or private, collective or individual.

It is not totalitarianism in that it does tolerate the existence of non-Communist thought and non-Communist groups, provided they are not significantly anti-Communist; i.e., a few political parties, such as the Democratic League, and certain churches and church groups. Theoretically it recognizes that a hundred flowers may bloom in the same garden, and it does encourage controversy and disputation within well-marked garden walls. In practice the People's Republic insists upon conformity or cooperation and tolerates some dissent about the means but *not* about the ends. While admitting personal fallibility it constantly asserts the infallibility of the system.

The temptation to claim a monopoly of the truth is not new. And perhaps no revolution can really succeed without absolute faith in itself.

The universalitarianism of the Maoist faith has a very important international consequence. The Chinese Communists are absolutely certain the peoples of South America, Africa and particularly Southeast Asia must necessarily travel not exactly the same road but a road to liberation and national development very similar to that taken by the Chinese. And they are prepared to provide more help in that direction than they themselves received from the Soviet Union, which was not very much.

To regard this phenomenon as proof of Chinese imperial ambitions or as a policy of world conquest would be an error. In appreciating Chinese policy today we must carefully distinguish between Maoist nationalism and Maoist ideology. Some Chinese territorial claims are strictly national and not ideological; on these Mao Tse-tung and Chiang Kai-shek have always agreed and always will. For example, they both hold that Formosa is part of China, that Tibet is part of Greater China, that the border with India is not where the Indians say it should be. On the other hand, it is the ideology of Maoism and its interpretation of so-called Leninism that has generated the bitter quarrel between Moscow and Peking and stirs the fears and apprehensions of the West.

Stripped of all the jargon, the quarrel with Moscow turns on a simple issue: Moscow has concluded that it is better to accept or tolerate the *status quo* than risk a nuclear war; Peking unyieldingly asserts that history inexorably demands constant struggle and the acceptance of risks rather than the acceptance of the *status quo*. What began as an argument about priorities has become a chasm, very wide and very deep.

The main point is that we must recognize that the Maoist faith is held by at least twelve million or more members of the Chinese Communist Party with utter certainty. They believe that the peoples oppressed by colonialism or neo-colonialism must be liberated from the imperialists, by their own efforts but with aid and comfort from China, and further, that the colonialists and imperialists never withdraw voluntarily but only when driven out by force. This belief is held with the same kind of certainty or fanaticism with which the Crusaders went forth to liberate the Holy Sepulcher. And it admits no compromise with imperialism, any more than the Pope could compromise or coexist with the Saracen in Jerusalem.

At the moment we need not debate the hoary thesis that history repeats itself. However, we know that other revolutions have had their periods of expansive missionary zeal.

For some time after the Reformation, British power, naval, military and political, was used, sometimes vigorously, to promote or defend Protestant interests in Western Europe.

The French Revolution declined to remain within the borders of France. Not only its armies but its ideas overflowed throughout Europe and the Western Hemisphere, and it was the ideas, not the armies, that left their imprint on Western civilization.

Obviously the American Revolution was much more than a military victory. It produced a Declaration of Independence and a Constitution embodying radical ideas that were contagious, and the contagion spread from the Rio Grande to Cape Horn.

We sometimes forget that the United States, to the extent possible in those days, gave considerable aid and comfort throughout Central America and South America to the eviction of the Spanish, Portuguese and other European imperialists. Among those liberated from Spain, and by *war,* was Cuba.

There is more to this than national pride. When any nation becomes strong, particularly after a revolution, it soon develops a sense of its historic role. The generals and the admirals acquire expanding horizons so that the nation takes a new and wider view of national security, and prepares to resist all interference in its own sphere of influence. In 1823, the United States, after a successful revolution, had become the strongest power in the Western Hemisphere. In that year President James Monroe announced a policy that became known as "the Monroe Doctrine" that is still American policy.

Monroe stated two principles in these words:

(1) The American continents, by the free and independent conditions which they have assumed and maintained, are henceforth not to be considered as subjects for future colonization by any European powers;
(2) We should consider any attempt on their part to extend their system to any portion of this hemisphere as dangerous to our peace and safety.

The attitude expressed in these words is exactly the attitude that will be taken by a powerful China in the Far East. The Peking Government has already demanded that the United States withdraw from the

Western Pacific. Of this we will hear a great deal more in the future. It is not unusual for a great power to take that attitude; and it is not necessarily an expression of communism. In fact, that has been the demand of all Chinese nationalists for a hundred years.

Whether or not history repeats itself, there is a cycle in the course of great revolutions. They begin with agitation and organization, often initiated by writers and intellectuals rather than politicians; they develop into armed revolt; they pass through a period of disorder and civil war. Then the successful revolution becomes intensely preoccupied with the vital necessity of remaining in power at all costs; its leaders are keenly aware of the retrogressive impulses in society and the dangers of counter-revolution.

The regime is led by men who have come to power the hard way, by risking their lives through the fires of war, and they do not wish to risk them again. They continue to be militant, intolerant, suspicious, but they are always supremely confident that they are right and that history will so recognize. Oliver Cromwell, George Washington, Robespierre and Lenin never doubted they were right. Nor does Mao Tse-tung.

But revolutions also mature. Then the convulsive social changes once painfully begun become so strongly established and consolidated that it is no longer possible to have a restoration—there is no danger of counter-revolution. By this time the original leaders are gone; they have been succeeded by other leaders and teachers—and preachers—who grew up in the new order and care nothing for the old, because the old order is only history and is no part of their lives.

Now, clearly, the Russian Revolution attained maturity some time ago, perhaps with the death of Stalin. The Chinese Revolution is still very much of a revolution. The point of maturity in China may be postponed or deferred for many years, and much longer than necessary, by the isolation of China, the embargoes, boycotts and other hostile acts of certain powers, by the constant threat of attack and the blockading of important ports on the South Coast. As long as these measures continue, we cannot realistically expect the Chinese leadership will cease to be militant, defiant, dogmatic.

Western churches, and particularly churchmen in the United States, have been greatly impressed by the anti-religious bias of Chinese communism.

To put this matter in some perspective, let us remember that religion has been deeply involved in every great revolution. Cromwell and his Puritans were hostile and repressive toward all those not Puritan, and Britain continued to discriminate against Roman Catholics until a century ago. The American Revolution had an anti-clerical bias and constitutionally separated Church and State, which most Americans forget until reminded of it by the Supreme Court. The French Revolution was anti-clerical or even anti-religious. Evidence is available that the Russian

Revolution, at least until recently, was more hostile to organized religion than the Government of Communist China.

While Chinese Communists remain anti-religious on ideological grounds, having in effect made Maoism their religion, the Chinese mind is realistic and does not expect people to renounce their faith. The Christian minority may have to surrender their schools and hospitals, but they are not required by law to give up their worship. The official position is stated in Article 88 of the Constitution of 1954: "Citizens of the People's Republic of China enjoy freedom of religious belief."

In practice the regime has been developing a strange modern variant of an established church. The Chinese Buddhist Association, the Islamic Association, the National Committee of Protestant Churches in China for Self-Administration have had official recognition. They are granted priorities for such essentials as printing paper and building repair materials. They sometimes get subsidized, and their leaders sit in the National People's Congress and in even higher bodies. Before becoming too indignant about this, perhaps we should remind ourselves that British bishops still sit in the House of Lords, and Her Majesty's Government has an effective voice in certain appointments.

By the same token, Western visitors to China have sometimes been shocked to see in church near the pulpit the brilliant red flag with the five stars. But have we never seen the Union Jack or the Stars and Stripes near a pulpit or altar?

Chinese Christians are faced with an acute form of a problem as old as the Church itself: How to reconcile the claims of patriotism with the claims of their faith. Before any judgments are passed on her Protestant clergy, or on certain of the Roman Catholic clergy, it would be proper to ask, "Has *anyone* ever really resolved the ancient Christian dilemma of just *how much* should be rendered unto Caesar?"

In China that dilemma is probably more acute than it has ever been anywhere, for important historic reasons.

In a few words, the Western impact on China in the nineteenth century and the first half of this century not only undermined an ancient society but subjected the Chinese people to a long period of national frustration, humiliation and despair. There is no need to detail the story of their crushing defeats in war, of the unequal treaties, foreign concessions and extraterritorial rights, foreign gunboats patrolling their rivers, foreign troops on Chinese soil. Or how they lost Vladivostok to Russia, Hong Kong and Weihaiwei to the British, part of Indochina to France, Formosa to Japan, Tsingtao and Kiaochow Bay to the Germans (as the result of the murder of two German missionaries), Manchuria to Russia —and then Japan.

Of course, this was the same period in which thousands of Protestant missionaries and a new wave of Roman Catholics arrived in China. Inescapably they fell under the protection of their own governments and the unequal treaties, sometimes under the protection of the gunboats.

They could not possibly renounce extraterritorial rights, their own nationality or their own obligations as citizens of foreign countries. Inevitably they came to be identified with imperialism not only by the Communists but also by many other Chinese patriots. They labored under handicaps the Western churches did not fully appreciate. One who has never been a missionary may be permitted to say that it is not remarkable they had so little success in China; what is really remarkable is that they had as much success as they did.

Now we face a period of tension, probably increasing tension, between Communist China and certain Western powers. We cannot expect much improvement in the near future.

March 8, 1965

Authoritarianism and Democracy in Asia

⟨ ✿ ⟩

M. M. Thomas

MILITARY REGIMES HAVE EMERGED IN several countries in Asia, most of which have attained national independence in the recent past. Egypt, Iraq, Sudan, Burma, Pakistan and Thailand have generals at the head of their governments.

The trends underlying the emergence of these regimes are interpreted differently. To Indians, the Western concern appears to pivot around the question: Has it strengthened or weakened the Western bloc militarily? There has been rather strong criticism here regarding this attitude and the unconcern of the "free world" for the democratic constitutions and free institutions in Asia.

Those people in the West and in Asia who assume that democracy cannot take root in Asian countries are doing a great disservice to democracy. For if this assumption becomes the prevalent mood, then it is easy for the West to be interested only in getting Asian nations on its side in its power struggle with the Communists. The problem of relating democratic forces to the new nations is ignored. At this point, Asians themselves begin to believe that their only choice is either an authoritarianism of the Right or a totalitarianism of the Left, thus further weakening the forces of democracy in the middle. The trend toward authoritarianism in the form of military rule has strengthened this general mood.

Democracy is a difficult form of government, and it needs a cultural basis that has always been hard to obtain in any country. But through the struggle for democracy, democratic institutions and values found cultural roots in the West; and through the impact of the West, Asian cultures are also in process of re-formation.

Anyone who despairs of democratic reorganization in Asia today is denying the sense of world mission of the best among the Western rulers in Asia and the vision of the best among the leaders of Asian nationalism. Such despair is a denial of the meaning of Asian political history of the last 150 years.

The difficulties involved in such reconstruction are great; but the advocates of democracy, either in the West or in Asia, should not let difficulties become an argument for giving up the struggle for free and responsible societies in Asia. This article takes for granted that the political goal for which Asia, strengthened by the West, must strive is the growth of democratic political structures with necessary modifications for its effective functioning in a dynamic situation and with roots imbedded in a re-examined indigenous culture.

The Christian churches of Asia, lacking an adequate theological orientation in the areas of politics, have alternated between a too-easy identification of Christianity with democratic ideology on the one hand and, on the other hand, a too-dangerous assumption that because democracy is not the Kingdom of God, Christians have no ultimate stake in the struggle for a democratic structure. This ambivalence is also shown by adherents of secular and non-Christian faiths.

Fundamental questions for democrats everywhere are raised by the current trend towards authoritarian military rule. Western democrats should ask themselves if their present system of military alliances in Asia strengthens or weakens the forces of freedom and responsibility in these countries. I believe these forces of national health, self-government and self-development have been weakened. Although in one or two cases these alliances were made necessary by the immediate situation, there was no such compulsion in other cases, and the tragedy imposed was not the inevitable resolution of the problem.

It is encouraging to learn that there seems to be a growing realization in the West of the necessity to relate more positively to plans for social change and economic development instead of concentrating exclusively on the military.

For democrats in countries now under authoritarian rule, the problem is to work in such a way that the military rulers will adopt policies in the social and economic realms sufficient to destroy the hold of feudal economy and religio-ethnic separatism while strengthening the new middle class that eventually may reinstate democratic regimes. Although most of the generals now in power consider their rule as "temporary" and promise to bring back democratic institutions, this does not guarantee it will happen. Yet, this makes it possible for democrats to work for the transformation to which the generals say they are committed. This is especially true in countries where the military has no totalitarian ideology and has not disturbed civil government and institutions of local self-government.

The advent of military regimes also has lessons for democratic parties and leaders in countries like India where faith in democratic values is still strong and democratic institutions are devoloping. Anti-democratic forces operating in these countries are similar to the forces that led to authoritarian regimes in Red China and elsewhere. When Nehru and Sukarno say "It can't happen here," they mean, I suppose, that their people can prevent it, if they want to. This requires implementation of national policies to effectively counter forces that may lead to the breakdown of democratic order.

What can countries like India learn from the problems of the newly independent countries that have fallen under military rule? I should like to deal briefly with several problem areas that I consider crucial.

It was imperialist rule, Western education and national struggle for freedom that instilled and developed the sense of nationhood into Asian countries. With independence, it has become necessary to develop this sense of national solidarity as the basis for the new nation-states. This *national* unity, however, comes into conflict with the only sense of solidarity that Asians have known for ages: the solidarity of narrow communal groupings based on religion, caste, language, provincial interest and family loyalty.

Moreover, these traditional communal solidarities have, with adult franchise, attained a new self-consciousness and are forging new political weapons so that today communalism has become more militant than ever. The franchise will no doubt weaken communalism in the long run by developing new loyalties and interests that cut across traditional communal ones. But in the short run, it gives these groups a new power, and the franchise is generally exercised on a communal basis. Thus the state has now become the arena of communal rivalries.

In India, after religious communalism had been weakened by the secular state, casteism and "linguism" have become real obstacles to the emergence of national community. In regard to the caste-communalism, it has been noted that today "no explanation of provincial politics in any part of India is possible without reference to caste." Sinhalese-Tamil riots in Ceylon, the insurrection of ethnic groups in Burma, regional revolts in Indonesia, East-West tensions in Pakistan and the prevalence of fanatic religio-political parties in most countries—all point to the strength of communalism in basic contradiction to the necessity for national unity.

In the face of such basic conflicts, the political unity that a centralized army can bring has a certain appeal. The army can bring order by force, but more than this, the army frequently has a national character and is capable of being impartial in intercommunal rivalries and of looking after national interest. A combination of factors, including emergencies, can bring the army to the top with popular acclaim as the only saviour of the nation-state.

Though military rule has a legitimate role in cases of communal violence or regional revolt, it cannot solve the problem of communalism. The road to national unity lies not in the suppression of communal self-awareness but in the give and take of intercommunal tensions in the context of living and growing together in freedom.

As R. W. Taylor recently wrote: "Perhaps a vital value of inter-group relationships in a democracy, which is 'live and let live,' can be fully accepted in any society only after passing through a period of un-resolvable opposition between groups none of which is able to dominate the other. . . . This may seem far-fetched but it is not too far from the kind of situation in which the Western democratic tradition of tolera-tion first grew."

The second problem involved here is the charge of "corruption" in government. Every general who effected a coup recently has sought to justify his action by pointing out the necessity to fight "corruption, in-efficiency and instability" created by professional politicians, self-seeking civil servants and merchants, and continuous party strife. This is a serious problem, and democracy cannot succeed anywhere if it cannot create stable, efficient and incorrupt government.

The problem is that the moral code and social disciplines of tradi-tional societies that once provided checks on self-aggrandizement and corruption have lost their authority and are becoming irrelevant. The new discipline of democracy and its ethos have not developed sufficiently to check the self-seeking made possible by the new freedom; widespread corruption results. Such new disciplines of responsibility are a matter of slow growth. Meanwhile corruption may become so acute that many question whether freedom is not a curse. And here lies the opportunity for an authoritarian answer.

There are two observations that must be made:

(1) Wherever there is freedom, we must grant the possibility of corruption. Asian peoples were too idealistic in their hopes for an incor-rupt state of affairs under democracy, and now they naturally swing to the other extreme of cynical exaggeration of corruption. Nothing has been more perilous for Asian democracies than a lack of understanding of its

realistic limitations. The resulting cynicism cuts the nerve of democracy.

This played a large part in the success of the Communist Party in Kerala. A consultation on "Christian Responsibility under Communist Rule in Kerala" in 1957 said:

> There is too much cynicism in Kerala regarding democratic political parties and their leaders. In part, it indicates a healthy reaction against utopian political hopes of an earlier day and a growth of political realism after independence. It also expresses a necessary condemnation by the people of corruption that prevails in our political life. But a sense of frustration has become so deep-rooted in Kerala today that the people suspect the integrity of political leaders without proof and exaggerate the picture of corruption. This saps the moral nerve of our politicians and of our political life. At present, the revival of healthy democratic political life requires that we see the weaknesses of democratic parties but at the same time not make them the means of increasing cynicism.

(2) Military rule may remedy certain evils at certain levels for a short while. But corruption inevitably returns, for the problem of building new ethical foundations for democratic living cannot be solved by military fiat. Further, what is the guarantee against the corruption of military authority itself?

Turning back to more general considerations, perhaps the most important problem that all newly independent nations face is that of finding a way to break the back of the rigid feudal socio-economic structure, thus setting the nation on the path of economic development. It is precisely in relation to this crucial problem that democracy is being tried in the extreme.

In the first place, it is a matter of creating a revolution in the traditional agrarian pattern of living. Traditional property relations and social institutions breed attitudes to land, labor and productivity that are obstacles to the utilization of science and technology in agricultural production and the development of an agrarian base for economic enterprise and social dynamism. Collective farming in Russia and the "People's communes" in China may be totalitarian, but they have strong appeal as they are more or less successful in breaking the hindrances of feudalism to economic development.

If the Communist or some other authoritarian path is to be avoided, democracy must discover a method that can revolutionize traditional social institutions and economic structures. In this connection the recent resolution of the Indian National Congress accepting cooperative farming as the goal has created strong debate. Opponents say it will destroy the traditional beliefs and social patterns of life and create a religious and moral vacuum perilous for India, leading inevitably to despotism.

These criticisms have substance, but they show no awareness of the fact that despotism may be inevitable if the static socio-economic structure is *not* radically broken. Although there may be perils in a revolutionary program even under democracy, democracy will not survive without showing its ability to make radical changes in the traditional society. If a certain measure of coercion is necessary, certainly it can be better exercised within a democratic system where it can be criticized and checked.

Military rule has played a part in the transition from feudalism to dynamic economy in several countries of the West. England had Cromwell, and France, Napoleon. In both, the military dictator was the instrument of a middle class out to destroy feudalism. And there are many who see a parallel here in the emergence of military rule in some Asian countries.

No doubt it is possible to argue that in Egypt the military accomplished much in land reform and in building the agrarian foundations for modern industrialization. Even in Pakistan, General Ayub Khan seems to realize that his rule has to be justified by policies of land reform. But the steps taken in Pakistan are too halting and, as Nehru has said, much less radical than the abolition of the *zemandari* system quite a few years ago in India. It is too early to say if the army in Pakistan stands for feudal *status quo* or change. Even if authoritarian rule is economically justifiable in some countries for a period of transition, the authoritarianism should be judged progressive or reactionary in the light of the socio-economic ideal it serves.

This does not answer the question of how a democratic order will emerge when the temporary justification for authoritarian rule ends— especially where a middle class committed to democratic values is of recent growth and where these values are alien to indigenous culture and perhaps would have been even further weakened during the rule of the military. Of course, Communists are anti-feudal, but as far as we can see there is less possibility for the "transition period" to end in Communist-ruled countries.

This is the dilemma of democracy in Asia. It must effect a revolution for its survival, but a revolution that can be contained within and controlled by its system.

This dilemma has been debated here a great deal in recent months with respect to the meaning of the rule of law in the Asian situation. The conflict between democracy's rule of law and the necessity for changes that outstep the slow due processes of legislation and implementation of law have been highlighted by the Communist regime in Kerala. The question raised has not yet been properly answered by the Congress Party.

The Congress Party is right in maintaining that order, freedom and social change should go together; this is a requirement of democracy. However, social change has a certain priority where people demand higher standards of living. No democracy in Asia can survive that does not recognize this priority. This has compelled recognition from even so conservative a body as the World Congress of Jurists, which met recently in Delhi to discuss the meaning of the rule of law. In defining it, they said it had to be interpreted dynamically in the modern world. What a dynamic rule of law means in the condition of rapid social change needs further inquiry.

The problem of sustaining the national intelligentsia within the spiritual and cultural climate of democracy is perhaps basic to all other problems in Asian democracies. The intelligentsia were produced by Western education; they were the leaders of independent governments in Asia. It is they who have imposed democracy on Asian countries. But skepticism about democracy has entered their soul, partly through the impact of Western totalitarianism and partly through the desire to overcome their cultural instability by identification with traditional culture.

Democracy must either reshape the traditional cultures to provide indigenous roots for itself and its votaries, or it must succumb to authoritarianism.

April 13, 1959

Africa, Christianity and the West

⌖

Alan Paton

This article was taken from the last speech Mr. Paton delivered in the United States. Upon his return to South Africa early in 1960, the Government withdrew his passport and forbade him to leave the country. He commented to us in a letter shortly thereafter: "I don't really care to have a passport from this Government. I wrote to them and told them that I hoped to have it returned one day by a Government more representative of the people of South Africa. I am accused of disloyalty, of course, but an accusation of loyalty would offend me much more."

Alan Paton

WE ARE LIVING AT THE END OF AN AGE—the end of the domination of the West—and Africans are experiencing the violence of being reborn. If we are to understand what is happening there, we must see the three striking characteristics of the modern African continent:

(1) The determination of every country and every people (and this Americans can well understand) to be free from any kind of external domination whatsoever. (2) Their determination to make their countries modern so that they can abolish illiteracy, disease and poverty; so that they can train their engineers, doctors, administrators and teachers. And this is not a materialistic motive. Rather this is a spiritual motive—the determination that these new countries should walk as equals in the company of the countries of the earth. (3) The bitter resentment of the arrogant rule of the West.

The tragedy of this arrogance is that it so often leads to hostility to Christianity, hostility to missions and missionaries, hostility to Western ideas of democracy and education, hostility sometimes even to the United Nations, hostility even to a man like Dr. Ralph Bunche (and the fact that he is not a white man does not save him from this particular kind of criticism). These are things that have their seeds in this arrogance of the past. And this factor must never be underestimated.

I would say that there has definitely been a decline in the self-respect and self-assurance of the people of the West. And I would say that this was the result of several very shaking experiences. When I look back on my own lifetime, I think of how it started in 1914 and was repeated in 1939. I think of the terrible shame that one of the great nations of the West should have murdered six million Jews; I think of the dropping of two atomic bombs, of the treatment of the Negro here in the United States, and of the treatment of African people in Africa.

I think also of an experience of my own: The realization that my own people, the white people of South Africa, would not yield one jot or tittle of their power or privilege until they were compelled to do so. And I must say that it is a sobering experience to realize that while individual man may turn and mend his ways, collective man finds it much more difficult.

However, I didn't come here tonight to speak to you about the sins of the West. I come rather to speak to you about the great opportunities to restore our self-respect and self-assurance and, at the same time, to render a service of a most magnificent kind.

In the past we have always gone to other countries and said: "We know what you need and we're going to give it to you." Now we have to learn a new lesson. We must say to them: "What kind of country is it that you want to build? What kind of use do you want to make of this new freedom that you have found?" And if we understand and sympathize with these things, then we must ask them further: "What can we do to help you to realize this modernity that you are so anxious to acquire? How can we help you to develop the resources of your country? How can we help you with the education of your children?"

Most Americans are astonished to learn how few universities there are in Africa. I just want you to realize that the university education in Africa is still a rare thing and that it might even be necessary for a country such as America to find some special, fresh kind of education that would enable people to learn in two years what they might at their leisure acquire in four.

I think there is one other great contribution that the people of the United States can make to the development of these new countries of Africa, and that is to restore the great damage that has been done to her own influence and authority by the fact that the deliberate speed enjoined upon her has been so much more deliberate than speedy. Undoubtedly one of the greatest things that you could do for us in South Africa would be to hasten the pace of the attempt to get rid of any kind of racial discrimination in your own society.

I have just been down to the state of Georgia, and I must say it is very fantastic to go into the Capitol and to see the state coat of arms and its wonderful motto: "Wisdom, justice and moderation." But don't think I'm pointing a finger at you because we also have a great motto in South Africa. Our motto, in the most divided country in the world, is: "Unity is strength."

I think it says a lot about ourselves and about human beings that we pick out these great slogans and mottoes. Although we are not just, we must pay this great homage to justice; although we are not free, we must pay this great homage to freedom. Quite a remarkable thing. But I think the thing that cannot be forgiven—any man can be forgiven for not being able to obtain the great ideals that he strives after—is to proclaim these great ideals and then to proceed in a contrary direction as so many of us do.

One of the reasons why it is almost impossible to speak about South Africa separately is that, while the rest of the continent of Africa is moving so firmly in the direction of liberation and independence, we in South Africa are moving in the opposite direction. There was one great mistake the British made when they gave a constitution to this new Union of South Africa, and that was that they didn't give us a written constitution and a bill of rights. Had they given them to us, we would not be in the deep distress that we are in today—the Nationalists would have been prevented from proceeding at the fast pace at which they have moved.

We like to give nice names to these laws of ours. When we say to the University of Capetown or to the University of Johannesburg, "You may not admit non-white students," we call that the University Extension Act. And when they take away a man's job because of his color, they call that the Industrial Conciliation Act. I am always so filled with anger when I think of these laws and when I think of the noble goals they are supposed to attain and of the cruel things they do to men and women that I cannot speak other than what I do now.

But one thing is quite certain, that our isolation from the rest of the world increases. I am sure there are many Afrikaners, including churchmen, who are very anxious and disturbed by the direction that their Government has taken. I just wish that they would more often exercise the prophetic role of judgment that a Christian is sometimes called upon to exercise.

It is a very interesting thing that the Afrikaner calls himself by a name which means a "man of Africa." It is tragic to record that he is the African who is afraid of Africa. And yet, they are a religious people, but I must say that we white people of South Africa have rewritten the great "second commandment" of Christianity, and it now reads: "Thou shalt love thy neighbor as thyself . . . so long as he does not live next door."

What is the future to be? I would like to say, first, that there is one thing that is certainly never to be the solution of our difficulties in South Africa, and that will be the policies of apartheid. They are completely unacceptable to the people of Africa—for that reason and that reason alone, their life is almost done.

Naturally I would like to have seen the people of South Africa come to their senses and I would like to have seen them open the door of opportunity to African people, not only in work and in education but also in the highest posts that could be available to them in government and in all of society. But I have come to the conclusion that whatever changes come will not come about that way. I don't suppose this is a disillusionment to American people because they must realize that if it had been left to the white people of the South to abolish practices of segregation, then who knows when they would have been abolished. You are very lucky in this country to have an additional force that you can exert—the power of the law. We cannot do that. The power of the law is against us.

Even if we do not experience a change of heart, there is still hope that we might experience a change of attitude. But this will only come about if the external pressures upon us become unendurable.

I do not exclude the possibility that one day our Government may be forced to say, "For God's sake come and help us." However, even if that were not to happen, if conflict and violence ensued and if the nations of Africa became more and more oppressive towards us, then it might still be necessary for the United Nations to intervene, to give us some kind of interregnum, the kind of government that would call out the best men from every race group and say to them, "Sit down and form a government; learn to work together. We'll give you a breathing space —ten years, fifteen years—to see whether you can come to your senses."

If that is not to be true, there is a third possibility: That we would go into an age of revolution, chaos and hatred of a kind that one hardly likes to contemplate. But that will only be if the United Nations has ceased to be the instrument of world authority. Thus you will see why people like myself in South Africa also look to the United Nations for some kind of help and support.

I call South Africa a land of fear. Well, in some ways that is true. In some ways it is a land of great courage also. It wasn't long ago that many of my friends were arrested and put into prison, and were released without the preferring of any charge whatsoever against them. One of my greatest friends had taught his children sanctity of the law, to respect the police as the arm of the law. At three o'clock one morning the police knocked on the door of his little daughter's room to say that they wanted her father; an hour later she saw her father taken away. One can just imagine the bewilderment and confusion.

When these people were released, they immediately took up the very same activities for which they had been sent to prison. While one has friends like that, there is still every reason to have hope. People ask me why I don't leave my country. And I always reply that if I saw no hope I would leave it.

And I might say that these people who went to prison didn't lose their sense of humor either, for some of them were very annoyed to think that they had gone to prison while I was still living at large outside. Now they made a plan to get me in. The plan was to take a piece of paper, tie it on a stone and to be seen throwing this stone over the walls of the prison to the street outside. And on this piece of paper was to be written: "Paton, for God's sake, hide those revolvers."

Although we are such a separated people, there are many white people who have the strongest possible bonds with African people; many African people have the strongest possible bonds with Indian people and Coloured people. There are still people who cross these lines.

And there is another thing which sustains us, the concern of our friends, the concern of the American Committee on Africa and its Africa Defense and Aid Fund, which I would like to commend to your attention. If it had not been for the help we had received from the Defense and Aid Fund, I do not know what we would have done. Four years ago, 156 people were arrested on charges of treason, and the case is still being tried. At first 60 were allowed to go, and then another 60, and finally 30 have been on trial for a period over four years. And so far this trial has cost us something like $300,000. I have no doubt that one of the intentions of the Government is to keep people tied up in trials of this kind. But I tell you that we couldn't have given them the defense that we did if it had not been for the generosity of our friends here and in other countries. I would like to give my thanks to all those who helped the Defense Fund of the American Committee.

I would like to say a word about the witness or lack of witness of the churches in South Africa. And you know that the Church has a prophetic role which it must exercise if it is to be true to itself. There are times when the most creative thing to do is to protest. We have been very fortunate in having men like the Bishop of Johannesburg, who was deported from our country some weeks ago. The reason he was deported was that his principles did not allow him to accept the principles of apartheid. We also have in the Archbishop of Capetown, in the bishops of the Roman Catholic Church and the leaders of other English-speaking churches a great deal to be thankful for.

There is a great struggle in the mind of the Christian person in South Africa because he derives benefits from the practices of apartheid, and yet, in his heart, he knows that it can't be true. So he erects these great hypocritical beliefs to assure himself that what he is doing is good and right. It is true that we no longer defend our practices on scriptural grounds (we gave that up 10 years ago) ; now we defend them on other grounds of Christian ethics.

You do not understand apartheid if you do not understand that there are at least two factors operating in it. One is fear for yourself, fear of being outnumbered, determination to keep your position of supremacy; the other is those good impulses struggling within you, and you want to do this in the best way possible. And so these two impulses—one evil and one good—must somehow be reconciled, and you all know that goodness and evil can never be reconciled.

A person like myself is often regarded as an extremist in South Africa. If it be extreme to choose justice and not injustice and not to seek some middle road between them, then I am happy to be called an extremist. If it is extreme to choose good and not evil, and not to seek some compromise between them, then again I am happy to be called an extremist.

Christians often imagine that the danger to Christianity and true religion is communism or something of that nature. The greatest danger to Christianity in Africa is pseudo-Christianity. And the marks of pseudo-Christianity are easy to recognize: it always prefers stability to change; it always prefers order to freedom; it always prefers the law to justice; and it always prefers what it considers realism to love. We as Christians should be rejoicing in the liberation of the people of South Africa; yet so many of us are afraid to do so.

As I say, pseudo-Christianity always exalts realism above love. It says, "You know, Paton, you are really talking a lot of bloody nonsense because human beings don't act in that way. You don't understand human nature. You are trying to achieve the impossible. It is all very well to say no compromise between justice and injustice, but it is politics to try to find some kind of compromise."

Seeing that this meeting is being held in a church, I would like to conclude with a few thoughts on the law of love. I think that ultimately if one wants to be a good man, one must live by the law of love no matter what the cost of it may be. If it means that suffering is the price that must be paid for it, then you must suffer. One simply lives by the law of love whatever the consequences may be. And if that is not the meaning of faith, then I don't know what is.

One must never identify suffering with love, nor must one seek suffering. One who seeks suffering is not loving, he is merely sick. But a person who shrinks from suffering when that is the price that must be paid is sick too. But, of course, there is so much more than suffering in love, for it is in loving that we are nearest to God; in loving we are most nearly like him.

I cannot think of any more important thing that you Americans can do than that you discharge this love and its responsibilities for your fellow men in Africa, who only now are beginning to look to a future where they will enjoy many of the bounties and blessings that you have enjoyed for so long.

December 26, 1960

Beware of Melancholy

༄

Alan Paton

ALL THE VISITORS ASK ME—the American, the British, the Scandinavian —what is the future? They ask me as though I had some special knowledge. South Africans ask me too. Experience has taught me the answer, and the answer is, "I do not know." At the moment it is possible to believe that nothing will change, that Afrikaner nationalism will never consent to any change that threatens its own position of power, however remote that threat may be. In its treatment of its enemies, it is becoming quite merciless. Those who openly oppose apartheid (or separate development, to give it its sweeter name) are going to suffer more, not less.

It is plain to me that the only opposition that will be allowed to continue will be an opposition that differs only in respect to the way apartheid is implemented. It is plain to me that ex-members of the banned organizations are going to face punishment even if they meet together as friends to discuss the events of the times. It is plain to me that the Government, believing that it has crushed subversive action, is prepared to move more ruthlessly into the field of ideas.

In the eyes of the Government, if you are a member of a political organization and that organization is banned, it is your plain duty to stop thinking politically. It is your plain duty, in fact, to change your character and personality; and if you do not, you will be put in prison. I have no doubt whatever that if the Government were to bring in a bill making it an offense to speak of separate development in a way considered by the Minister to be contrary to the public interest, it would be passed by a large majority, Helen Suzman and a few others opposing.

There is another thing that is plain to me, and it is not a pleasant thing either. Any person who, at the expiration of his or her ban, picks up public life where he or she left it off will be banned again immediately. This person, too, has to change his or her character and personality, or has to accept a life cut off from the life of society.

The full meaning of a ban and the full legal implications of a ban have not yet been clearly established, but there is the shocking possibility that judicial interpretations will become stricter and stricter, and that ultimately a ban will be interpreted as meaning a complete severance of all personal relations outside the immediate family, if the banned person has one.

These facts are shocking. Much more shocking than the facts of Stellenbosch sex and municipal corruption. In a way I hesitate to write them down, but write them down I must, and look at them we all must, for this is the immediate future that I see.

For how long will this future last? My answer is, "I do not know." To me there is another question: how long can I last? and there is still another question: is it worth trying to last?

People answer this question in different ways. Some leave the country. Some leave politics. Some stick to their course, even if they expect certain consequences. And even this last group is diverse, for some would face *any* consequences and some would not.

What is my own answer to this question? I must give my own answer, because I would not dare to answer it for anyone else. I think it is worth trying to last. It is worth something to me, even if it apparently achieves little.

If someone were to ask me, "What would you and your wife do if you had young children?" I would answer—"We would have two choices, to stay here and to give our children a father and mother who put some things even above their own children's safety and happiness; or to leave, and give our children a father and mother who put their safety and happiness above all else." Which would I choose? They are both good courses, are they not? I hope I would choose the first.

To those who want to stay, whether out of love or duty or plain cussedness, I direct these words.

Stand firm by what you believe, do not tax yourself beyond endurance, yet calculate clearly and coldly how much endurance you have, don't waste your breath and corrupt your character by cursing your rulers and the South African Broadcasting Corporation. Don't become obsessed by them, keep your friendships alive and warm, especially those with people of other races, beware of melancholy and resist it actively if it assails you, and give thanks for the courage of others in this fear-ridden country.

November 1, 1965

Speaking to New Realities

IV

Secularism's Impact on Contemporary Theology

ᚙᚖᚖ

Langdon Gilkey

THE PECULIAR CHARACTER OF THE CURRENT theological situation lies in the fact that it is dominated by the massive influence of secularism. Secularism is, so to speak, the cultural *Geist* within which all forms of thought, including the theological, must operate if they are to be relevant and creative. It functions in our period much as idealistic dualism functioned in the Hellenistic world, providing basic attitudes to reality, categories of thought and evaluations of meaning and goodness.

This is not to argue that all of the implications of secularism must or could be accepted by theology, any more than all the implications of idealistic dualism were accepted by the thinkers of the early Church. But there is no question that the creative forms of patristic thought, as well as the "heresies," were set within the fundamental structures of Hellenism. My own feeling is that our theological relation to secularism as the

127

basic mood of our age is roughly analogous, and that our task is in this sense similar to theirs.

Secularism is not so much a philosophy as the pre-rational basis of all potent contemporary philosophies. Like all fundamental cultural moods or historical forms of consciousness, it exists on the level of what are called presuppositions and thus is expressed *in* the variant forms of a given culture's life rather than being one of these forms. It is, therefore, not easy to characterize briefly.

Four terms seem to me helpful in describing it: naturalism, temporalism, relativism and autonomy. These words express an attitude that finds reality in the temporal flux immediately around us, effectiveness solely in the physical and historical (or human) causes in that process, knowledge possible only of that passing flux from the position of one within it, and value only in the fulfillment of its moments. This attitude emphasizes the here and now, the tangible, the manipulatable, the sensible, the relative and the this-worldly.

This cultural or historical viewpoint, practically synonymous with the modern mind, has been expressed with progressive radicality in a wide variety of philosophies beginning roughly 200 years ago: empiricism, Kantian *criticism,* Hegelianism, evolutionism and process thought, pragmatic naturalism, and now existentialism and positivism. What is significant about the historical development of this *Geist* is that all the elements of what we might call "ultimacy," with which it began in the eighteenth and nineteenth centuries, have steadily vanished from it: The sense of an ultimate order or coherence in the passage of things, of a final purpose or direction in their movement, and of a fundamental goodness or meaning to the wholeness of being.

We are thus left with a kind of "raw" or radical secularity in which no ultimate order or meaning appears. This is expressed both by positivism and by secular existentialism, especially in the latter's literary forms. However different these two points of view may be, each in its own way reflects a concentration solely on immediate knowledge or value, and asserts either the meaninglessness of ultimate metaphysical or religious questions (positivism), or the complete absence or irrelevance of ultimate answers (existentialism). Man is no longer felt to be set within an ultimate order or context, from which he draws not only his being but the meanings, standards and values of his life; he is alone and alien in the flux of reality and quite autonomous with regard to meaning and value.

This is almost as vast a departure from the "secular" evolutionary philosophies of a century ago as it is from the classical Christian world-view. It is no accident that the phrase "God is dead" is taken as the symbol of present-day secularism. But since for this mood existence also "is the absurd," we should add that *all* the gods are dead—that is, all those structures of coherence, order and value in the wider environment of man's life. Darwin and Nietzsche, not Marx and Kierkegaard, are the real fathers of the present mood.

This developing modern mood has, of course, had increasing influence on the theology of the last two hundred years. At first this was largely confined to (1) the acceptance of naturalistic causality and, by extension, the methods and results of science with regard to spatio-temporal facts; (2) the appropriation of the attitudes of historical inquiry, resulting in at least a qualified relativism with regard to both scriptural writings and doctrines; (3) the emphasis on religion as of value for *this* life and on ethics as having relevance only for one's concern for his neighbor's welfare. In the nineteenth century these and other elements of the modern mentality began to transform traditional theology completely.

Liberalism succeeded in relating itself to the earlier forms of this secular mood by using the remaining elements of ultimacy (an ultimate order of process, the progressive direction of change, etc.) as the ontological bases for its theological elaborations; but this broke down in the twentieth century with the general loss of faith in these immanent structures of ultimate meaning.

Neo-orthodoxy rejected these "secular" ways of talking of God and used the older non-secular biblical categories, while accepting the whole modern understanding of the spatio-temporal process now de-sacralized of all ultimacy. Out of this came an uneasy dualism, with a naturalistically interpreted world and a biblically understood God giving meaning and coherence thereto.

The developing problem of this God's historical activity—where the two diverse worlds were joined in his "mighty acts"—became more and more evident. One might say that, not unlike today's Roman Catholics, the neo-orthodox thought they could accept secularism "secularly," i.e., as exclusively an attitude toward ordinary history and nature, without compromise to the autonomous biblical superstructure that was set upon that secular base. The present crisis in theology illustrates the increasing difficulty of that strange marriage of heaven and earth, of *Heilsgeschichte* and *Geschichte*.

What is the form of this crisis? In theology the crisis has revealed itself in the virtual disappearance of discourse about God, surely a crisis in *that* discipline if there ever was one! This was first evident in the aforementioned difficulty of relating the biblical God to a naturalistically interpreted process. Then in Bultmannian theology, where the problem was made explicit, God was shoved farther and farther into the never-never land of sheer kerygmatic proclamation.

Theological understanding contented itself with an existential analysis of man and a hermeneutical analysis of a relativized Scripture and experienced "word-events"—though why such analyses should be called "theological" without the inclusion of God remains problematic at best. For if only the effects of divine activity in history, documents and experience can be spoken of—but not that activity itself—one is very near to sheer secularism.

It is not surprising that at this point a "religionless Christianity" should appear powerfully in our midst, a Christianity that seeks to understand itself in some terms other than man's dependence upon God, and to realize itself totally in the "secular," in the service to the neighbor in the world. The end result has been the appearance of the "God is dead" theologies, which openly proclaim the truth of the new secularity described above, reject for a variety of reasons all language about God, and in a thoroughly secular way concentrate on life and action in the modern world. The power of secularism is vividly revealed here; for in these most recent theologies secular presuppositions and attitudes have utterly infected those formerly inoculated against them.

Probably, however, the purely intellectual difficulties of neo-orthodoxy did not themselves lead to its sudden demise but were reflections of a more basic problem: the fundamental mood of secularism in all of us with which neo-orthodoxy was in the end unable to cope. Apparently what has happened has been that the trans-natural reality that neo-orthodoxy proclaimed—the transcendent God, his mighty acts and his Word of revelation—became more and more unreal and incredible to those who had learned to speak this language. Younger enthusiasts began to wonder if they were talking about anything they themselves knew about when they spoke about God, of encounter, of the eschatological event and of faith. Do these words point to anything, or are they just words, traditional symbols referring more to hopes than experienced realities?

Because of this experience of the unreality, or at least the elusiveness, of the divine, younger theologians began to listen anew to positivist accusations of "meaninglessness" and existentialist affirmations of the death of God. And since, it seems to me, this sense of elusiveness remains the predominant reality of the present religious situation, the questions of the reality of God and the possibility of language about him are our most pressing current theological problems, prior to all other theological issues.

I say this for two reasons. (1) The effort to interpret Christian theology without God is a failure. Such efforts have had vast significance in revealing the power of secularism inside as well as outside the Christian community. But they show themselves to be halfway houses to humanism and thus unable to maintain, without some category of deity, any peculiarly Christian elements.

(2) Other contemporary theological problems—for example, the question of the Christ of faith, the historical Jesus and their relation to the words of Scripture, or the issues centering around the Word of revelation, our reception of it and its relation to Scripture and to the modern mind (i.e., the currently popular "hermeneutical problems")— are clearly secondary to the problem of God. While the Bible remains in *any* theological atmosphere a book of immense historical, literary and linguistic interest, it is of direct *theological* concern only if it is first pre-supposed that through it a divine word comes to man. Only if we know already that the Bible is the word of God can theology unfold its concepts without further prolegomena from its contents. And only then does the question of the meaning of its message for our day become the logically primary theological question.

At present, however, serious questions are being asked about the reality of God, and all the more about the reality of *any* revelation, let alone one through these documents. In such a situation these questions must be settled before we can treat the Bible as the source of truth and, therefore, of theological truth.

Of course it is possible that the question of the reality of God may be answered in relation to our hearing of the biblical word—but then that "word-event" becomes a category in philosophical theology and not merely in hermeneutics. That is to say, "word-event" becomes the argued basis for our assurance that we have here met something real we must call "God"—and such an argument has infinitely transcended the hermeneutical question of interpretation into the philosophical-theological question of what ultimate reality is.

One result of this change of theological concentration will be a separation for the next few years between biblical studies and theological concerns. No longer can the theologian or biblical scholar merely appeal to the "biblical view" as an assumed *theological* authority, since the questions of whether there be a revelation or a revealer at all are the ones he must deal with. And it surely begs *these* questions to cite only what the Bible says about them! This may seem to take the zip out of biblical studies—but a goodly number of eminent scholars will welcome for a while this cooler atmosphere in which to do their work.

Above all, dealing with the question of God in the radically secular atmosphere we have described will not be easy. For if the starting point of "biblical faith" is under question, so are the other two starting points of recent theology. In the first case the effort is to begin with "the stance of Christian faith" and to unravel theological conceptions from an "encounter or faith situation" of some sort. But secular acids have touched this foundation too, and rendered the questions "Do I *have* such faith?" "Have I experienced an encounter?" pressing questions for contemporary theologians. No one can start from a faith that is itself in question; the felt unreality of faith is an inevitable correlate to the felt unreality of God, and thus is also an aspect of our secularism.

The other starting point has been metaphysical inquiry à la process philosophy. But such a metaphysical knowledge of God itself presupposed the coherence of reality and the correlation of our thought to that orderly reality—else the metaphysical enterprise has no ground or legitimacy. Clearly radical secularism, whether in its positivistic or its existentialist forms, doubts that coherence and the relevance of our thought to such ultimate questions as firmly as it doubts "God" and the reality of faith. I do not pretend to know where the new theology will go; but I am sure that in dealing with the question of God, as it must, it can now neither be purely biblical nor simply metaphysical. This means a very new day for all of us.

I said initially that theology must reflect the secular consciousness of our time if it is to be relevant. This means that whatever language it uses must be both discovered in and related to the experiences of man's natural, temporal and communal life in this world. It is true that the latter-day secular denial of all categories of ultimacy makes theology impossible. But I also think it reflects a false analysis of man's secular experience, of nature, of himself, of community and of historical existence. A more valid analysis, probably of a phenomenological sort, of those realms of ordinary experience that we call secular will reveal dimensions for which only language about God is sufficient and thus will manifest the meaningfulness of that language. Such a prolegomena to discourse about revelation, word-event, Christ-event and Church is necessary if these forms of theological discussion are to be meaningful in our secular age.

April 5, 1965

Playboy's Doctrine of Male

~~~

Harvey Cox

SOMETIME THIS MONTH OVER ONE MILLION American young men will place sixty cents on a counter somewhere and walk away with a copy of *Playboy*, one of the most spectacular successes in the entire history of American journalism. When one remembers that every copy will probably be seen by several other people in college dormitories and sub-urban rumpus rooms, the total readership in any one month easily exceeds that of all the independent religious magazines, serious political and cultural journals, and literary periodicals put together.

What accounts for this uncanny reception? What factors in American life have combined to allow *Playboy's* ambitious young publisher, Hugh Hefner, to pyramid his jackpot into a chain of night clubs, TV spectaculars, bachelor tours to Europe and special discount cards? What impact does *Playboy* really have?

Clearly *Playboy's* astonishing popularity is not attributable solely to pin-up girls. For sheer nudity, its pictorial art cannot compete with such would-be competitors as *Dude* and *Escapade*. Rather, *Playboy* appeals to a highly mobile, increasingly affluent group of young readers, mostly between eighteen and thirty, who want much more from their drugstore reading than bosoms and thighs. They need a total image of what it means to be a man. And Mr. Hefner's *Playboy* has no hesitancy about telling them.

Why should such a need arise? David Riesman has argued that the responsibility for character formation in our society has shifted from the family to the peer group and to the mass media peer group surrogates. Things are changing so rapidly that one who is equipped by his family with inflexible, highly internalized values becomes unable to deal with the accelerated pace of change and with the varying contexts in which he is called upon to function. This is especially true in the area of consumer values toward which the "other-directed person" is increasingly oriented.

Within the confusing plethora of mass media signals and peer group values, *Playboy* fills a special need. For the insecure young man with newly acquired time and money on his hands who still feels uncertain about his consumer skills, *Playboy* supplies a comprehensive and authoritative guidebook to this foreboding new world to which he now has access. It tells him not only who to be; it tells him *how* to be it, and even provides consolation outlets for those who secretly feel that they have not quite made it.

In supplying for the other-directed consumer of leisure both the normative identity image and the means for achieving it, *Playboy* relies on a careful integration of copy and advertising material. The comic book that appeals to a younger generation with an analogous problem skillfully intersperses illustrations of incredibly muscled men and exces-sively mammalian women with advertisements for body-building gim-micks and foam rubber brassiere supplements. Thus the thin-chested comic book readers of both sexes are thoughtfully supplied with both the ends and the means for attaining a spurious brand of maturity.

Playboy merely continues the comic book tactic for the next age group. Since within every identity crisis, whether in 'teens or twenties, there is usually a sexual identity problem, *Playboy* speaks to those who desperately want to know what it means to be a *man,* and more specifically a *male,* in today's world.

Both the image of man and the means for its attainment exhibit a remarkable consistency in *Playboy.* The skilled consumer is cool and unruffled. He savors sports cars, liquor, high fidelity and book club selections with a casual, unhurried aplomb. Though he must certainly *have* and *use* the latest consumption item, he must not permit himself to get too attached to it. The style will change and he must always be ready to adjust. His persistent anxiety that he may mix a drink incorrectly, enjoy a jazz group that is passé, or wear last year's necktie style is comforted by an authoritative tone in *Playboy* beside which papal encyclicals sound irresolute.

"Don't hesitate," he is told; "this assertive, self-assured weskit is what every man of taste wants for the fall season." Lingering doubts about his masculinity are extirpated by the firm assurance that "real men demand this ruggedly masculine smoke" (cigar ad). Though "the ladies will swoon for you, no matter what they promise, don't give them a puff. This cigar is for men only." A fur-lined canvas field jacket is described as "the most masculine thing since the cave man." What to be and how to be it are both made unambiguously clear.

But since being a male necessitates some kind of relationship to females, *Playboy* fearlessly confronts this problem too, and solves it by the consistent application of the same formula. Sex becomes one of the items of leisure activity that the knowledgeable consumer of leisure handles with his characteristic skill and detachment. The girl becomes a desirable, indeed an indispensable "Playboy accessory."

In a question-answering column entitled: "The Playboy Advisor," queries about smoking equipment (how to break in a meerschaum pipe), cocktail preparation (how to mix a "Yellow Fever") and whether or not to wear suspenders with a vest, alternate with questions about what to do with girls who complicate the cardinal principle of casualness, either by suggesting marriage or by some other impulsive gesture toward permanent relationship. The infallible answer from the oracle never varies: sex must be contained, at all cost, within the entertainment-recreation area. Don't let her get "serious."

After all, the most famous feature of the magazine is its monthly fold-out photo of a *play*mate. She is the symbol par excellence of recreational sex. When play time is over, the playmate's function ceases, so she must be made to understand the rules of the game. As the crew-cut young man in a *Playboy* cartoon says to the rumpled and disarrayed girl he is passionately embracing, "Why speak of love at a time like this?"

The magazine's fiction purveys the same kind of severely departmentalized sex. Although the editors have recently dressed up the contents of *Playboy* with contributions by Hemingway, Bemelmans and even a Chekhov translation, the regular run of stories relies on a repetitious and predictable formula. A successful young man, either single or somewhat less than ideally married—a figure with whom readers have no difficulty identifying—encounters a gorgeous and seductive woman who makes no demands on him except sex. She is the prose duplication of the cool-eyed but hot-blooded playmate of the fold-out page.

Drawing heavily on the phantasy life of all young Americans, the writers utilize for their stereotyped heroines the hero's school teacher, his secretary, an old girl friend, or the girl who brings her car into the garage where he works. The happy issue is always a casual but satisfying sexual experience with no entangling alliances whatever. Unlike the women he knows in real life, the *Playboy* reader's fictional girl friends know their place and ask for nothing more. They present no danger of permanent involvement. Like any good accessory, they are detachable and disposable.

Many of the advertisements reinforce the sex-accessory identification in another way by attributing female characteristics to the items they sell. Thus a full page ad for the MG assures us that this car is not only "the smoothest pleasure machine" on the road and that having one is a "love-affair," but most importantly, "you drive it—it doesn't drive you." The ad ends with the equivocal question, "Is it a date?"

Playboy insists that its message is one of liberation. Its gospel frees us from captivity to the puritanical "hat-pin brigade." It solemnly crusades for "frankness" and publishes scores of letters congratulating it for its unblushing "candor." Yet the whole phenomenon of which *Playboy* is only a part vividly illustrates the awful fact of a new kind of tyranny.

Those liberated by technology and increased prosperity to new worlds of leisure now become the anxious slaves of dictatorial tastemakers. Obsequiously waiting for the latest signal on what is cool and what is awkward, they are paralyzed by the fear that they may hear pronounced on them that dread sentence occasionally intoned by "The Playboy Advisor": "you goofed!" Leisure is thus swallowed up in apprehensive competitiveness, its liberating potential transformed into a self-destructive compulsion to consume only what is *au courant*. *Playboy* mediates the World of the most high into one section of the consumer world, but to me it is a world of bondage, not of freedom.

Nor will *Playboy's* synthetic doctrine of man stand the test of scrutiny. Psychoanalysts constantly remind us how deeply seated sexuality is in the human self. But if they didn't remind us, we would soon discover it anyway in our own experience. As much as the human male might like to terminate his relationship with a woman as he snaps off the stereo, or store her for special purposes like a camel's hair jacket, it really can't be done. And anyone with a modicum of experience with women knows it can't be done. Perhaps this is the reason why *Playboy's* readership drops off so sharply after the age of thirty.

Playboy really feeds on the presence of a repressed fear of involvement with women, which for various reasons is still present in many otherwise adult Americans. So *Playboy's* version of sexuality grows increasingly irrelevant as authentic sexual maturity is achieved.

The male identity crisis to which *Playboy* speaks has at its roots a deep-set fear of sex, a fear that is uncomfortably combined with fascination. *Playboy* strives to resolve this antinomy by reducing the terrible proportions of sexuality, its power and its passion, to a packageable consumption item. Thus in *Playboy's* iconography, the nude woman symbolizes total sexual accessibility, but demands nothing from the observer. "You drive it—it doesn't drive you." The terror of sex, which cannot be separated from its ecstacy, is dissolved. But this futile attempt to reduce the *mysterium tremendum* of the sexual fails to solve the problem of being a man. For sexuality is the basic form of all human relationship, and therein lies its terror and its power.

Karl Barth has called this basic relational form of man's life *Mitmensch,* co-humanity. It means to me that becoming fully human, in my case a human male, necessitates not having the other totally exposed to me and my purposes—while I remain uncommitted—but exposing myself to the risk of encounter with the other by reciprocal self-exposure. The story of man's refusal to be so exposed goes back to the story of Eden and is expressed by man's desire to control the other rather than to *be with* the other. It is basically the fear to be one's self, a lack of the "courage to be."

Thus any theological critique of *Playboy* that focuses on its "lewdness" will misfire completely. *Playboy* and its less successful imitators are not "sex magazines" at all. They are basically anti-sexual. They dilute and dissipate authentic sexuality by reducing it to an accessory, by keeping it at a safe distance.

It is precisely because these magazines are anti-sexual that they deserve the most searching kind of theological criticism. They foster a heretical doctrine of man, one at radical variance with the biblical view. For *Playboy's* man, others—especially women—are *for* him. They are his leisure accessories, his playthings. For the Bible, man only becomes fully man by being *for* the other.

Moralistic criticisms of *Playboy* fail because its anti-moralism is one of the few places in which *Playboy* is right. But if Christians bear the name of One who was truly man because he was totally *for* the other, and if it is in him that we know who God is and what human life is for, then we must see in *Playboy* the latest and slickest episode in man's continuing refusal to be fully human.

April 17, 1961

Toward a New Definition of Obscenity

⮾⮾⮾

Howard Moody

IT WAS NO ACCIDENT THAT ONE OF the issues in the Presidential campaign was the "breakdown" of morality and the "deterioration of decency." We are obviously in the midst of what is simultaneously a moral and an artistic revolution, and it is usually difficult to tell where one leaves off and the other begins. All the way from the police department "put-down" of "dirty poetry" in coffeehouses in the early Fifties to the recent persecution of that most tragic of all shamans, Lenny Bruce, we have felt the reverberations of a battle that is as old as the country itself.

In the last few years slick-paper sex magazines like Ralph Ginzburg's *Eros,* as well as classics like *Fanny Hill,* have been banned and unbanned with disarming regularity. More recently the new wave of off-beat film makers experimenting with weird and strange themes have been arrested and their films banned from public places. Everything from topless bathing suits for women to bottomless bathing suits for men (in a Greenwich Village sportswear shop) are subjects for legal action.

To some people the foregoing is merely evidence of the decadence and coming destruction of American civilization, while to others it is the dawn of a new day of freedom of expression and the demise of shackling censorship. Whatever one's point of view as to the significance of the present revolution, it will be impossible to understand the present situation without knowing something of the history of the problem. How continuously, and sometimes obsessively, we as a people have been bent upon what Morris Ernst and Alan Schwartz have called "the search for the obscene." *(Censorship: The Search for the Obscene* [Macmillan] is their valuable study of this question from which I have drawn much of the legal-historical material in this article.)

Though the Puritans have often been blamed for "blue laws" and censorship, they actually were a great deal freer than they are often given credit for. In his revealing volume *The Not-Quite Puritans* Henry Lawrence refers to no fewer than sixty-six *confessions* to fornication in one small town between 1761 and 1765 (that was only those who confessed).

As a matter of fact, our first anti-obscenity law did not come into existence until the nineteenth century. Our forefathers, the Revolutionists and fashioners of the Constitution, did not seem so concerned with obscenity or pornography (and don't think there wasn't plenty around; cf. *The Fyfteen Plagues of a Maidenhead* and Ben Franklin's *Advice to a Young Man on Choosing a Mistress,* a ribald essay not published but freely circulated). Their concern is contained in the words of the First Amendment about Congress making no law abridging freedom of speech, religion and the press.

The real beginning of censorship—the establishment of prudery by legal sanctions—was the work not of Puritans and Pilgrims but of nineteenth-century Protestants. This will come as a surprise to those who label Roman Catholics as the book-banning "bad boys" of censorship and the first antagonists of pornography. After all it was Anthony Comstock, a fanatical twenty-four-year-old grocery clerk, who with the decisive help of the YMCA badgered the country and the Congress into passing a law that still governs obscenity in the mails. State after state followed the Congress and enacted "Comstock Laws." The major support for Comstock came, ironically enough, from the Babylon of sin and iniquity, New York City. The crusaders were not Irish Catholics; their top leadership was from the Protestant social hierarchy of New York, and J. P. Morgan's name led all the rest.

The leaders of censorship crusades used several means to gain their end, beginning with the law. From the late 1880's on, the crusaders have been confounded in attempts to get a definitive ruling on the meaning of obscenity in the courts of the land. The definition in the Comstock Law was terribly unclear, and since that time the courts have played the "synonyms game" (obscene is "dirty," "lewd," "lascivious," "scurrilous").

The protesters seemed to be disturbed by several matters as they pressed by law for the banning of books, and later films. They were deeply offended by "dirty words." One of the most important court cases was the Woolsey case, named after Judge John M. Woolsey, which dealt with the question of whether James Joyce's *Ulysses* might be distributed in this country. The basic objection to this book was the use of "four-letter words." The counsel, Morris Ernst, gave a historic exposition. The following is his dialogue with the judge.

> *Counsel:* Judge, as to the word "fuck," one etymological dictionary gives its derivation as from *facere*—to make—the farmer fucked the seed into the soil. This, Your Honor, has more integrity than a euphemism used every day in every modern novel to describe precisely the same event.
> *Judge Woolsey:* For example . . .
> *Counsel:* "They slept together." It means the same thing.
> *Judge Woolsey:* (smiling) But, Counselor, that isn't even usually the truth!

The final opinion of Judge Woolsey was that *Ulysses,* in spite of its vulgar language, did not excite sexual impulses or lustful thoughts and that its net effect was only that of a somewhat tragic and very powerful commentary on the inner lives of men and women.

This was the beginning of a whole series of significant legal cases on "obscenity" and attempts to control pornography.

One of the most important cases on obscenity was the Roth case, which involved an outright challenge to an obscenity law and its constitutionality under the First Amendment. Justice Harlan's decision in this case ought to be read by every fair-minded person interested in the problem of freedom and censorship.

Roth had been convicted by a lower court for selling books that "tend to stir sexual impulses and lead to sexually impure thoughts." This would, of course, condemn much of the world's great literature, and, moreover, Justice Harlan asserts: ". . . in no event do I think that limited federal interest in this area can extend to mere 'thoughts.' The federal power has no business, whether under the postal or commerce laws, to bar the sale of books because they might lead to any kind of 'thoughts.' "

And in sections of the decision Justice Brennan's understanding of human nature is comparable to his judicial wisdom. He says:

> However, sex and obscenity are not synonymous; obscene material is material dealing with sex in a manner appealing to prurient interest. The portrayal of sex, e.g. literature, art and scientific works, is not itself sufficient reason to deny material the constitutional protection of freedom of speech and press. Sex, as a great and mysterious moving force in human life, has indisputably been a subject of absorbing interest to mankind through the ages; it is one of the vital problems of human interest and public concern.

The culmination of the long court battle was the Supreme Court's decision last June declaring *Tropic of Cancer* and the film *The Lovers* not to be obscene.

The peddlers of prudery also used another technique for the enforcement of their morality on the community as a whole: social and religious sanction. This was an effective weapon as long as a people dominated by a common Protestant ethos or Christian moral understanding controlled both legally and socially the normally accepted standards of behavior for the society. However, with the "passing of Christendom," and the accompanying breakdown of religious authority, control has become much more difficult.

The censors in more recent years have used more desperate techniques such as that of quasi-legal and police action. Since the higher courts keep refusing to make irrevocably clear what is obscene, censors are driven to vigilante tactics that are extra-legal, highly undemocratic and probably unconstitutional. Self-appointed citizens' clean-books councils are springing up all over the country. Their tactics are intimidation, and their appeals are sloganeering. Operating under the very appealing objective of "keeping filth and smut from our children," they move on to cleaning from libraries such books as *Brave New World, Black Boy, Catcher in the Rye* and others.

One of the more renowned private citizens' groups in this country is an interfaith organization in New York City called *Operation Yorkville,* which has garnered financial support and the backing of religious and political leaders for its task of guarding the morals of the city's youth. Most recently its chief targets of "malignancy" are the American Civil Liberties Union, the Supreme Court of the United States and every Court of Appeals judge who refuses to accept their "book-burning" standards. In order to punish the "pushers of pornography," methods are used, including accusations, that violate the rights of others.

One would not for a moment deny the right of these individuals acting in concert to make their point of view felt by means of persuasion. But when they use intimidating threats and slanderous name-calling as in the recent attack on the Supreme Court Justices for their June 22 ruling as "nurturing degeneracy," then these groups have gone beyond the boundary of what constitutes responsible citizens' action.

The question that comes to the Church and to individual Christians at this point is what should be our posture in the midst of these revolutions going on about us? I think Christians should look carefully at the confusion regarding the meaning of obscenity and then make a major contribution by raising our own standard for judging obscenity. The Supreme Court, in its most recent case prior to last June's decision, defined it as follows:

> Obscene material is material which deals with sex in a manner appealing to prurient interest, and the test of obscenity is whether to the *average* person, applying contemporary community standards, the dominant theme of the material appeals to *prurient* interest (Justice Brennan: *Roth* v. *U.S.,* 1957).

Howard Moody

The dictionary defines *prurient* as "having an uneasy or morbid desire or curiosity: given to the indulgence of lewd ideas; impure minded." It is almost too obvious to say that even the wisest gods, let alone mortal men, would have an exceedingly difficult time deciding under this definition what is obscene, who is an average person, whose community standard, and what constitutes dominant theme. More basic than such highly ambiguous matters is the larger question of the legitimacy of using sex (even in a prurient way) as the sole basis for determining what is obscene. Here we are up against the most important aspect of the definition of obscenity: at least two of the important grounds for censorship are "dirty words" and "sexual subjects."

Relative to the matter of vulgar language, what righteous indignation can we Christians muster about our Anglo-Saxon forebears? Can we really pretend that the use of "coarse" and "vulgar" words is somehow tantamount to an affront to God Almighty? (Do we have to be so ashamed of the "bawdy" talk of Martin Luther?) Vulgar speech and four-letter words are not blasphemous or immoral, and our shame and prudery over them are basically class matters. (Even the derivation of the word "lewd" is interestingly traced to a *lewdefrere*, a lay brother; unlearned, unlettered, rude, artless, belonging to lower orders.) Vulgar and bawdy language may well be objected to on the basis of aesthetics and social manners, but it is hardly justifiable to make a moral or theological case against raw language as the Church has tended to do.

I remember my father telling me as a youth that uttering the profanity "Goddamn" was the unforgivable sin of blasphemy as well as the breaking of the Third Commandment. It is the Christian's devious manner of avoiding the hard truth that "taking God's name in vain" is a far more profound sin than profanity. It is not the vulgar utterance from our lips but our deeds that truly profane human life. Christ always warned that you can't judge a man by his speech. Not everyone who says words like "Lord, Lord," even spoken with great reverence and piety, "does the truth" of those words; conversely many people who speak roughly in the raw language of vulgarity live in awe of and respect for the mystery of humanity.

The true profanity against God is to refuse to take him seriously; the truly "dirty" word is the one used to deny and to denigrate the humanness of another person. Language is symbolic, not literal; when a person speaks in raw language he may be trying to say something that nice and prosaic words will not communicate.

My point here is that, from a theological or ethical perspective, "dirty words" are a terribly inadequate base from which to write a definition of obscenity.

In the same way, we do not do justice to the Christian perspective upon human evil and immorality if we see *sex* as the dominant and determinative factor in the judgment of what is obscene. Sex, by our understanding of creation, is vital and a potent force in human behavior, though shot through with human sin and distortion. To make sex the sole determinative factor in defining "obscenity" or "pornography" or "filth" is to relegate it to the shadowy regions of immorality (depending on who says it in what community and how much). This completely fails to explain what all Christian faith and tradition teaches us is really *obscene* in this world.

For Christians the truly obscene ought not to be slick-paper nudity, nor the vulgarities of dirty old or young literati, nor even "weirdo" films showing transvestite orgies or male genitalia. What is obscene is that material, whether sexual or not, that has as its basic motivation and purpose the degradation, debasement and dehumanizing of persons. The dirtiest word in the English language is not "fuck" or "shit" in the mouth of a tragic shaman, but the word "NIGGER" from the sneering lips of a Bull Connor. Obscenity ought to be much closer to the biblical definition of blasphemy against God and man.

The censors tell us that "filth" must be stopped because it is leading our children into acts of violence, rape, narcotic addiction and prostitution. They say that young minds are being poisoned and perverted by "pornographic books."

Are we really worried about the pornographic pictures peddled by shady characters on street corners? I remember all those "dirty" comic books in high school, i.e., *Popeye, Maggie and Jiggs*—they made me feel I was "illicit" and they made me laugh, but I wasn't moved to ravish my teacher as a result.

I do not conceive that a picture is "dirty" because sex is its dominant theme. (The tragic disservice of slick-paper sex magazines is not that they display nudes in suggestive poses but that they become anti-sexual by pushing sex to the point of satiety, thus making it a deadly bore.) A picture is not dirty that shows a man and woman in one of the fifty-seven recommended positions for intercourse (unaesthetic perhaps, possibly bad taste, but hardly obscene!). The dirty or obscene is the one that shows the police dogs being unleashed on the Negro demonstrators in Birmingham. The "lewdest" pictures of all—more obscene than all the tawdry products of the "smut industry"—are the pictures of Dachau, the ovens and the grotesque pile of human corpses.

Let us as Christians write a new definition of obscenity based on the dehumanizing aspects of our contemporary culture. Can we not see the hypocrisy of our prudery when we spend time, words and money trying to prevent the magazine *Eros* from going through the mails and never raise an eyebrow about the tons of material that vilify human beings and consign whole ethnic groups to the lowest kind of animality? Do we not have to admit the duplicity that allows our police to *guard* George Lincoln Rockwell as he mouths blasphemous obscenities of the most inhuman order on public streets, while the same police are used to *harass* Lenny Bruce in the confines of a night club while he vulgarly satirizes our human hypocrisies?

Should we not as Christians raise a new standard of "obscenity" not obsessed with sex and vulgar language, but defined rather as that material which has as its dominant theme and purpose the debasement and depreciation of human beings—their worth and their dignity. Such a definition might include some material dealing with sex but this would be a minor aspect of pornography. The "words" that would offend us and from which we want our young protected would not be "Anglo-Saxon" but English, French, German, which carried within their etymology and meaning outrages against human individuals and groups.

The pornographic pictures would be those that showed humans being violated, destroyed, physically beaten. (The prize obscene film might be a three-minute documentary of a fully clothed man, twitching and writhing as the shock of electricity applied by our officials burns through his body.)

All the resources of our Christian teaching and tradition, all the theological armament in the Church could be called up in the warfare against "the new obscenity." The significant concomitant of this is that it would lessen the distortion and perversion of sex in our society that the present definition of obscenity has created. A further advantage to this new understanding would be that the Church and many literary critics would be saved the embarrassment of having to defend every mediocre form of literature and art against the wild attacks of the book-banners.

We would be saved the somewhat ludicrous spectacle of "far-out ministers" and "hip theologians" eloquently testifying in court for what may be lousy literature or atrocious art. (There was a laughable scene in the recent court case against Lenny Bruce when a minister was forced into justifying why he didn't use four-letter words in his homiletical exercises on Sunday. I can already see some enterprising seminary developing a new course in "The Use of Pornography in Preaching.")

Norman Podhoretz has stated the matter succinctly: "It is the extent to which law has forced criticism into hypocrisy that, in order to defend freedom of expression, one must always be exaggerating the literary merits of any piece of erotica that happens to get published."

If it is asserted that this position skirts dangerously close to "license" and the accompanying breakdown of moral order, I can only reply that it is one of the hard truths of Christian tradition that we have been released to a freedom whose burden is a terrible risk. This freedom of the Christian man has already sent Christians in our time against the law, to prison and even to death. With this new definition of obscenity we will run a risk by allowing our children and ourselves to see "obscene pictures" of the instant destruction of two hundred thousand persons at

Hiroshima with one bomb—the risk that we may come to accept this as a natural and realistic way of solving conflicts between men and nations. This is a real danger, but the alternative is mental slavery, a restricted thought process, a closed society. Consequently in the battles of censorship in a pluralistic society Christians may find themselves coming down regularly against the inroads of censorship at the risk of being called licentious and immoral.

It may be, as some politicians claimed in the past campaign, that this nation is in a state of moral decadence. If so, I am convinced that the evidence of this is not to be found in salacious literature, erotic art, or obscene films, but in the "soul-rot" that comes from the moral hypocrisy of straining at the gnat of sexuality and swallowing the camel of human deterioration and destruction.

Protestant Christian liberals in this country have been very adept at accommodating Christian faith and ethics to the social and economic revolutions of the past thirty to forty years. However, we display every evidence of being ill at ease and unprophetic in relating our Christian insights and teachings to the moral and sexual revolutions in American life. There are a few clues that the wind is changing, but much more study and reflection in honesty is needed.

January 25, 1965

On Taking Sex Seriously

❧

Tom F. Driver

HEADLINES WERE MADE IN England last winter by the publication of a 75-page pamphlet titled "Towards a Quaker View of Sex." Of all the revolutions through which we are passing, the revolution in sexual mores is the one that receives the least thought. I do not mean that it gets the least attention but that the attention it gets is least informed by objective and radical thinking.

The Quaker pamphlet deserves the critic's praise and the public's reading because it is one of the few recent documents written by Chris-

tians that attempt to look at sex dispassionately and at human beings
compassionately. The group that prepared the statement proceeded on the
honest Quaker assumption that Christian ethics must be founded primarily upon conscience, not primarily upon law sacred or secular, and
they have spoken conscientiously. As a result, their conclusions are very
liberal with respect to the letter of the law. A society that finds much of
its sexual pleasure in breaking the received code cannot help, therefore,
giving headlines to a statement by Christians that puts the ultimacy of
that code in question.

The pamphlet is not an official statement of the Religious Society of
Friends in Great Britain. It is the result of a six-year study carried out
by eleven individuals, six of them elders in the Society. Their discussions
began in response to problems of homosexuality "brought by young
Quaker students . . . who came to older Friends for help and guidance."

The group discovered that this one type of sexual problem could
not be clearly seen apart from other types: "a few pieces of the jigsaw
puzzle could not be identified without the whole picture." Thus the
pamphlet includes an "Introduction and Basic Assumptions" and chap-
ters on "Normal Sexual Development," "Homosexuality" (both male
and female), a call for a "New Morality" and "A Word of Counsel to
Counselors." There are also appendices, a glossary and a book list.

The reader looking for surprises may find them. For instance, we
read the following about triangular heterosexual relations:

> This is too often thought of as a wholly destructive and irrespon-
> sible relationship. . . . Not sufficient recognition is given to the fact
> that a triangular situation can and often does arise in which all
> three persons behave responsibly. .`. . It is worth noting that in the
> two-woman/one-man situation, the very happiness of the marriage
> may attract a young girl or a sensitive and responsible woman. . . .
> By the same token, it could surely help a nervous youngster to fall
> in love with a happily married woman. (p. 20)

On homosexuality, the group supports the recommendation of the
1957 *Wolfenden Report* that such acts between consenting adults in private should no longer be a criminal offense. It follows the Bishop of
Woolwich in his 1962 appeal for reform of "our utterly medieval treatment of homosexuals," which he called "a peculiarly odious piece of
English hypocrisy." The group adds:

> Surely it is the nature and quality of a relationship that matters:
> one must not judge it by its outward appearance but by its inner
> worth. Homosexual affection can be as selfless as heterosexual
> affection, and therefore we cannot see that it is in some way mor-
> ally worse. (p. 36)

In its section on a needed "new morality," the group writes:

Nothing that has come to light in the course of our studies has altered the conviction that came to us when we began to examine the actual experiences of people—the conviction that love cannot be confined to a pattern. The waywardness of love is part of its nature, and this is both its glory and its tragedy. If love did not tend to leap every barrier, if it could be tamed, it would not be the tremendous creative power we know it to be and want it to be. (p. 39)

The utterances of the group on particular problems, such as those cited, are courageous and debatable. What interests me, however, is the basic assumption that gave rise to them. This assumption is that the cardinal ethical virtue of responsibility can be made the norm for regulating and judging sexual behavior. Sexual acts are thus to be evaluated by whether they express and encourage the responsible behavior of the whole person, negatively by whether they involve exploitation.

Using this as its criterion, the group finds no reason to condemn premarital, extramarital or homosexual relations *as such*. Sexuality, regarded objectively, is "neither good nor evil." The Christian sees it as "a glorious gift of God," which can indeed be misused; but misuse is not synonymous with infringement of the moral code, not even when that code is called Christian and seems to have biblical sanction. "It seemed to us that morals, like the Sabbath, were made for man, not man for morals. . . ."

I am going to criticize this approach, but I would like first to say that the group's obvious concern for "what is happening to people, what they are seeking to express, what motivations and intentions they are satisfying, what fruits, good or bad, they are harvesting" is of great importance and commends their report to every person who is seeking light on sexual ethics in our time.

The issue for Christian ethics raised by the pamphlet is a particular case of the relation of Law and Gospel. The Friends group was right to see that in our present cultural situation it is no longer sufficient to reiterate traditional standards, not even if this is combined with a Christian compassion for the offender. For the problem is that the traditional standards are no longer felt by the society to be derived from a genuine authority. This is so not only because of the alienation of the multitudes from the Church but also because within the Church—among pastors and other counselors—there is a widespread feeling that to insist upon "pure" sexual behavior may lead to neglect of "weightier matters," may jeopardize the communication of that profounder thing, man's freedom in Christ.

This feeling may not be based upon the deepest sort of insight, but it *is* based upon one accurate opinion: namely, that when traditional religious authority is not felt by a man to be binding upon his conscience, then it is not possible to preach to him the Law and the Gospel at the same time. Well aware of the disasters created by preaching the Law only, ministers tend to say more about the Gospel. But in the long run this has the effect of undermining the Law itself, at least in so far as the Law must be spelled out as a specific guide to conduct.

The last fifty years have witnessed most churches steadily liberalizing their views on divorce, softening their condemnations of many sexual practices, particularly homosexuality, and at the same time failing to provide a new formulation of the Law as it pertains to sex. No area of life is so neglected by specialists in Christian ethics as is sex. In no field have we done less to re-examine our basic assumptions, "Bible in one hand and newspaper in the other."

The Quaker group calls for a "new morality" of sex. It affirms that "there must be a morality of some sort to govern sexual relations." It insists very cogently upon the social character of even the most private sexual acts. But it says nothing that might lead directly to the enunciation of the "new morality" for which it calls.

The call had to be made, however, and I want now to add to it a few considerations that ought to be taken into account by Christian ethicists when they consider, as they must, the problem of sexual morality anew.

The aim of the Quaker group is to pass beyond an insistence upon conformity to a code by urging that sexual relations, conformist or not, be brought into line with authentic selfhood. This is, of course, commendable, especially in a time when so many people treat sex as a commodity. But I am convinced that it is insufficient and even highly misleading. It is at once too idealistic and too somber to fit the facts.

Sex is a force that streams impersonally through nature. If we ask that this force be an expression of love, we must be aware of the several realities that are signified by this one English word. Love is not only responsibility and *agape.* It is also *eros,* which means desire. Sexual desire is not only desire of the "other" for the various kinds of beauty and good he, she or it may possess. It is also desire for self-gratification. The great power of sexual desire comes from the fact that it combines desire for the other with desire to gratify the self. If we are not speaking of this Janus-force we are not speaking of sex but of other things that are deemed good in association with it.

No sexual ethic, including a Christian one, can be valid if it does not recognize the sex force as a power in its own right and in both its other-directed and self-directed aspects. Whatever we say of the Church's time-honored view that marriage is a license for the outlet of sexual passion (and the Quakers' report is adamant against it), at least it had the virtue of realism in regarding the sex-force as a given and not fully tamable fact of human nature.

It is a mistake to assume that sex can be entirely personalized or, as a new book by a Protestant tells us, that "it is inseparable from the realization of one's humanity."* Sex is not essentially human, it is not inseparable from the human in us, and it cannot be fully humanized. It can be *personified,* as Aphrodite or Brigitte Bardot (I prefer Aphrodite), but these personifications have imaginative power because they represent as personal that which overrides personality. Did we not laugh when Thurber and White asked us, "Is sex necessary?"

It is, indeed, from sexual humor that Christians have at present most to learn. We should distrust any pronouncement about sex, including the Quakers' report, that does not allow for the humorous side of the subject. Volumes of ostensibly Christian literature may in this way be swept from the shelves, with good riddance.

Misplaced seriousness has wreaked more havoc on modern sexuality than all the films of Hollywood, most of which are themselves soddenly lugubrious as a "concession" to the pious. A return of ribaldry, now virtually absent from Broadway and Hollywood, would do much to clear the air.

Laughter at sex is about the only way to put sex in its place, to assert one's humanity over against that impersonal, irrational, yet necessary force that turns even the best of men into caricatures of themselves. Not only "sinful" sex does this: lawful sex, safely within the limits of marriage and love, does it too, as everybody knows; and he who does not laugh about it must be humiliated by it.

To be sure, there are various kinds of laughter. I hold no brief for snickering. Quite the opposite. A snicker is the unhappy result of a healthy impulse to laughter being partially suppressed by an unhealthy sense that laughter is forbidden. Also the giggle, which comes from embarrassment.

What I proclaim is the Christian freedom to treat an impersonal aspect of creation lightly. What I deplore is that almost every book and article written on sex by a Christian leaves one with the feeling that sex must be a serious business. What has happened to our common sense?

Part of the answer may lie in the negative attitudes St. Paul seems to have had, part in the Church's long-held view that flesh belongs to sin. But I believe there is a simpler explanation closer to hand, especially as regards recent writing. It is that writers on sexual behavior tend to have

* Roger Mehl, reviewing in *Le Monde* (May 29, 1963) *Amour et Sexualité* by Robert Grimm (Delachaux et Niestlé: Neuchatel and Paris, 1962).

in mind the needs of adolescents and other persons who are disturbed about their sex life.

Laughter at sex comes naturally to the blessed, by which I mean young children and grown-up people, but not to the adolescent and the disturbed. To children the human body is neither a temple nor a prison: it is just odd, like the frog in the garden.

The girl child's laughter at male physiognomy is no rejection of the body but simply a subordination of it to common sense. And her mother, if she has left adolescence behind her, will find the subject even funnier because she knows the sex act and all its disproportions. (Males usually do not find as much to laugh at: proud man does not like humor to cut him down to size.)

In the whirlwinds of puberty the body becomes a serious matter. Loss of chastity looms up, longed for and feared, and even after that happens there is a long road to travel before those many adjustments are made that allow the sex life both to flower and to be separated from the centers of anxiety. While this is going on, laughter seems too cheap for sex—though by an assumed toughness the adolescent can invert his natural feelings.

A special problem is therefore posed as to how one discusses sex with the adolescent and the disturbed. Telling a homosexual who is a potential suicide that his situation is comic is obviously not going to help him. That doesn't change the fact that this is actually what he most needs to know. Had Oscar Wilde considered his own emotions to be as humorous as he considered other things, he would not have gotten into all that trouble. Of course he *wanted* trouble; and the law, being as serious as he, obliged him. If Wilde lost his sense of humor at this point, at least one old lady maintained hers. Asked what she thought, she replied, "I don't care what they do, as long as they don't do it in the street and frighten the horses."

What we say to the adolescent and the disturbed is a pastoral question or, if you like, a question of therapeutic strategy. (Adolescence is a disease: if one is cured of it, he becomes immune.) The strategy will often be decided, as the Army says, "by the situation and the terrain." But this particular question is to be separated sharply from the problem of framing a basic Christian sexual ethic. The psychology of the adolescent and the disturbed cannot be normative.

The adolescent is endemically romantic: he idealizes sex, sometimes inverting this idealism into scorn and fear. But Christianity should no more idealize sex than it should scorn or fear it. It sees sex as a fact of created nature. This natural force can no more be made fully "human" than can mountain goats or ocean currents. Like them it can, if accepted, be used by man for his own good within a life of faithfulness and praise. Only, however, if the *mystique* of sex, a holdover from paganism, is blanched away. For the idealization of sex is merely one face of the coin that shows on its other side the disparagement of sex.

Among the topics in the Quakers' report that could be improved with the leaven of humor is homosexuality. Society regards homosexuality between consenting adults as a crime. Opposing this, the Quaker group sees it as tragedy or potentially as a serious and responsible sexual relation. Now a crime it certainly should not be. A tragedy it need not be. It is neither of these essentially. I would not deny that it *can* be a serious and responsible relation. But the matter cannot be left there, as the report leaves it.

Let us go on to say that homosexuality is odd. All sex is odd, but homo-sex is odder than most. And funnier. The homosexual doesn't know what he's missing. Bigger joke: for emotional reasons, he *can't* know. The guy is trapped. The question now is: are we to take this trap as fate (bad), or destiny (potentially good), or as a devil of a predicament from which there might be a way out? The minute we opt for fate and/or destiny we play acolyte to the bogus rituals that surround homosexuality. There is a whole literature and psychology built on this, and it's just plain cockeyed. Psychiatry, as it sheds its doctrinaire determinism, is waking up to this fact.

Since we are not to idealize heterosexuality, neither are we to acquiesce in the idealization of homosexuality. The first step to health is to remove from it the aura of forbidden (therefore exalted) mystery. And I submit that homosexuality brought fully into the light of day and stripped of its exotic defenses will appeal to only a fraction of the people now swept along by it.

I do not mean to say that the ethical dilemmas of sex can be overcome by purely social and psychological means. Whatever we do to dispel by laughter and common sense the *mystique* of sex, whatever we do to make the statutes of the land more wise, there will always remain an area in which one's moral response is decisive and in which codification is necessary. But the area of decision-making will remain obscure as long as the laws and the prevalent attitudes of society are out of touch with human nature.

Let us not try fully to humanize, let alone to sanctify, sex; but let us assert a human transcendence over it. Such a plea does not add up to a Christian ethic of sex. It only asks that specialists in ethics deal with sex as the thing it is and not as the bearer of either our salvation or our damnation. The Quakers did not make that mistake, but they were so serious in their approach that they came close.

Sex is necessary, but it is not necessity.

October 14, 1963

Evangelical Ethics and the Ideal of Chastity

෬෨෮

Harvey Cox

WHEN JOHN U. MUNRO, Dean of Harvard College, warned his students last fall that their sexual conduct in dormitory rooms was "getting closer and closer to outright scandal," other university officials added the somewhat less than surprising comment that traditional religious teaching seemed to offer students little guidance in sexual behavior. The Harvard furor came on the heels of a recommendation by British Quakers that traditional Christian sexual ethics be totally overhauled, sanctioning sexual relationships before and outside of marriage under proper conditions. Meanwhile, back at the Key Club, *Playboy* editor Hugh Hefner's wearisome attack on the religious repression of sex has reached its sixteenth turgid installment.

In short, the whole vexing question of the Christian estimate of sexuality seems to have crept out from under the rug where it had been so carefully swept.

In view of the immensity of this erotic Augean stable, the best one more article can hope to do is to ventilate one small corner. I propose therefore to limit my discussion to a single issue: The traditional ideal of premarital chastity.

I choose this not because of any belief that this is really the key issue. It does seem clear, however, that for many young adults today "to bed or not to bed" *seems* to be the Big Question, and I believe the reasons they press it so vigorously merit exploration. Three aspects of the problem require particular attention: (1) Why the yes or no of premarital chastity is more critical for young adults today than in the past; (2) why the answers we usually give to this question are either not heard or provide little guidance; and (3) what, if anything, we should be saying about the matter.

The question of premarital chastity is not the only one in which the yawning disparity between what we *say* and what we *do* in America is being questioned and examined. Negroes are calling us to *do* what we *say* about equality and justice. Young adults are challenging us to *say* what we really *do* in the area of sex. In both areas the contradictions have about reached their limit.

Let us reject at the outset any Kinseyian inference that what *is* being done should determine what *ought* to be done. But let us candidly admit that our culture has undergone drastic changes. Though our Puritan style of life has vanished almost completely, the Puritan sex ethic remains, at least on paper. We have exchanged ankle-length dresses for bikinis. We hold blanket parties instead of apple-bobbing. But the people caught up in these epochal changes are still taught, albeit with winks and evasions, the selfsame code of total premarital abstinence that was instilled into Priscilla Alden.

We have thus fashioned for unmarried young adults a particularly unfortunate combination of emotional environments. They are constantly bombarded—through clothing styles, entertainment, advertising and courtship mores—with perhaps the most skillfully contrived array of erotic stimulants ever amassed. Their sexual fears and fantasies are studied by motivational researchers and then ruthlessly exploited by mass media hucksters. Elizabeth Taylor's Brobdingnagian bosom decorates billboards, and throaty songstresses hum their hoarse invitations from transistors.

Yet we pass on to our youth, unaltered, a set of behavioral taboos that, in a sex-saturated society, seem diabolically created to produce a high level of duplicity and desperation.

Why have we deliberately constructed such a bizarre disbalance in our moral and psychological milieu? Obviously because we want to have our cake and eat it too. We want to gorge ourselves at the table of an affluent society whose continued prosperity, we are told, necessitates a constantly expanding market. And sex sells anything. At the same time we want to cherish our national memories of Pilgrims and piety, including the sexual code of Massachusetts Bay. The inherent contradiction comes home to roost in the already tormented psyche of the unmarried young adult.

The essential contradictions of any society, as the Marxists say, are concentrated in its proletariat. In a sexually exploitative society, youth sub-culture becomes the psychological proletariat. It picks up the tab for our hypocrisy. Exposed to all the stimulants married people are, young people are forbidden the socially acceptable form of fulfillment. The refusal is expressed both in the laws of the realm and in the official taboos of the culture. Enforcement, however, is sporadic, and, because the signals are so confused and contradictory, adolescents suspect that it is all one vast dissimulation.

No wonder the "beatnik," who rejects *both* the signals of the mass media and the sexual mores, becomes the secret hero of many young adults.

To make matters just a bit more trying, we have thoughtfully provided Jane and Joe with more privacy and permissiveness in dating than ever before. This extends far beyond Harvard dormitory rooms. I wonder if Henry Ford ever realized that his invention would be viewed by many not primarily as a means of transportation but as the urban society's substitute for Keats' "elfin grot."

Remember also that dating (and with it various types of petting) now reaches back to the sixth grade. Youngsters are thus exposed for a longer period and much more intensely to the mutual exploration of erogenous regions, which is the American courtship pattern. The only advice they get is "don't go too far," and it is usually the girl who is expected to draw the line.

By the time a girl who begins petting at thirteen has reached marriageable age, she has drawn an awful lot of lines. If she is especially impressed with her religious duty to avoid coital intercourse, she will probably have mastered, by age twenty-one, all the stratagems for achieving a kind of sexual climax while simultaneously preventing herself and her partner from crossing the sacrosanct line.

What this border-skirting approach does to inhibit her chances for a successful adjustment in marriage is a question now engaging the attention of psychologists and marriage counselors. One psychologist who specializes in sexual behavior remarked recently that if Americans had consciously set out to think up a system that would produce maximal marital and premarital strife for both sexes, we could scarcely have invented a more sexually sabotaging set of dating procedures than we have today. This may be an overstatement, but I suspect the inherent hypocrisy of the cultural taboo and the patterns of behavior it engenders must have considerable negative influence on marriage.

Add to this the fact that penicillin and oral contraceptives will soon remove the last built-in deterrents to premarital coitus and the reason for the recent rumblings of discontent with traditional standards becomes clearer. Not that the young adults themselves are guiltless. They share the blame for perpetuating the same values. But they also consider themselves to be the victims of a kind of cultural charade. They are shown one thing, told another, and they never know when the society will wink and when it will whip them. Their suspicion that they are the fall guys in a giant collusion is expressed in their growing demand that we come clean on this matter.

Now we can turn to the question of why, amidst this schizophrenic carnival of prurience and prudery, the Christian Gospel seems to offer so little positive guidance. I believe the answer to this question is that most young adults do not perceive Christian sexual ethics as "evangelical," that is, *good news*. They are not hearing the Gospel as good news and therefore they are not hearing the Gospel at all, but something else.

This may in part be their own fault. We all have ways to avoid hearing what we do not want to hear. But much of the blame lies with those of us who bear the responsibility of seeing to it that the real Gospel and not some distortion of it is preached.

Friedrich Gogarten (in *Der Mensch Zwischen Gott und Welt,* p. 34) states that the two most serious dangers from which the Gospel must be protected are (a) its being dissolved into a myth, and (b) its being hardened into a religion of Law. In either case it ceases to be the Gospel. When we examine what has happened to the Gospel as it touches the area of sex, it is evident that both of these distortions have set in.

The Gospel comes to the sexual puzzlement of most young adults not as a liberating "yes," not as God's Good News freeing them for personhood and community. It comes rather as a remnant of cultural Christendom and an assortment of confused conventions. To be heard once again as the Gospel it must be de-mythologized and delegalized.

Let us turn first to the task of de-mythologizing it from odd bits of sexual folklore with which it has been confused. I shall refer to only two of the many mythical motifs that obfuscate the Gospel in its bearing on sexual conduct. First the ideal of romantic love, which Denis de Rougement has traced to paganism and which is almost always fused with any young American's ideas about sex. Second, the Western obsession with coital intercourse as normative sexuality and hence as that which defines the content of "chastity" and "virginity." The idestification is now so complete that, as Theodor W. Adorno recently pointed out, "intercourse" now *means* coitus.

Both the romantic ideal and the identification of intercourse with coitus are cultural accretions that have been coalesced with the rule of premarital chastity. The combination has so beclouded the liberating power of the Gospel that it can scarcely be heard because of them, and the Gospel is frequently perceived to be saying almost the opposite of what is intended.

The ideal of romantic love is the most obvious mythical excrescence. It leads often to the belief, especially among girls, that certain forms of intimacy become progressively less objectionable the more you "love" the boy. The snares in this curious amalgam of Our Gal Sunday and St. Teresa are manifold. Among adolescents of all ages "love" has come to mean nothing more than a vague emotional glow. It's "that ol' black magic," "those icy fingers up and down my spine."

The belief that "love" is the only honest basis for sex forces countless maidens into anguished efforts to justify their sexual inconstancy by falling in and out of love with a passing parade of partners. Naturally, opportunities for self-deception are almost endless, and the outcome is often an acid cynicism about the possibility of ever really loving anyone.

Furthermore, the sex-and-romantic-love question sets up an inevitable collision course. The conflict occurs because, although girls tend to "go the limit" only with a boy they believe they "love," many boys, as sociologist Winston Ehrmann shows in his *Premarital Dating Behavior,* will stop short of intercourse with girls they "love" or "respect," though they will go as far as possible with a girl they do not. Thus girls associate sex with romantic love far more than boys do, and emotional scars emerging from this built-in contradiction often last far into married life.

Since girls feel they must be swept into sexual experience by something "bigger than both of us," they often fail to take the precautions against pregnancy they might otherwise take. Somehow it doesn't *seem* romantic to go out with a boy having prepared in advance to be swept off one's feet. Consequently many instances of intercourse are not "planned" but occur more or less spontaneously at the end of an evening of progressively heavier necking. Unwanted pregnancies, abortions, shattered family relations and forfeited careers are the inevitable result.

One solution is to admonish everybody to avoid any physical contact that could spiral toward intercourse. But how sane or compassionate is this advice in a society where various types of petting are the only socially approved way of handling tensions exacerbated by a sexually saturated culture? Petting does sometimes lead to intercourse, but not always. In fact, most of the time it does not. To try to abolish it while still retaining our prosperity and our aphrodisiacal advertising would be even less honest than the preach-and-wink pharisaism.

Another antidote is simply to de-romanticize sex. This would mean urging young people who are going to have intercourse anyway (and who, under layers of unsuccessful self-deception, know they will) to accept the full responsibility for their behavior and to take the necessary steps to avoid pregnancy.

Such a solution, although more realistic, has almost as little chance of acceptance as the first. It would necessitate dispelling the illusions of romantic love and suggesting that young people ponder soberly in the light of day what they are really doing. But it would also require our society to face up to the cant and flimflam of its sexual folkways, and this no one really wants to do. So the black magic, petting and pregnancies will probably continue.

A more stubborn and deceptive segment of folklore that has been equated with the doctrine of premarital chastity is one that is rarely discussed openly: The curious presumption that a person who has not experienced coital intercourse remains a virgin—no matter what else he or she has done. This popular piece of legerdemain explains in part the discovery by Kinsey that, although the incidence of premarital intercourse among women has merely mounted steadily, premarital petting of all varieties has skyrocketed.

Kinsey's finding could be substantiated by the most casual observer of the American college scene. The number of students who do not pet at all is virtually negligible. An increasing number regularly carry their necking to the point of heavy sex play and orgasm. A pert young graduate of a denominational college assured me recently that although she had necked to orgasm every week-end for two years, she had "never gone all the way." Her "premarital chastity" was intact.

Or was it? Only, I submit, by the most technical definition of what it means to preserve virginity. True, some writers actually advocate such non-coital orgasm as the "safest" way for unmarried people to achieve sexual climax. (See Alex Comfort in *Sexual Behavior in Society*.) However distasteful this idea may seem to some, it is extremely important to realize that the Church's traditional teaching actually functions in such a fashion as to give considerable support to this view.

The idea of premarital chastity is generally understood to mean that, although necking is somewhat questionable, the fragile gem of virginity remains intact so long as coitus is avoided. This myth has helped to open the floodgate to a tidal wave of non-coital promiscuity.

Here the de-mythologizing process might be helped if we note St. Paul's insistence (in I Corinthians 6:15-16) that liaisons intended to be highly casual, for example with prostitutes, nevertheless involve us in a relationship that is inevitably much deeper than we bargained for. We "become one flesh." D. S. Bailey calls this "a psychological insight . . . altogether exceptional by first century standards."

St. Paul saw the striking fact that as human beings we both *have* and *are* bodies. This is an issue that has been explored at length by such contemporary philosophers as Gabriel Marcel and Maurice Merleau-Ponty. St. Paul saw that sex, unlike excretion for example, is not simply a physiological but a "bodily" (somatic) activity. It involves us at the deepest levels of our personal identity.

But why limit St. Paul's insight to coital intercourse alone, or to contacts with prostitutes? The mere avoidance of coitus does not exempt anyone from becoming "one flesh" with another. All "virgins" who are promiscuous neckers should know that. Also the "one flesh" phenomenon cannot be restricted to the bordello.

St. Paul knew that no sexual relationship could be kept merely physical without ceasing to be really sexual in the fully human sense of the word. This is why the "playmate-of-the-month" domestication of sex as a purely recreational pursuit just doesn't work. Paul really appreciated sex more than Hugh Hefner does. He expected more from it. Sex is certainly fun, but to make it *simply* fun is to eviscerate and enfeeble it. And then it eventually ceases even to be fun.

When it is de-mythologized, the evangelical sexual ethic turns out to be an invitation to life together in a community of personal selves. The Gospel frees us from the need to cling to romantic self-deception and the works righteousness by which we clothe our promiscuity in the costume of technical virginity. By delivering us from mythology into history, Jesus Christ allows us to see that the marvelous skein of privileges and responsibilities in which we find ourselves as human beings is something for which we are responsible. But how do we exercise this responsibility?

At this point the going becomes more difficult. Any effort to arrest the generation of the Gospel into some form of Law will be viewed in some quarters as "antinomianism," the belief that the precepts of the Law are not binding for Christians. A Gospel ethic, however, demands more maturity and more discipline than a Law ethic. Evangelical ethics are by nature riskier. This risk must be run since the New Testament insists unequivocally that it is the Gospel and not the Law that saves. How then can we begin to "delegalize" the Gospel when sexual behavior is the question at issue?

The Gospel is addressed to persons; the Law sees acts. One weakness of the traditional ethical formulation on premarital chastity is its sweeping inclusiveness and total lack of discrimination. Reduced to a precept, the ideal of premarital chastity permits no distinction between intercourse by engaged couples, for example, and the chilling exploitation of high school girls at fraternity parties. Both are transgressions of the Law, and there is no middle ground between virginity and non-virginity.

Consequently there emerges alongside the technical virgin her shadowy counterpart, the technical fallen woman, the girl who, because she once consented to intercourse, now feels she is permanently pastured among the goats. She has crossed the sexual Styx, and there is no way back. Because she can no longer present herself to her husband in purity on the wedding night anyway, why shouldn't anything go?

Her self-condemnation arises in part because she has not heard the *good* news. She has perceived the traditional teaching as a *law*. Law without Gospel is arbitrary and abstract. It cannot discriminate among cases. And it has nothing helpful to say to the transgressor. Consequently for the increasing proportion of young people who have already had sexual intercourse, the rule of premarital chastity is simply irrelevant. And since for many it appears to be the only record the Church ever plays on this subject, they conclude the Church has nothing to say to them.

But preaching the Gospel also entails preaching the Law, i.e., exposing the false absolutes from which one is liberated. Negatively this means making clear the distorted images of sex from which the Gospel delivers us. Positively it entails protecting sex as a fully human activity against all the principalities and powers that seek to dehumanize it. In our day these include the forces, both within and without, that pervert sex into a merchandising technique, a means of self-aggrandizement, a weapon for rebelling against parents, a recreational pursuit, a way to gain entrance into the right clique *or*—let the reader beware—a devotional act with some sort of religious significance.

To be freed from the "bondage of the Law" means to be freed from these dehumanizing powers. It also means to be freed from those diabolical pressures toward sub-cultural conformity that push so many adolescents into whatever is "in" at the moment. Sexual freedom in Christ, in one concrete case, means that a harried co-ed can say "no" to a cloying Romeo without feeling she is being hopelessly square.

Evangelical ethics cease to be Law and once again become Gospel when the Word liberates people from cultural conventions and social pressures, when persons discover their sexuality as a delightful gift of God that links them in freedom and concern to their fellows. But how do we make *this* Gospel heard by young adults in today's sexually rapacious society?

Before answering this question we must admit that we have created a set of cultural conditions in which sexual responsibility is made exceedingly difficult. In our American Xanadu, exhortations to individual continence are almost as useless as urging businessmen to eschew the profit motive.

It is strange how even people who see most clearly that crime, illegitimacy, narcotics addiction and poverty are largely structural problems, still interpret the increase in premarital sexual experience as a breakdown in personal morals.

But the jig is nearly up. Our feverish effort to paper over a society propelled by drives for sex and status with a set of Victorian courtship mores is breaking down badly. We must direct our fire more toward the "feminine mystique" and the cynical misutilization of sex by the public relations culture than toward the hapless individual offender.

This may involve some searching questions about limiting the deliberate use of sexual stimulation in selling or, even more radically, about the merit of an economic system that seems to require a constant perversion of sexuality in order to survive. Commercial exploitation of sex drives—not the call girls—is our most serious form of prostitution today.

When we do turn from the society to the individual, especially to the unmarried young adult, we must avoid giving a simple yes or no answer to the question of premarital chastity. Of course, this will sound like evasion, but any simple answer panders to the cheap attempt to oversimplify the issue, to reduce all the intricacies of premarital sexuality to one decision. And churchmen, by allowing the Gospel to deteriorate into folklore and fiat, have contributed to this fatal oversimplification.

I do not believe that an evangelical ethic of premarital sex can be chopped down to a flat answer to this freighted question without impoverishing and distorting it. Instead of registering an answer, the Gospel poses a question of its own (as Jesus himself frequently did with such questions). It asks how I can best nourish the maturity of those with whom I share the torments and transports of human existence.

The Gospel liberates men from mythical taboos and rigid concepts for a purpose: So that the full and untrammeled resources of the human imagination can be exercised in responsibility for others within the patterns of public and private life. In the freedom of the Gospel, we arrive at decisions by utilizing norms that themselves must always be open to criticism and transformation, and are therefore never final. Traditional Christian sexual norms are no exception. They do not stand above history. They have arisen as Christians attempted to live faithfully through constantly changing social systems. Like all human codes they stand in continuous need of revision so they will help rather than hinder God's maturation of man.

Christians believe God is at work in history bringing man to adulthood and responsibility. Within this framework the norms by which we make our decisions are fashioned and discarded in a continuing conversation with the Bible and with the culture, a conversation that is never completed. The Christian knows he is free only as a partner in this conversation and as a member of this community. This means, among other things, that his decisions about sexual conduct inevitably involve more people than he would sometimes like to involve. Sex is never simply a "private matter."

To refuse to deliver a prepared answer whenever the question of premarital intercourse pops up will have a healthy influence on the continuing conversation that is Christian ethics. It moves the axis of the discussion away from the arid stereotypes by which we oversimplify intricate human issues. It gets us off dead-end arguments about virginity and chastity, and forces us to think about fidelity to persons. It exposes the promiscuity of sexual pharisees and the subtle exploitation that poisons even the most immaculate Platonic relationships.

By definition "premarital" refers to people who plan to marry someone someday. Premarital sexual conduct should therefore serve to strengthen the chances of sexual success and fidelity in marriage. And we must face the real question of whether avoidance of intercourse beforehand is always the best preparation.

This question includes consideration of the appropriate degree of sexual intimacy during increasingly extended engagement periods. The reason it cannot be answered once and for all is that circumstances vary from couple to couple. Guidance must be given with specific persons rather than with general conventions in view.

Admittedly this approach requires more resourcefulness and imagination than relying on universally applicable axioms. Principles are useful, perhaps indispensable in ethical thinking, but all too often "sticking to principles" can become just another way to avoid seeing persons. It can signify a relapse from Gospel into Law.

Perhaps one day we in America will put away childish things. Perhaps one day we will outgrow our ridiculous obsession with sex, of which our fixation on chastity and virginity is just the other side of the coin. Until that time, however, we should rejoice that in Jesus Christ we are freed from myth and from Law. We are placed in a community of selves, free to the extent that we live for each other, free to develop whatever styles of life will contribute to the maturation of persons in a society where persons are often overlooked as we scamper to pursue profits and piety all at once.

April 27, 1964

The Gospel According to St. Hereticus—Scripture Lesson for Easter

IN A PREVIOUS INSTALLMENT I offered a new text for the Advent lesson, a kind of prologue to a fifth gospel, on the assumption that the canon is not closed and that future church councils will want to take all new manuscripts into account. It seems to me that something of the sort is also called for in the Easter season. In what follows, therefore, I offer the Easter story as it has come to be told in the oral traditions of modern culture-religion. While some will urge that it belongs to the *genre* of saga, folklore, tradition or myth, others will want to insist that it is not, for all that, the less true. It should be clear, at all events, that this is not something that I have "made up." It is sober and straight-forward reporting of the various strata of twentieth-century religion. Students of the *Formgeschichte Schule* who want to disentangle the various sources can start from the fact that the extant versions draw on at least the following sources: SS (Sunday Schools), ss (sermons by seminarians), Ss (Sunday supplements), Pp (Protestant pulpits), RC (Radio Commercials), and StSp (Sermon topics in Saturday's papers).

The Gospel According to St. Hereticus

CHAPTER 23

[1]But on the first day of the week, toward dawn, they arose and went to the garden in convertibles, ranch wagons, and Corvettes, wearing on their persons the spices they had prepared for the occa-

sion. [2]And behold, as the sun burst forth there was a great blast from four trumpets, drawn from the local high school marching band. And at the blast of the trumpets, an Easter bunny, wondrous large, stood before them. [3]His appearance was like lightning and his fur was white as snow. [4]And he did carry a sign affixed to his hat bearing the words "Courtesy of Jones' Department Store."

[5]And in great joy at his appearing, all the children began to clamor and to shout, [6]saying as with one voice, "Who will roll away the eggs for us?" [7]For at his appearance it was as though the miracle of spring had been enacted once again, and that from the belly of the Easter bunny had come forth many eggs, some green, some yellow, some chocolate; and red, white and blue ones not a few.

[8]And the parents were grieved and afraid for the children, that they would pick up the eggs and pelt one another therewith. [9]For it was the custom in that place that on Easter morn all believers were to dress in new raiment. And the parents were afraid not only for the children's raiment but for their own as well, [10]for verily all those assembled were believers and were wearing new and shining apparel for which they had paid beyond their means, some thirty, some sixty, and some an hundred fold.

[11]Then all with one cry took up the refrain, "Behold the miracle of spring!" [12]And those on the left did cry aloud, "I believe in the deep greenness of the new-grown grass," [13]while those on the right were heard to say, "Verily once again from out the earth hath come forth shoots," [14]and all together raised their voices in a mighty chorus to repeat together, "As it was in the beginning, is now and ever shall be, world without end. Amen."

[15]But certain scoffers there were among them who did say, [16]"Ye know not what ye do. [17]Is this not the great miracle of the irruption of eternity into time? [18]Know ye not that the eschatological moment of all the aeons is here compressed into the facticity of the concrete, specific and unrepeatable?" [19]But they said unto them, "We will hear of this another time," [20]and they turned their backs on them. [21]Whereat the scoffers said one to another, "It is as we have always heard. The multitudes will not hear gladly the simple word of the Gospel, for their ears are verily stopped by the sin of their *hubris*." [22] And they went away content among themselves.

[23]And others there were in their midst who did speak on this wise: "Easter is the season of joy. Be joyful in the God of your choice, all ye lands. Serve the God of your choice with earrings, come before his presence with new clothes, and show yourself glad in him with raiment and new finery." [24]And then, with scarcely a change in intonation, the voices went on to say, [25]"For a small down payment you can own the hat of your choice with which to worship the God of your choice. Show your faith in the future by buying now and paying later." [26]And all with one impulse did go

forth, and he that had no money went, bought and did eat, and they all with one accord did sing forth praise to one another's raiment. [27]But privily each one said to himself of the other, "Why did she buy that ghastly hat?" [28]And some did carry placards with words of cheer inscribed thereon, for the hope and consolation of the multitudes. [29]And affixed thereto were words for the season, to wit: [30]"There Is No Death," [31]and "Make Every Day Easter Day," to which latter sign was appended in smaller letters inscribed beneath, "By Banishing All Thought of Death." [32]And one there was whose banner went, in a glorious affirmation of the entire festival, "The Miracle of Easter is the Miracle of Spring." [33]And many there were who carried words too small to read, but whose meaning was writ large by pictures affixed thereto, of green leaves, pansies and new ploughed fields. [34]And through it all none was discouraged save three. [35]And they went out and fled. For trembling and astonishment had come upon them. And they said nothing to anyone, for they were afraid.

Some of the textual critics have suggested that the MSS has broken off in the middle of a sentence. I'm willing to let it stand as is. It seems a fit conclusion.

March 16,1959

Morality and Democratic Decision

V

The Church and Power Conflicts

John C. Bennett

MUCH OF THE DEBATE ABOUT THE Church and power conflicts now going on in many American cities seems very familiar because it is a replay of discussions in which I was involved in the 1930's when the chief issue was the relation of the churches to the labor movement in its early struggles to achieve power. Almost the first article I ever published was on the subject "Christianity and Class Consciousness." (It was published in 1932 under the auspices of the Fellowship of Reconciliation.) Re-reading it recently, I found it quite relevant to the present discussions.

I might say some things differently today, but I would still hold to the basic principle that an important aspect of Christian social responsibility is the organization politically of the victims of social injustice so that they can use their power to change conditions.

It was often assumed in certain circles in the Thirties that there should be labor churches, though it was also assumed that the Church at large should find ways of including all classes. In those days many of us thought in a more doctrinaire way about social classes than we do now. Those were the days of the Great Depression when the whole of American society was so stricken that one could think of organizing the many against the few. Such a pattern is no longer needed.

Rather, we need to find ways in which the comparatively few who are most neglected can combine the strategic forms of power they still have with persuasion in order to change those conditions in our cities that cry to heaven. In this process we need to find ways in which churches can help both in organizing political pressures and in using this as part of a broader strategy of persuasion—often persuasion of consciences within the Church.

Let me now mention several presuppositions that underlie what follows.

(1) Christian love must seek justice for the neglected and oppressed in our nation and the world.

We all take this for granted, but it has not generally been assumed. It probably would not be as widely accepted in the Church as it is if the neglected and oppressed had not in this country gained a voice and considerable power to make themselves felt. I doubt if the churches themselves have done very much to inspire the revolutions of our time even though the inspiration of the Gospel has been behind them.

One hardly needs to argue today for the revolutionary implications of our faith. God, as known to us in Christ, is seeking to raise the level of life everywhere. (I like the phrase of my colleague Professor Paul Lehmann, "God is seeking to make humanity more human.") God is acting in the "revolution of rising expectations" on other continents. But he is also active in the revolution of rising expectations in American cities where millions live in shameful ghettos.

Our civil rights revolution is a part of this worldwide revolution. While it must go on in Mississippi and the hard-core South, for most of us this revolution is concentrated in Northern cities where the racial factor is important but where there is also a broader rebellion against slums, schools that do not educate, poverty and unemployment. One of the most startling facts about America is the contrast between our great prosperity as a nation and these islands of misery in our cities. Why, with all our resources, initiative and ingenuity, do we do so little to solve these problems?

We seem to sacrifice these millions of people on two altars—the altar of prejudice and the altar of economic individualism. In the name of freedom of the individual, we sacrifice them to that caricature of Christianity that some people call "the Protestant ethic," an ethic that finds no way of dealing directly and massively with large-scale social problems.

(2) The Church should not choose to be a sect made up of those who belong to any one class or social group, or of those who hold the same opinions.

I am not suggesting that the Church should include everyone, all the slum landlords and all the members of the John Birch Society. If some people choose to leave the Church because it has come to stand for racial integration and for a dynamic approach to social problems, that may be a good sign. But let the Church still seek to be the mother of us all. Let it not exclude those who, because of many confusions, differ from one or another of its declared positions. Let it include people on all sides of the conflicts of power, seeking to be a pastor to them all. Let it go out to all men—poor and rich, in city, town and suburb—with the Gospel, seeking to change and heal them.

Think for a moment of what a policy of exclusiveness would mean. If we were to begin to divide the Church over differences of opinion about current issues, it would be split in the 1960's over one set of issues and in the 1970's over another. This is madness, and it must not be. We must still have a church that seeks to be all-inclusive and yet stands for something.

(3) We should be guided by a doctrine of man that sees our humanity as made in the image of God and as distorted by pride and egoism, and especially by that form of both that causes people to try to exalt themselves by keeping others in an inferior position.

All too often people are corrupted by the crudest form of greed, though they are skillful in covering this up with high-sounding defenses of the rights of property. My emphasis here is on the fact that all of us are strange mixtures of virtue and sinful distortions.

I want to stress two implications of this general view. The first is that people who have advantages and are complacent about their situation do not usually change unless pressure is put on them by those who, because of their suffering, need to have things changed. It doesn't mean that those who bring the pressure are subjectively better people than those who have the pressure brought on them. The latter are in a different position, and it may well be that those who bring this pressure are, on the whole, on the side of an objective justice.

Persuasion is seldom an adequate lever; people do not even see the facts until they are forced to look at them. And the defenses of complacency are endless. In our society, pressure by itself is not enough either. One of our chief interests should be *to make interpreted pressure an instrument of persuasion.* Certainly this has happened on a very large scale in this country since the Montgomery boycott and the first sit-ins. People all over the country, North and South, were forced to attend to the problem; issues became clearer; many minds and hearts were changed. Sometimes the changes have been accepted grudgingly, but they have come. There is a combination of pressure and persuasion when a candidate discovers that he lost because ninety-five per cent of the Negroes in his state voted against him. A shifting of gears is necessary, and then people can learn by doing. We need not take a cynical attitude toward this process.

The other implication of this way of thinking about human nature is that we must not separate groups, classes or races of men by assigning to one the image of God and to the other the effects of the fall. Martin Luther King's strong statement in London expressing alertness to the danger of black racism as well as white racism is to be welcomed. In one moment almost all the virtue may be on one side in a conflict, but that moment will not last long, and it is the responsibility of the Church to help people on both sides realize that they have common temptations and weaknesses and sins. The outward expressions may be different, but the Church stands for the common humanity across the lines that divide people.

Herbert Butterfield in *Christianity and History* (Scribners) emphasizes the contribution of Christianity as an antidote to self-righteousness:

> The more human beings are lacking in imagination, the more incapable men are of any profound kind of self-analysis, the more we shall find that their self-righteousness hardens, so that it is just the thick-skinned who are more sure of being right than anybody else. And though conflict might still be inevitable in history even if this particular evil (of self-righteousness) did not exist, there can be no doubt that its presence multiplies the deadlocks and gravely deepens all the tragedies of all the centuries. At its worst it brings us to that mythical messianism—that messianic hoax—of the twentieth century which comes perilously near to the thesis: "Just one little war more against the last remaining enemies of righteousness, and then the world will be cleansed, and we can start building Paradise." (p. 41)

The optimism of the last words has faded, but we still are inclined to assume that victory in this last battle against the one enemy in our minds at the moment will destroy the major threat to our society.

One of the major problems in Christian theology and social ethics is to relate this warning against the danger of self-righteousness on all sides to the necessity of taking a stand. We may have to risk a little self-righteousness to get a necessary job done, but if people recognize the problem, this will reduce the effects of self-righteousness.

So much for presuppositions:

> Love must seek justice, often revolutionary justice.
> The Church should seek to include those on both sides of most conflicts.

166

Our doctrine of man should help us to remember the need of combining pressure with persuasion, and it should warn against the self-righteousness on both sides of a conflict.

The most general definition of power is in Paul Tillich's *Love, Power and Justice* (Oxford): "Power is being actualizing itself over against the threat of non-being." Another rather general definition is in Bertrand Russell's illuminating book *Power* (W. W. Norton): "Power is the production of intended effects."

These definitions do not help us much with concrete problems, but they may help us to realize that power as such is neutral; it is always present when any of our purposes are actualized. Also, we need to remember the wide range of the forms of power, from pure persuasion at one end of the scale to what Russell calls naked power at the other.

One of the most important distinctions is between covert and overt power. The established forms of power are no less coercive because they get their way without very obvious use of power. Such power is exercised by the almost automatic enforcing of the accepted rules in the society. Those in power discharge employees; they evict tenants; they refrain from taking any positive remedial steps by dragging their feet.

They might take drastic action to change many things, but they prefer to do nothing or to take delaying or token action. It is in their power to do so, and it avoids the appearance of naked power. Protection of interests by foot-dragging is often the most pervasive form of power in our cities. Behind it is control of votes, property, corrupted investigators and many opinion-forming agencies.

This power of the strong to protect their interests may be just as coercive as the most obvious form of violence. The weak who are trying to put together forms of power and to gain political strength are constantly forced into positions in which they have to demonstrate, strike, boycott or initiate events that may be accompanied by violence. This use of power may appear more bloody, but it is less coercive and less destructive than the power to prevent change.

In labor disputes the workers are the ones who cause inconvenience to the public by denying services or perhaps creating a scene in which there may be some violence. Yet the employers may be the cause of the strike, or the responsibility may be divided.

Boycotters, sit-ins, freedom riders, demonstrators have for years been seeking to develop power in a weak minority to counteract the power of employers, local law-enforcement officers and state governments. They are accused of making a disturbance, of risking violence; but their activities have been a relatively weak form of power, in intention nonviolent, against the institutionalized violence of the police system of many a community, against the pervasive intimidation that is the next thing to violence.

Our Protestant constituency by and large does not understand this distinction between the overt force of the weak and the covert force of the establishment. They are all too ready to give low marks to the former and high marks to the latter. They can see the former because it occurs on the streets.

The famous study of Harlem entitled *Youth in the Ghetto* has a significant subtitle: "A Study in the Consequences of Powerlessness" (published by Harlem Youth Opportunities Unlimited, 2092 7th Ave., N. Y., N. Y., $4.50 donation). Harlem "can best be described in terms of the analogy of a powerless colony." As a result, "the basic story of academic achievement in Central Harlem is one of inefficiency, inferiority and massive deterioration." How can this be true of a city in which there is so much wealth and which is sophisticated and liberal in so many ways?

I realize that the conditions described are not only the result of deliberate defense of greed or prejudice or foot-dragging. They also result from the sheer complexity of many problems, but this fact of complexity too easily becomes a kind of umbrella under which the more deliberate efforts to prevent change are the more effective.

The churches have the responsibility to help develop forms of power among the powerless in order to counteract the pervasive power of the strong. It is at this point that I reject the *a priori* arguments against the community development programs in Chicago and elsewhere. To say that they increase conflict need not be a valid criticism. (I do not deny the force of such criticism when this is done without restraint.) But there is a stage in which hidden conflict needs to be brought out into the open. It is a great advance when people who have been powerless and plagued by apathy or fatalism organize to improve their lot, and this means creating instruments of political and economic power that enable their interests to be felt by the community at large.

I realize that such methods have some unfortunate by-products: Concentration on a single issue, the tendency to use oversimplifying slogans, the tendency to turn other parties into provisional devils. But the intensification of conflict may be a necessary stage in the movement away from apathy and submission to injustice and oppression.

This was true in all of the early struggles of the industrial workers. It has been true in all the struggles of the new nations for independence. Anti-colonialism creates many devils; yet it is a by-product of a basically constructive impulse. This is true of the awakening of the younger generation of Negroes who decided that they have taken conditions of deprivation and humiliation long enough, and some of them are tempted to believe no good of any white man.

Most of the criticism of the community development movements is what might be called pre-Niebuhrian. The year 1932 is an important date in American theology and church history. It saw the publication of Reinhold Niebuhr's *Moral Man and Immoral Society,* which contains basic diagnoses of tendencies in human history that are still true: One cannot escape from sin by refusing to relate oneself to movements that seek to develop the power of self-defense among the powerless. One becomes involved in some evil by-products, but one should also count up the evil by-products of refusing to do this: Hypocrisy on one side, apathy on the other, and the injustice that pervades it all.

Some critics charge that many of the processes of community development are "sub-Christian." Doubtless they are, and in some cases particular methods may be justly condemned. I am not asking for an uncritical acceptance of any policies, methods or movements. What I am saying is very similar to what Walter Rauschenbusch said in the context of the struggle of the industrial workers for justice:

> We started out with the proposition that the ideal of a fraternal organization of society will remain powerless if it is supported by idealists only; that it needs the firm support of a solid class whose economic future is staked on the success of that ideal; and that the industrial working class is consciously or unconsciously committed to the struggle for the realization of that principle. It follows that those who desire the victory of that ideal from a religious point of view will have to enter into a working alliance with this class. (*Christianity and the Social Crisis,* Harper Torchbooks, p. 409.)

As we look back on all that has happened since 1907, we would now speak differently of "class." Many qualifications need to be made as a result of hindsight. But at the core of social advance there must be the dynamism that comes from the interests of those who know in their own lives the necessity of change. Today Negroes are the most readily organized group among those who feel the need for change. Their welfare depends upon broad solutions to the problems of urban poverty, unemployment, housing and education that will benefit all races. Here we do not want to play up the racial factor; yet we do need to allow the solidarity of a deprived race to open doors into which many others can enter.

This should not be a struggle involving the use of naked power. Organization to give dignity and morale so that the apathetic can help themselves, organization to bring economic pressure on the community, organization to make effective political decisions—these are all necessary, but we must remember that the world that needs to feel this pressure is itself very complex. Such organization would have many allies and potential allies; it may also count on others who have enough of a bad conscience or who are open enough to accept a changed situation without continued resistance. Also, our Federal Government can be a mighty force in taking the side of the weak and the poor.

The Church can bring essential resources into this struggle: Resources for the organizing of power and for the correction of the idolatries that often go with power. The local church in a neighborhood of deprivation and injustice should not hold aloof from this struggle. I admire what I have read of the work of some local churches in Chicago. Ministers and congregations have identified themselves with this struggle.

To be sure, this creates problems. Their action is no different in principle, however, from what many Negro congregations have done in Montgomery, Birmingham and many other places, for which they have been widely praised. It is no different from what happens in new nations where the Church identifies itself with the aspirations of the people.

The minister may play a provisional political role in these situations, since he is a visible spokesman for his own people who need his leadership. The ambiguities of this role are less than the ambiguities that surround the political silence of the minister in a homogeneous church that resists change, who allows the people to think that he agrees with them when he doesn't.

The church needs many ministers who identify themselves with the efforts of the poor to gain power to balance the thousands of ministers who, implicitly, give their blessings to the way the strong keep their power. There are no clear roles in this area.

A person may rightly choose a role that has its limitations, its dangers, its by-products, all of which are ambiguous, but let us bring this out in the open; let him know about the ambiguities. And let the person who doesn't know what his role is, except that he ministers to those who hold on to the *status quo,* also learn the ambiguities of his role and try to correct some of these.

But there are other dimensions: In no church should the Gospel be reduced to simple advocacy of this or that social goal. The preaching and the liturgy should clearly transcend the immediate teaching about social issues. The minister and laymen who have been exposed to the full teaching of the Church should keep alive resources for criticism of their political involvement. They should not become intransigent in facing complexities that emerge as any community moves toward concrete solutions. Slogans are less and less helpful as guides as soon as real, constructive possibilities emerge.

The local church or a group of churches may move into various forms of action that from some purist position may seem problematic, but at a given moment these may be actions of enormous importance in giving dignity and opportunity to the people of the various congregations and their neighbors. Yet the local church should remain a part of a larger Christian community.

Here we return to the emphasis upon the more inclusive church— inclusive of people in suburbs and inner city, of all races, of people of many different opinions and on both sides of most conflicts. Churches must live with the problems created by inclusiveness.

But such inclusiveness may be good for both community and church. It may temper the partisanship on both sides. On central issues it may reveal many allies. But it may also help to correct one-sidedness in the understanding of the Gospel and prepare for a future in which the lines of conflict may well be drawn differently and perhaps modify future forms of intransigence. It may help Christians in many different situations with different experiences and interests to remain under a common judgment, to be open to each other in a common fellowship, and to recognize that they are objects of a common redemption.

March 22, 1965

The Plight of Seasonal Farm Workers

Wayne C. Hartmire, Jr.

SEASONAL FARM WORKERS in California and the rest of the United States are poor and exploited, and most of us don't want to hear about it. We eat well and suffer the "burdens" of overweight while those who harvest our foodstuffs struggle for the basics of life. It is a deep cancer in our national life that compares in intensity, if not in scope, with racial injustice.

That farm workers are poor is well known. The average migrant worker earns around $1,000 per year. In areas where they are settling down things appear to be better. A settled worker in California may earn $1,500-$2,000 per year. With the help of his wife and children, the income may go above $2,500.

But, with the exception of her agribusinessmen, California is not bragging. The March 1963 Welfare Study Commission report concluded: "One occupational group is so deeply locked in poverty that it is set off from all others. . . . The median income of others [seasonal occupational groups] is two to three times that of the farm laborer, whose median income is $1,940."

California is an important place to look at because the state epitomizes the booming affluence that caresses most of us. Median family income is $6,726 even though the unemployment rate hovers around five per cent. The Golden State is also the world's richest agricultural area with annual cash farm income of $3.6 billion.

There are many things to be said about the seasonal farm workers' situation. Most often one hears about filthy labor camps, poor health, educationally deprived children, unattended babies sleeping in hot cars, and people on the move in dilapidated trucks and cars. The natural public response is to remedy these visible evils with special programs to provide compensatory education, establish health clinics, upgrade sanitation, develop or extend child care centers and crack down on old trucks and buses. The list could be extended.

Farm workers are polite and they will not object to such programs. But when given an opportunity, they speak about better jobs, higher wages, a home of their own and better opportunities for their kids.

Perhaps one example will show the basic power reality that underlies their visible sufferings. The United States Sugar Act provides among other things subsidies to sugar beet growers and requires that laborers engaged in the production of sugar beets receive at least a minimum wage. In 1964 and early 1965 that hourly minimum was $1.15.

In the southern San Joaquin Valley the thinning and weeding of sugar beets takes place in early spring when there are many workers and not much work. Wages frequently do not reach even the indecent minimum. Paid on piece rates this year, workers earned from sixteen to eighty-five cents per hour. Finally, they rebelled. They knew that a new organization called the Farm Workers' Organization (FWO) of Tulare County was being formed (organized by staff from the United Church of Christ and the California Migrant Ministry working together). The workers brought their complaint to the FWO office.

The officers and staff of FWO went into action. A formal complaint was filed. A hearing was scheduled before the County Agricultural Stabilization and Conservation Board, which is charged by the Department of Agriculture with local enforcement of the minimum wage. The board is composed of sugar beet growers elected by other sugar beet growers. The workers were not too hopeful, but they certainly were not prepared for an inquisition.

Instead of the grower and his labor contractor being called to answer charges, the workers were brought in one by one to answer a barrage of hostile questions about their complaints. The FWO staff person had to force his way into the room. A local labor commissioner was ejected from the meeting. The workers were humiliated and frightened by the day-long proceedings. Because they were affiliated with an active, militant organization, they carried the complaint to the State Labor Commissioner's office and may yet get some back pay for their trouble.

The night of the sugar beet hearing, Secretary of Labor Willard Wirtz was in Tulare County taking testimony about the use of foreign

.abor in agriculture. The FWO farm workers told him in essence: 'Foreign workers are not needed; rather we need decent wages and working conditions *guaranteed by a legal contract*. Government promises are not enough (the State Department of Employment was recruiting labor for other counties with promises of $1.25 per hour and other guarantees). We can't get the legal $1.15 per hour in our own county; why should we believe you when you say we can get $1.25 per hour in another county?"

Mr. Wirtz was visibly irritated by this challenge. To his way of thinking, the successful end of all foreign labor importation depended on effective recruitment based on government guarantees. The workers were in no mood to agree.

The story illustrates one basic reality: Farm workers are disorganized, weak and poverty stricken, while their employers are highly organized, affluent and powerful. The latter unilaterally make almost all decisions about size of work force, wages and working conditions. They exercise determinative influence in county and city governments. Through a variety of boards and advisory committees, they influence public agencies that are supposed to serve and/or protect the workers.

A lone worker has no chance against this power array and he knows it well enough to swallow his anger. An affiliated worker will at least get far enough in his protest to discover the interrelatedness of the forces opposed to his best interests.

It is this radical power imbalance that is at the root of the injustices experienced by seasonal workers. Community leaders and agricultural employers, who are often the same, have too much power over the workers. Like most other men, they have tended to use that unchecked power irresponsibly.

The key issue, therefore, is *the organization of workers* into effective civic and labor organizations that can deal with basic injustices, particularly low wages and inferior working conditions. Given a fair return for their labor and some security in employment, farm workers will buy for themselves and their children the services we want to give them through special programs.

The importation of foreign labor is part of the system that has kept domestic workers poor and disorganized. They have contributed to the power imbalance that exists in agriculture. At their best, these programs have robbed domestic workers of the little bit of bargaining power they have had as individuals. At their worst, they have displaced American workers and been used to undercut attempts to unionize them.

Agriculture in California has depended on a ready supply of docile foreign workers for nearly a hundred years. Chinese, Japanese, Filipinos, Mexican immigrants, wetbacks and *braceros* have all been part of an established system that has maintained an oversupply of hungry workers.

Public Law 78 is only the latest chapter in the foreign labor story.

The law was passed by Congress in 1951 to end the wetback traffic and meet the emergency need for labor during the Korean War. It provided for the temporary importation of Mexican nationals under a contract between the U.S. and Mexican Governments. PL 78 was extended again and again; finally in 1963 it was extended for a one-year final phaseout period. At its peak use in 1959, 447,000 Mexican nationals were contracted for work in the U.S.; California got 182,000 *braceros*. The numbers dropped each year until the law expired at the end of 1964.

The battle this year has been over the proposed use of PL 414 (McCarran-Walter Immigration Act), which in one section provides for the temporary importation of foreign nationals to do needed work. The Secretary of Labor, with approval from the Attorney General, has the power to decide whether the labor is needed.

Mr. Wirtz established certain minimum standards that would have to be offered domestics and Mexican nationals (including $1.40 per hour after April 1st in California) and set his people to finding enough domestic workers to harvest the crops. (Farm worker groups, however, have protested that the domestic recruitment programs will, like the *bracero* program, produce an oversupply of workers.) He made it clear that in accordance with congressional intent there would be a sharp reduction in the importation of foreign workers.

The outcry from growers in California was heard around the world; it was claimed that disaster threatened the lettuce, date, lemon, orange, strawberry and asparagus crops. Housewives were warned to look for astronomical price increases. Newspapers thundered, "Is one man going to allow California's $3.6 billion agricultural industry to be ruined?" Governor Brown and Senators Kuchel and Murphy joined the outraged reaction.

But Wirtz held the line and with few exceptions refused to allow the importation of foreign nationals in California. Of all the public officials involved he alone was at least partly tuned in to the farm workers. He knew that the Department of Labor wage and working condition standards were not being met by growers. A trip through California confirmed his belief that domestic workers would be available in sufficient numbers when they were treated decently and not harassed and pushed off as poor substitutes for *braceros*.

In January 1965, as compared to January 1964, there were ten thousand fewer *braceros* employed in California and eight thousand more domestics. In June the employment of domestics was up thirty-five thousand over the same period in 1964. The crops were getting harvested despite the earlier cries of anguish. *The Los Angeles Times* found that "over-all farm gains are outstripping losses so far despite the end of the *braceros* program."

The fall tomato harvest is the next major hurdle. Secretary Wirtz unexpectedly softened his stand and certified 18,400 *braceros* for this crop. Last year thirty-seven thousand *braceros* were used. Apparently this part of the battle for justice is not over. (Some twenty-five thousand foreign nationals are currently at work in the United States, according to the National Sharecroppers Fund.)

The present situation poses a difficult dilemma for the churches. Charitable services, long the mainstay of Protestant penetration into poverty areas, are now problematic. The expectations of low-income people are revolutionary and not evolutionary. They want justice now and not special services for an unjust interim. Farm workers want to be organized so they can have enough power to change their situation. They will not for long tolerate programs that either evade the issue of power or get in the way of organizing. This fact of life is especially relevant for service programs planned outside their community and imposed on them.

But this new situation is also an opportunity for the churches. English classes, health education, child care, etc., in the labor camps will now be carried on by public programs under the Economic Opportunity Act; these public penetrations are not likely to be revolutionary in focus. City Hall, public agencies and most social welfare groups are more interested in keeping the people pacified with partial measures than in upheaval.

Churchmen could lead the way in approaching the underlying social, economic and political issues. A good beginning point is to understand and give support to basic attempts at organizing workers.

This controversial approach to the farm labor problem is probably more honest for Protestant churchmen. The basic relationship between that part of the community we represent and the labor camps and fringe areas is one of exploitation. We live well at the expense of these field workers and their families. They provide cheap labor for our farms, stores and homes. The exorbitant rent they sometimes pay is money in the bank for our church members and eventually money in the church budget. Lower food prices benefit all of us, but only the workers sacrifice dignity to keep those prices low. Their low status feeds our sense of well-being. Our pride is their humiliation.

If this is an accurate analysis of the way things are, our first task is to deal with that basic relationship, i.e. with the structural evils that continue our inhumanity to our fellow men. It is dishonest to evade the structural issues and carry ameliorative programs into the camps. Our consciences may be salved, but the people are not fooled; and our efforts are neutralized by continued exploitation.

I spend a good deal of my time with rural churchmen, and I know how difficult implementation of these words will be. How are local congregations, dominated by agribusinessmen and their close associates, to relate creatively to organizing activity and other programs aimed at social change? For some congregations it is *institutionally* impossible.

Martyrdom and institutional chaos is the certain outcome for pastors who lead their flocks in this direction, and I am not sure the result will be worth the effort.

Perhaps we should sit looser in the institutional saddle. Christians can operate independently of denominational and local church programs. Those concerned about justice for farm workers can band together outside the normal channels and support the farm worker in his struggle.

Those unwilling to separate Christ's witness from the institution will have to agonize long and hard about concrete ways to relate a static institution to revolutionary events. Out of common commitment and much mutual suffering local churchmen may find a way. But it will not be apart from the "dirty" arena of organized power.

For those congregations and/or ad hoc Christian groups that are ready to act, some hints can be offered. First, we must go slowly and quietly because the farm worker's community is alien to most of us. Second, we should not go to the people with questions or programs without a genuine invitation.

The Santa Clara County Council of Churches operating on this premise asked for a consultation with the people of East San Jose. The churchmen made it clear they would come as equals to listen and learn. They got an earful of "things as they are." As a result, the council is involved in a basic community struggle to protect hundreds of poor families being displaced by a freeway.

Third, we need to find out what organizations serve the farm workers. Paper organizations that serve the pride of two or three "doers" should be bypassed. Where no effective action groups exist, ways of providing organizing services to low income people should be considered. Catalytic staff services will be needed and someone will have to pay for them. Churchmen can provide initial financing but only with the understanding that within a specified time the organization will be financed and controlled completely by the people.

Where labor organizations or neighborhood action groups exist, a number of key issues arise. Community police power is too often used unjustly and effectively against such organizations. Christians should be informed about this and be active in protesting the use of public funds to perpetuate an unjust balance of power in the community.

In the case of labor organizations, farm employers will generally refuse to bargain with any organization of workers. While recognizing the theoretical right of these people to be organized, agribusinessmen deny the existence or the validity of specific organizations as they appear. The key issue here is the extension of the National Labor Relations Act to agriculture so that both workers and employers will be legally required to bargain and will be protected in the process. *No other piece of protective legislation is so important to farm workers.*

Christians also have a responsibility to sort truth from falsehood. Organizers are often personally maligned and their methods distorted and ridiculed. This always happens when longstanding community and employer practices are challenged. The facts should be determined and proclaimed. It is true that distortions occur on both sides of a conflict, but the one that churchmen hear most often will be aimed at mobilizing community support to maintain an unjust *status quo.*

A final word about "services" that depend on outside skill and resources. They may be needed in the same way a suburban locale needs a mental health clinic. But the people to be served should define the need, request the service and dominate the planning process. That is the way we want it in *our* communities; so it should be for farm workers and other low income people.

But what of Gospel proclamation and life in the community of faith? The denominations in California are attempting to extend the life of existing congregations and to develop indigenous congregations in these communities. It is an enormously frustrating task. Our forms do not fit. Our fellowship is often too shallow and fearful to encompass the real life problems of these families. ("You are welcome here, but we can't discuss such things as wages and police harassment.")

Perhaps this is not the historical moment for extending the institutional life of the Church here. The truth is that there is probably more practical atheism where our churches are strong than in the farm worker communities where our churches are absent. But beyond that observation, our corporate sin against farm workers is so great that the only word that can now be heard is the incarnate word—the word proclaimed by deeds of justice and mercy. In the doing of those deeds, Christians may discover those forms of corporate life that can include men on both sides of the tracks.

October 4, 1965

Saul Alinsky and His Critics

❧

Stephen C. Rose

CHICAGO IS REGARDED AS a great natural laboratory of the social sciences. Graham Hutton once declared, "Chicago has the best human virtues and the worst vices. It is, therefore, more truly human than any city, and it tells more about humanity." This opposition of best and worst is *the* literary approach to this "city of the big shoulders." G. W. Stevens called Chicago "the queen and guttersnipe of cities, cynosure and cesspool of the world."

One thinks of Al Capone *and* Jane Addams. The achievements of its great universities are set against all-Negro public schools whose valedictorians are thrust into remedial reading classes in college. An unseen force forbids unambiguous judgments, and one delves into the stuff of the laboratory, hoping for whatever truth ambiguity will yield.

Chicago is the center of an emerging crucial debate among custodians of public and private welfare enterprises as they seek to forge what President Johnson is calling the Great Society. The debate is basically about who calls the shots in urban development, and it involves the future of democracy in the metropolis, the basic structure of the social work endeavor, the place of the Church in the city and the nature of voluntarism within a pluralistic society.

The protagonist in the debate is a well-publicized, outspoken community organizer named Saul D. Alinsky, who heads the Chicago-based Industrial Areas Foundation (IAF). A prominent antagonist is *Christian Century* Editor Harold Fey, who has pinned a Marxist label on Alinsky and all his house. Alinsky's house includes the nation's largest Roman Catholic Archdiocese and the United Presbyterian Church in the U.S.A.

Lutheran planner and church executive Walter Kloetzli emerges as the *advocatus diaboli* in proceedings that would either canonize Alinsky as the one true guide to urban church strategy or vilify him as a Machiavelli who has turned Luther's doctrine of the two realms upside down, casting the radiant light of theological approval upon a series of contemporary Peasants' Revolts.

An occasion for noting the debate is the recent publication of *Fortune* Editor Charles Silberman's book *Crisis in Black and White* (Random House, $5.95). Alinsky emerges as Silberman's hero, as the man who offers the best hope to the apathetic, poverty-stricken urban Negro whose greatest need is a sense that he has some control over his destiny. "The only difference between Alinsky and his enemies," says Silberman, "is that Alinsky really believes in democracy." Meanwhile Dr. Fey says that Alinsky's concept of community organization, in which power and the creative use of conflict are prime ingredients, is a "totalitarian" implementation of "class war" techniques.

To date Alinsky and the IAF have organized four communities in Chicago, not to mention others across the country, including effective coalitions of migrant workers in California. At least two further communities in Chicago are slated for possible organizational efforts.

The object of Harold Fey's charges is a greying, largish man in his mid-fifties whose office perches above Chicago's Lake Michigan. Louis Sullivan once said that the lake and the prairie enfold Chicago "as a wistful mother holds a subnormal child." Saul Alinsky believes that the hope of democracy, and of the city, lies in a rejection of the "subnormal child" image of the poor and disinherited. "I do believe in the democratic faith," says Alinsky. "If not, I have nothing left to believe in."

One visits Alinsky's IAF office half expecting to hear an elaborate political and economic thesis, a sort of mid-century *Weltanschauung*. Instead one finds a man who despises dogmas of any sort and insists there are no panaceas. One looks for radical solutions to automation and all the other "ations" that are replacing the "isms" and finds instead a man whose vision is an almost sentimental picture of a mountain path paved with external threats. Man's faltering climb to the top may someday be completed. He may vanquish the externals of hunger, inadequate housing, economic and racial injustice. Alinsky's world is centered upon the climbing of the mountain. On the ultimate question, the question of life's meaning, he professes only an inability to answer. A friend calls him an existentialist in the true sense of the term.

His basic perceptions are of the imminence and finality of death (the product of personal tragedies in his own life) and of injustice. He professes an almost instinctive siding with the underdog. His anger at injustice becomes somewhat wistful when it crops up in an organization he helped to create.

Perhaps a self-portrait emerges when he describes the way he chooses community organizers to work with IAF. Recruiting begins, he has said, "When we hear of a guy who is mad and organizing on his own. We ask, 'What kind of anger is it? Is it a neurotic anger that could be cleared up by eliminating some personal cause? Or is it an anger at injustice that will stay with him?' Then we see whether he will take advice, whether he has a passion for anonymity, and whether he wants to learn." The organizer must combine the Old Testament's prophetic anger with the cool detachment of the Greeks. Alinsky feels that Saul of Tarsus ("your Paul") fits this description—Saul, the organizer.

Under Alinsky's tutelage—he sees himself as a teacher—the recruit begins to see "the opposition" as an integral element of the organizing strategy. For example, Bull Connor was a great asset to Birmingham Negroes. Alinsky believes in the strategic cultivation of Bull Connors.

The IAF organizers—the number varies with the number of communities being organized—are "all prima donnas in their own way," says Alinsky. "The only way I manage to keep their respect is that they know I can go out and out-organize them." Alinsky normally spends only a week each year in actual grass roots operations. The rest of the time is spent consulting various IAF-organized projects. Now, with Silberman's book, about three-fourths of his time is devoted to explaining his work to reporters ranging from national magazine staffers to German TV documentary personnel.

Alinsky's detractors accuse him of running a well-oiled publicity machine. He responds that his most useful publicity is provided by his critics. A series of derogatory editorials in *The Christian Century* apparently inspired a number of Protestants to investigate the IAF and to see for themselves that "the charges just weren't true."

The range and diversity of Alinsky's personal associations is somewhat amazing. He has been a friend and informal consultant to Michigan's Governor Romney. At the urging of his long-time acquaintance Jacques Maritain, Alinsky had several cordial sessions with the Archbishop of Milan before he became Pope Paul. He advised the Archbishop on means by which the Church might combat Milan's strong Communist party. Alinsky's financial support comes from liberals and conservatives; IAF's Board of Directors includes Presbyterian executives, the president of a major life insurance company and an official of the Southern Christian Leadership Conference. His dinner guests may be partisans or friendly critics like the University of Chicago's urban expert Dr. Philip Hauser.

Alinsky's first organizing effort was in the neighborhood Upton Sinclair described as *The Jungle*. There in 1938 he welded together antagonistic national Catholic groups and packing house workers into what is now the powerful Back of the Yards Neighborhood Council. A Chicago Building Department official calls the work of the council in community upkeep "consistently tremendous." Recently this neighborhood has shown considerable resistance to the possibility of residential integration. Alinsky hopes various IAF-spawned community groups may be able to negotiate the orderly movement of Negroes into such all-white areas. If not, he says he is willing to organize a community to fight Back of the Yards on the integration issue.

Accusations are made that Alinsky organizes communities on a basis of fear and hostility that can ultimately lead to the polarization of neighborhoods and the destruction of patterns of metropolitan consensus. Alinsky insists, however, that what is seen as apathy and dependency in depressed urban areas is really the suppression of deep resentment over a sense of impotence. The mobilization of community pride and of the impulse to self-help involves arousing these resentments and providing, through a mass organization, the instrument by which bad conditions can be changed.

In a 1962 speech he outlined the basic characteristics of an effective community organization. These constitute his personal acknowledgment of what IAF strives for in its own efforts.

The organization must attract and involve most of the groups in the community.

Its program should be "specific, immediate and feasible" in order to create self-respect through success.

The organization should see power for what it is, and use it. "The power concept must be seen nakedly, without the sordid raiment which serve more as disguises for our own inability or unwillingness or timidity to get involved in controversy in which we may get smeared or hurt."

"An action group . . . has two primary considerations in selecting a means for operation towards an end. First, what means are available and, second, what means are most effective? . . . Any so-called organization which spends a great deal of its time discussing means and ends always winds up on its ends without any means!" (It should be pointed out that the tactics of Alinsky organizations have never gone beyond occasional instances of civil disobedience. Most tactics have combined clever "symbolic" demonstrations with the threat of economic or political coercion.)

"Controversy has always been the seed of creation." No vital community organization can exist without it. In an organization of "have nots" it is inevitable that resentment will focus on the "prevailing dominant interests of the status quo," particularly when these interests inhibit the self-determination of the organization.

The organization must recognize self-interest as its basic *raison d'etre,* but to be effective it must aim at a multiplicity of goals. This will insure a broad base of support. "In effect," says Alinsky, "everybody makes a deal: You support me in this, and I'll support you in that."

IAF's enemies charge that these organizing principles result in the creation of totalitarian super-organizations, controlled from the outside, and dedicated to such varied motives as keeping Negroes out, keeping Negroes in, fronting for Roman Catholicism's vested interests, and even, according to Dr. Fey, splicing together enough IAF-organized neighborhoods to gain control of a whole city. Silberman, in *Crisis in Black and White,* has made a thorough investigation of such charges, and he also points to the need for more detailed study of Alinsky's efforts in community organization. Unfortunately, IAF's critics, particularly within the Protestant Church, have made little effort to substantiate their allegations. Opinion has superseded reporting.

One of the most emotion-laden charges against Alinsky is that IAF organizations are dominated by and subservient to Roman Catholic interests. There is no question that the Roman Catholic Church has supported IAF, nor is there reason to believe that it has not benefited from IAF's efforts.

The most direct challenge to Catholic motivation has been that of the Rev. Walter Kloetzli in his book *The Church and the Urban Challenge* (Muhlenberg Press). Writing in 1961, Kloetzli suggested that the Chicago Archdiocese was using IAF to "freeze" neighborhoods—to halt migration from areas of Catholic strength and to limit the migration of Negroes into these areas. He also criticized the Catholic Church for espousing Alinsky's organizing techniques and offered some alternative principles of organization that are critical of the power concept and "the tactic of deliberately stirring up community animosities." The same observations have appeared in a number of *Christian Century* editorials.

The man who will respond to these charges if given the chance is Monsignor John Egan, head of the Office of Urban Affairs of Chicago's Archdiocese. "If *that* [racial containment] was our policy, we sure have failed," he said recently. Monsignor Egan's willingness to speak openly and at length about the relationship between the Archdiocese and IAF places the burden of proof squarely on the shoulders of the critics.

Alinsky first met Monsignor Egan in 1954 at the behest of Jacques Maritain. Shortly thereafter the Archdiocese became involved in an effort to develop a self-help program among Puerto Rican newcomers to Chicago's Woodlawn area. Monsignor John O'Grady, then the executive director of the National Conference of Catholic Charities, suggested that Monsignor Egan and others consult with Alinsky about the new program.

Subsequently Alinsky was asked by the late Cardinal Stritch to study conditions affecting Puerto Ricans on the city's North Side. The satisfaction of the Archdiocese with this study gave rise to yet another request, this time for a survey of the effects of the large scale relocation of Negroes made necessary by the clearing of Chicago's Lake Meadows area for middle income housing. Monsignor Egan was freed to work with Alinsky, and during the summer of 1957 he tramped through the all-Negro area south of Lake Meadows. "I really got to know the effects of poverty and discrimination in this town," he recalls.

The report concluded that relocation had resulted in an aggravation of slum conditions in the study area. Monsignor Egan remembers that Cardinal Stritch was "terribly upset" by the findings.

During 1958-59, the Archdiocese was critical of the first major urban renewal plan to be implemented in Chicago, the Hyde Park-Kenwood Project. Monsignor Egan recalls that some twenty-two persons of both races were slated for "urban removal." The brunt of the relocation was upon the poor Negroes of the area. Today Hyde Park-Kenwood bills itself as a liberal-minded, integrated area, but this has been achieved at the expense of low income Negroes. A hopeful sign in recent months has been the willingness of Hyde Park residents to endorse the construction of low rise, small density public housing in the community.

Monsignor Egan states that three basic convictions came to him during this period. First, the need throughout the City of Chicago for community organizations that were "strong and tough." "We had lots of weak organizations that were avoiding or afraid of controversy." Secondly, "any organization had to represent and serve all the people." Finally, "if urban renewal programs were going to succeed in reflecting the mind of the people, we needed community organizations as a strong voice to supplement and speak to the political arm." Monsignor Egan adds that he "felt the political organization in Chicago was not using tools to give people enough voice in the democratic process."

And so, in the wake of the Hyde Park-Kenwood dispute, the Archdiocese became involved with Alinsky, the organizer. (Monsignor Egan stresses that Alinsky "had absolutely nothing to do with our entry into the Hyde Park-Kenwood fight.") In 1959-60 a coalition of Protestants, priests and businessmen called IAF in to organize a large area of Chicago's Southwest Side. Although the Archdiocese kept informed about the development of the Organization for the Southwest Community (OSC), Monsignor Egan says that all financial support of the organization came from parishes within the community.

In a thorough report on OSC in November 1961, the Rev. Robert Christ, then pastor of the Seventh Presbyterian Church of Chicago, made the following observations:

Neither Protestants alone or Catholics alone could have established OSC; the necessity for joint action has resulted in a corporate effort by twenty-five Protestant congregations and eleven Roman parishes. . . . The coalition of churchmen has been largely responsible for the structure, policy and success of the organization.

It was the combined church voice that secured non-gerrymandered boundaries (thereby including areas of Negro residence). The presence of priests and ministers on the membership committee secured the admission of Negro institutions at the organizing community congress.

The novelty of the Protestant-Catholic coalition explains part of its effectiveness; opponents have not yet learned to respond when both . . . stand together on issues. The still-tenuous nature of the coalition provides a built-in safeguard which will prevent the coalition from over-extending itself and abusing its power in the city.

Christ's report is persuasive on two points. Both Protestant and Catholic clergy took the lead (sometimes at considerable cost) in affirming a racially inclusive community. Checks and balances were provided to insure that neither group would dominate the organization and that the two groups acting together could not dominate it. Christ also points to the genuine ecumenical sense that emerged among Catholic and Protestant participants. The same observation has been made by numerous participants in IAF-spawned organizations. The range and diversity of OSC is indicated by an enumeration of its various program committees: Real Estate Practices, Home Loan, Home Modernization, Law Enforcement and Safety, Education, Health and Welfare, Traffic and Transportation, Community Relations, etc.

This seems to confirm that Monsignor Egan is justified in his assertion that Catholic involvement is based on the recognition of the need for strong grass roots organizations whose main objective is to create self-determination in a given neighborhood. One can generalize that Catholics are as sinful as Protestants when it comes to self-interest. Surely one of the motivating forces in Catholic participation in the Northwest Community Organization, IAF's latest effort in Chicago, was the desire to stem migration from an area served by twenty-two Roman Catholic parishes. But the success of NCO will involve restoring community pride and better living conditions to an area that otherwise might have continued downhill. This is a desirable goal since continued out-migration of middle class elements will only sharpen the evident rift between city and suburb. Finally, it seems rather inconsistent to fault Catholicism merely because it, unlike Protestantism, elected long ago to remain in the inner city.

Kloetzli has also criticized the Chicago Archdiocese for its implicit acceptance of IAF's organizing technique. "I'm not saying Alinsky is the only organizer," says Monsignor Egan, "but I don't know of another. . . . If I'm going to build a building, I'll hire a professional contractor." Alinsky's credentials are those of performance. Egan adds, "It is peculiar that people will accuse Alinsky of using power, and then use power themselves. In order to achieve peace and tranquillity and order, you may have to go through certain conflicts. But in my ten years' association with Alinsky, I have never seen him violate the moral law or advocate the violation of it."

Some observers dismiss Dr. Fey's charge that IAF embodies "totalitarian" principles and "class war techniques" as "just plain silly." Julian Levi, who directs urban renewal efforts for the University of Chicago and who has done battle with the IAF-organized Woodlawn Organization, says he "would not go as far as that." Dr. Franklin Littell, Chicago Theological Seminary professor and lecturer on totalitarian ideology, feels Dr. Fey's fears stem from a "basic misunderstanding of the nature of freedom." Dr. Littell sees adequate checks and balances existing in Alinsky-style community organizations and suggests that merely because they are highly disciplined is not adequate grounds for charges of dictatorship.

Totalitarianism involves a sinister effort to gain control of the masses. It is dangerous to charge that any institution or person espouses totalitarian principles without documentation. And all the evidence suggests that IAF lacks both the cynicism and the means to implement such an approach. In the first place, it is IAF practice to pull its organizers out of a community as soon as possible and sever all financial ties to the organizations it helps create. In the case of OSC, the IAF withdrew after nine months.

The structure of IAF-founded organizations provides for wide community participation in the decision-making process. After the initial organizing period a constitutional convention is held at which each member group is represented on a proportional basis. The constitution is debated clause by clause before it is approved.

A similar congress is held annually at which a program committee presents resolutions that will determine the work of the organization for the coming year. Alinsky calls this annual congress "the House of Representatives." "The Senate" is an executive board made up of one representative of each group. This board divides into various smaller groups with responsibility for implementing program. The annual meeting is the final authority in all matters of program and policy. Officers are elected yearly, and the number of permissible consecutive terms is determined by the constitution.

At this year's convention, The Woodlawn Organization turned down a proposal that would have thrown support to Negro candidates for public office only. This significant vote was generally acknowledged by all present, including Dr. Fey, to be an example of the democratic process at work. The only difference is that Dr. Fey clung to the reasoning that the proposal's defeat stemmed from the failure of the "ruling clique" to "brainwash" a majority of TWO's constituency.

The accusation that IAF uses "class war" techniques involves one in semantics. If the notion of the class war is accompanied by visions of Bolshevist insurrections and the dictatorship of the proletariat, the specter of IAF becomes one of sheer fantasy. Alinsky has never professed or implemented the ideas necessary to a notion of class war. If, however, the concept of class war is liberated from its militaristic imagery and seen as part of the continuing effort of American "outs" to become "ins," Alinsky and the facts would confirm the proposition. Such a notion is not foreign to democratic soil, and the rationale for conflict of this sort is found in such documents as the *Federalist Papers* and Reinhold Niebuhr's *Moral Man and Immoral Society*.

What Alinsky's severest critics have done is to magnify the old American town-gown conflict (TWO vs. the University of Chicago) into a class war. They might better focus their fears on the Black Muslim Temple located in Hyde Park or the John Birch Society, which is explicitly totalitarian in concept.

The American underdog has always tended to elevate the class concept only for the purpose of obliterating class barriers. Today it is the rare union member who would sing the militant (and eminently class conscious) labor songs of the Thirties. And if there is any criticism to be made on this score, it is that IAF's organizations may (as in the case of Back of the Yards) grow away from sympathy with the underdog as they attain a greater measure of affluence and "middle class" status.

The unsubstantiated charges of Catholic domination, totalitarianism, etc., should not be permitted to obscure a number of genuinely important questions. Some observers have suggested that the IAF approach is overrated in terms of actual results; also that it is possible to upgrade depressed communities without cultivating hostility toward the "dominant interests of the *status quo.*"

It is both the nemesis and the salvation of the social welfare community to be forced to consider results. Unfortunately neither the journalistic nor academic method of determining results is entirely satisfactory. Nevertheless, let us examine the results of IAF's organization in a Chicago community. In 1960, IAF organizers entered the Woodlawn area, directly south of the University of Chicago.

Woodlawn is practically all Negro. It is one of those neighborhoods in which old, middle class homes have been sliced up to accommodate part of the vast migration from the South that may ultimately provide Chicago with a Negro majority. Slum landlords have been among the few beneficiaries of the pervasive myth that the Northern city would provide a vastly more abundant life than might be eked from Southern soil. Rents for comparable units are about fifty per cent higher for Negroes. Woodlawn has everything one would need to create a macabre picture of slum life: High school dropouts, crime, unemployment and a high percentage of welfare recipients. And like most similar areas, Woodlawn has a number of institutions, including more than thirty churches, that have tried with limited success to stem the tide of slum culture.

IAF entered Woodlawn after receiving a formal invitation from a group of local clergymen. The organizing effort was supported by the Emil Schwartzhaupt Foundation, the Roman Catholic Archdiocese and the United Presbyterian Board of National Missions. To date the total financial outlay for The Woodlawn Organization has been $177,500. Of this amount $27,000 was raised within Woodlawn. The Schwartzhaupt Foundation contributed $74,000, the Archdiocese $50,000, with the remainder coming from the Presbyterians. Alinsky says that IAF will probably withdraw by the end of 1964 and TWO will operate on an annual budget of $30-40,000, all of it raised within the community.

IAF's policy of withdrawing after the organizing phase has the effect of forcing indigenous support of the organization, thus assuring self-determination. The total allocation for TWO over a four-year period is about half the annual budget of the Church Federation of Greater Chicago and one-third the annual budget of the Chicago City Missionary Society. By any standards, particularly those of institutions working in slum areas, the IAF dollar has gone a long way in Woodlawn. (Alinsky speculated recently about what the IAF could do with five million dollars. With such resources, he said, IAF could organize depressed areas in five large cities and have enough left over for Harlem. It is doubtful that Alinsky, who says the Founding Fathers would have had rough going with the Ford Foundation, will ever get his five million.)

The history of the organizing effort in Woodlawn is fully re-counted in Silberman's book. In brief, the organizers had little difficulty in locating community resentments. Residents were embittered over the high-handed aplomb with which Chicago School Superintendent Benjamin Willis has consistently disregarded the pleas of the Negro community. They were aroused against some local merchants who gave short weights and overcharged. Merchants and residents alike were fearful that the University of Chicago's stated plan to extend its campus southward would be carried out with no regard for the people.

Then too, the organizing of the community coincided with the great upheaval that we have come to call the Negro Revolution. This was an unquestionable asset in community mobilization, but it should be pointed out that TWO became a spearhead of the Chicago protest movement well in advance of the catalytic events in Birmingham and Mississippi. The IAF approach here was completely free-wheeling in terms of strategy. The emergent Woodlawn Organization had no suburban board of directors urging it to go slow or to eschew direct action. It was an institution financed by the *status quo* in order to fight the *status quo.*

The initial organizing was not without conflict, and there were elements in the community that responded negatively to what must have been considerable initial pressure to join. The West Woodlawn Council of Block Clubs and the Student Woodlawn Area Project (sponsored by the University of Chicago) are among the groups that chose to work independently. This reflects some criticism of TWO from within the community, but it also dispels the notion that the organization is an all-powerful monolith. Despite Dr. Fey's fears, it is not THE Woodlawn organization.

Early in TWO's history five pastors withdrew from the Greater Woodlawn Pastor's Alliance, criticizing the alliance for endorsing tactics "based on the cultivation of fear, hatred and useful antagonisms." A flurry of charges and countercharges followed. One of the pastors, the Rev. C. Kenneth Proefrock, wrote that the alternative to IAF was an "insistence upon careful planning, orderly change and legal processes."

In order to determine the extent of church support of TWO today, the writer made contact with nineteen of the thirty-six churches in the community. Of the seventeen churches not contacted, four had no phone, five no longer existed and eight did not answer after three days of repeated calling. Each church was asked its reaction to TWO and the extent of its participation in the organization.

Of the nineteen churches contacted, eleven indicated a positive response to TWO and the active support of church members; three respondents indicated opposition; two were inactive in the organization but favorable toward its aims; one minister said his church "just sits back and watches"; one church was inactive but expressed awareness of what

TWO "has been and can be"; and, finally, with the noise of a mid-week Pentecostal service in the background, one respondent said that he had "never heard of it." Most of the favorable responses echoed the belief that TWO's program was consistent with the aims of justice and that association in the ministerial alliance had been a spur to ecumenicity.

Initial programs of TWO included rent strikes and a march on local merchants accused of short weights. What Alinsky calls "our entrance into the community of atomic powers" took place on Saturday, August 26, 1961, when more than two thousand Woodlawn residents rode in a cavalcade of buses to Chicago's City Hall to register to vote. The demonstration had a tremendous effect on community morale, and observers say that even the least articulate Woodlawn residents gained a feeling of participation. Incidentally, the only election in which TWO has participated vigorously resulted in a three-to-one victory for a TWO-backed white alderman over a Negro lawyer who ran with the backing of the Democratic machine.

Today TWO, through its representative membership, claims to speak for some thirty thousand Woodlawn residents. In a time when the illusion of power (created largely by extended news media coverage) seems almost as determinative as actual power, TWO can rightfully contend that it has power. The *Chicago Daily News* once ran an ad promoting a series of favorable articles on TWO that included a picture of the former president, the Rev. Arthur M. Brazier. The headline-sized caption read, "This man has POWER." The ad went on to indicate that Brazier could, by his leadership, dictate the future course of urban renewal in the Woodlawn-University area.

The claim may have been extravagant but it underlines a fundamental precept of IAF-style organization: The creation of a strong indigenous leader. (Brazier is minister of a Pentecostal church in Woodlawn but doesn't live there.) One observer suggests that a prime achievement of TWO has been, through emphasis on leadership, to restore the image of the strong, purposeful male within the matriarchal Negro community.

What has TWO's "power" yielded in terms of tangibles? There is no question that TWO was able to force the university to negotiate its proposal to move into the north edge of Woodlawn. By an agreement forged in Mayor Daley's office last summer, the university will not begin demolition of the area until housing has been built to accommodate relocated residents.

A fortuitous circumstance was the recent agreement of TWO and the Kate Maremont Foundation to sponsor jointly the construction of 762 units of middle income housing in Woodlawn. Rents in these units will be very modest and a TWO spokesman claims that persons relocated from the university clearance area will have first choice of the new units.

Almost two thousand units of housing will be demolished, however, and some observers wonder what will happen to the remaining relocatees.

The city will not pass the ordinance designating the proposed middle income housing site until a pending study proves that there is no urgent need for public housing in the same area. TWO has set itself against the construction of public housing adjacent to the proposed middle income housing. The Rev. Lynwood Stevenson, currently president of TWO, says his organization is not opposed to public housing *per se,* but would prefer that additional low rise public housing units be scattered throughout Woodlawn to accommodate relocatees who can neither afford nor otherwise qualify to live in the proposed middle income housing.

This emphasis on middle income housing has led some, including a local paper, *The Woodlawn Booster,* to suggest that the organization is reneging on its commitment to the low income residents of the area. The paper holds that TWO is growing more and more middle class in its outlook and that its object is to create "another Hyde Park."

It is undoubtedly true that, with success, an institution will begin to assert the self-interest of its most powerful elements at the expense of the less powerful. Indeed, in my opinion, the acid test of TWO's considerable and commendable success in gaining a strong voice in urban renewal policy will be the extent to which it lives up to its original determination to serve *all* of its constituency. It would be a tragedy if Woodlawn were to become another Hyde Park at the expense of its low income residents.

Today, TWO members seem justified in scoffing at such speculations. Practically every observer of Woodlawn acknowledges that TWO has implemented grass roots democracy in the area. Dr. Edgar H. S. Chandler, executive vice president of the Church Federation and an acknowledged leader in the ecumenical movement, says this year's TWO convention was a remarkable successor to the town meetings he knew in his New England boyhood. In addition to its success in combating the university, slum landlords and unfair merchants, TWO can rightfully claim the following laurels.

City-wide influence in the struggle for integrated, higher-quality schools. TWO was instrumental in inaugurating an important court case in this area.

The relaxation of employment barriers in several stores.

The creation of a better understanding of welfare problems through meetings with public aid officials and cooperation with the local welfare office.

The creation of an ecumenical spirit within the community and on a city-wide level through interfaith contacts.

The formation of a strong citizens' group to watch over future urban renewal programs in Woodlawn—with a majority of the representation from TWO.

Woodlawn, through TWO, will soon be the beneficiary of what may prove a more significant venture than the University of Chicago fight. The Federal Government has given TWO a grant of $76,000 and a big challenge. Can TWO, with its indigenous base, select, counsel and provide training for the indigent unemployed? Similar programs have foundered on the rocks of paternalism and poor communication. TWO claims that it can use the grant to turn unemployables into employables. Success in this venture would be a powerful argument against welfare colonialism and in favor of the indigenous, self-determination approach of TWO.

TWO members acknowledge that there is much more to be done in Woodlawn. It is still a slum, but as Silberman suggests, a slum with hope. If Woodlawn's achievements have been overrated, it is only because they stand in such stark contrast to the failures of other similar communities, where millions of dollars have been spent to get slum dwellers to confirm the stereotype that they are somehow unable to control their own future if given the chance.

The tactics of TWO have included everything from sit-ins at the office of Mayor Daley to prearranged mass walk-outs at School Board meetings. Unquestionably there are well intentioned persons—ministers, social workers and citizens of Woodlawn—who have been deeply hurt by the raucous and rude attitude of those who advance TWO as the ultimate savior of the community. Nothing is more upsetting than to be told that for thirty years your method was wrong. At times the disciplined anger of TWO organizers has erupted in personal assaults on critics which, whether justified or not, merely proves that mixture of motives that Reinhold Niebuhr has so often and ably perceived.

And yet there is a spirit to the operation and to Alinsky that leads one to conclude that IAF's cardinal sin has been that of impoliteness, a quality that most Americans are attracted to only in secret. Indeed, what may alarm the critics most of all is IAF's elevation of impoliteness to the policy level. In a facetious memorandum, Alinsky recently advised his staff to cease referring to slums as slums and to call them "grey areas."

The controversy over Alinsky has created a number of important issues within the church and the social welfare community. One of these, raised by some Protestant clergy, is whether a local congregation is justified in joining an IAF organization as a congregation. Some churches that are quite active in TWO have not joined officially in order to maintain their priestly function as a mediator in conflict situations. It can be argued that TWO is a political instrument and that, for this reason, a church should refrain from identification. Most persons who hold this position, however, endorse the enthusiastic participation of laity and ministers through other institutional structures, such as the block club or the ministerial alliance.

Another theological issue for some is the reconciliation of Christian ethics with the use of self-seeking power. It seems to me that the Christian citizen must judge the points at which power benefits only the one who seeks it and speak out against the perversion of power solely for personal gain. IAF organizations seem less susceptible to this perversion of power because they are organized around a multiplicity of goals. The perils of power, however, do not justify the avoidance of power when the end is just.

This concept of power is tied in with the revitalization of voluntarism implied in IAF's organizing policy. Because these organizations lack police power, nothing prevents their dissolution save the will of their members. It strikes me that most of the organizations that we call voluntary (including the church) are really involuntary. We lack clear reasons for joining; we perceive little difference in our lives whether we are in or out; and in many so-called voluntary organizations the structure that might encourage controversy and debate is corroded by the pervasive sense that controversy is a bit more sinful than change.

One could begin a diatribe on the loss of national purpose, the frustration we are beginning to feel at cybernation (one of the few big words that is existentially understood by the rank and file), and the general breakdown of responsibility implied in last spring's knifing in Queens when neighbors, fearing involvement, did nothing. The basic point is that IAF's insistence on power in the context of a democratic organization has given people some sense that they matter. Alinsky says he would never be able to organize the leisure class. I suspect that the future of democracy, however, is somehow dependent on infusing the affluent society with the sense of purpose that emerges when one is forced to make clear-cut decisions. Is not the good psychiatrist's role to release in his patient the capacity to exercise the will?

The tyranny of the minority in America will be made possible only by what James Reston has called "the indifference of the majority."

Another issue involves the nature of urban government. Dr. Fey feels that IAF organizations are a judgment on the urban power structure for its failure to provide the education and tools for democratic decision-making. He contends with justification that Chicago is a city without a plan (although the City Fathers say there *is* a plan) and that, in this setting, the squeaking wheel gets the grease. TWO squeaks loudly, gets headlines and gains a victory, while some docile communities accept their lot. The judgment has merit. Even those who condemn TWO indicate that Chicago's urban renewal authorities have failed miserably in providing a voice for those who are to be affected by the bulldozer. Unless the city realizes this, urban renewal programs are destined to failure.

Meanwhile the urban renewal officials cite the ease and extent of citizen participation in stable Hyde Park. Which means that urban renewal has benefited the articulate at the expense of the "have nots." Which is precisely the point at which IAF entered Woodlawn. It is true that other cities have developed less controversial programs of citizen involvement, but controversy can become consensus only when there is genuine partnership between the administrators and the community. TWO is not, as some have claimed, anti-urban renewal. But it does demand a voice in it.

In conclusion, I would like to make two brief observations.

First, the social work community must put up with IAF's rudeness long enough to consider the tremendous implications of the theories of power and self-determination in the renewal of slum culture. In a provocative speech to the Child Welfare League of America in 1962, David R. Hunter provided a masterful analysis of the basic problem faced by every agency from the smallest community service to the largest welfare operation:

> Somehow today it is hard to escape a feeling of powerlessness and ineffectuality. The big things are getting away from us. We seem to be occupying ourselves in the recesses and eddies of the main stream. . . . [Social work] has shopped too exclusively at the stores of the psychic sciences and too rarely dropped in at the supermarket to select from the sociology, political science, anthropology and economics shelves. . . . The public is entitled to know what can't be accomplished by present methods. . . .

Finally, it seems to this writer that IAF's achievements ought to be studied thoroughly and dispassionately, particularly within the Christian community, to see whether they do not offer a way by which churches might better express their mission in the city. There are many pitfalls, and it cannot be doubted that some of IAF's more sophisticated partisans have seized on it as a means of proving to themselves that they have a righteous cause, or to solve identity problems. But this is understandable in an age when Holden Caulfields are more prevalent than Saul Alinskys.

July 20, 1964

John David Maguire

When Moderation Demands Taking Sides

୭~ତ~ଏ

John David Maguire

LIKE MOST MEN, I resent the destruction of the myths by which I have lived. By birth from Montgomery, by temperament moderate, I had convinced myself—until the Freedom Rides—that the complexity of Southern segregation patterns, suffused by unspeakably dark, blood-boiling emotions, signalled a "Stay Out" to those of us now living in the also discriminatory North, with plenty of local problems on our hands. "Local problems, to be solved locally, by moderation"—that was the myth by which I lived.

The Freedom Rides, however, began to break that myth, for there were interstate travelers (by definition not to be confined to a single locale) seeking no more than what had already been guaranteed them by Federal law[1]—desegregated access to all public interstate conveyances, and the non-discriminatory use of all interstate terminal facilities, waiting rooms, rest rooms, lunch counters and restaurants. Since I have to return south often to visit relatives, since I have Negro friends, colleagues and students, since I have to live on a professor's salary, I felt half-jokingly when the rides commenced that I had a stake in their success.

A few days later, all smiles had vanished. For, seeing violence in my birthplace and mobs momentarily ruling in my boyhood home, I was confronted by the fact that discrimination, and the hysteria in which it is grounded, was no longer simply an isolated local problem. Middletown, Connecticut, was suddenly so close to Montgomery, and indeed I had a deep human stake in it all.

In that moment, my version of the myth of stay-at-home moderation shattered. I saw that we moderates, by our failure to forge an

---

[1] In 1945, the case of *Morgan* v. *Virginia* resulted in a ruling that states cannot burden interstate commerce by the segregation of interstate passengers on common carriers. In 1955, in the case of *NAACP* v. *San Francisco Railway Co.*, the Interstate Commerce Commission prohibited segregation of interstate passengers in trains and railway stations. In December, 1960, the U. S. Supreme Court ruled that restaurants in Richmond bus stations must serve any passenger. In February of the same year, the Fifth District Federal Court of Appeals, sitting in Montgomery (the same court and the same site in which we have been heard) ruled, on a case growing out of an arrest at the Birmingham Terminal Station, that segregated waiting rooms and segregation of passengers were illegal. In March a similar decision covered the Greenville, S. C., airport restaurant.

effective instrument for the instantaneous registration of political pressure in crises, had no way for stemming the tide of the mob, nor for
restraining exasperated extremist governors who impetuously elect to
teach "outsiders" a lesson by withdrawing police protection and leaving
them to the crazed crowd.

The conversion of Time into an agent, the metaphysical fallacy
on which my version of moderation was founded, became transparent.
I had told myself that Time would effect change, that Time would
reconcile, that Time would tell. But I saw that Time is simply a
neutral receptacle within which men and movements shape society, its
defining characteristic being its waiting for no one. Had we moderates
been making the most of our moments in Time?

Hoping to avoid conflict, to avoid taking sides, I had sought, in
the name of Christian mediation, to stand in the gap between the much
discussed extremes. But it became clear that, in this situation, there is
little or no middle ground. One is either for law or against it. Hand-
wringing deplorings of violence are no substitute for the open support
of law. Violence can in large measure be averted when the body politic
does not siphon off its energies in these diversionary gestures. Indeed,
the failure of us moderates to identify openly and concretely with the
seekers and upholders of law was silently, but no less really, to cast
votes against it. For me there was suddenly no middle ground.

I could not settle for peace within the church, especially within
the Southern church in which I still hold membership, at the price of
keeping out someone human and ripping open the nation. I saw at last
the meaning of Martin Luther King's declaration that "Peace is not the
absence of tension, but the achievement of actual justice." I could no
longer settle for peace at any price.

Suddenly, going on the projected Atlanta-New Orleans journey
became a very natural act. The adventitious meeting of our group—a
Negro law student, the chaplain, and a divinity school teacher from
Yale, a Wesleyan faculty colleague and myself—with two Negro
theological students from North Carolina seemed parabolic of the way
in which all interstate travelers meet. Discovering mutual interests and
a common destination, they decide to travel together. And so began that
strange, stare-filled, frightening ride across my native South.

With each mile, I became clearer about why I had come. Every
day when I studied abroad I had been importuned for an explanation
of how America justified the gap between its constitutional guarantees
and professions and its actual practices—the same kind of explanation
Dean Rusk must give to African diplomats barred from Maryland
beaches, that Adlai Stevenson must give to dark-skinned UN delegates
for whom finding housing in New York is next to impossible, that the
Institute of International Education must give to black students as-
signed to Southern schools when they begin their travels within

America, that I had often sadly given to Negro fellow graduate students when asked why we could not have a cup of coffee or a meal together while waiting for a train in the middle of Montgomery.

I was convinced that this trip would narrow the gap between law and practice, perhaps by symbolizing that the safest profession in the country—the academic—must on occasion act as well as talk. Perhaps other conservative professionals might be encouraged to become involved. Perhaps everyone could be reminded that it is respectable to identify with decency.

I was assured that we were breaking no law.[2] A test between archaic social customs and existing national law always produces momentary tension and rivets floodlights on the testing ground. Publicizing the total events *might* embarrass the President, but surely the embarrassment is not caused by folk who have been humiliated all their lives and are only now seeking their established rights. Surely it is those law-defying folk bent on denying fellow human beings their Constitutional privileges who are the agitators. We were not the law-breakers, the provocateurs.

Morally, I had to make this journey. Segregation, withholding as it does recognition of the humanity of fellow creatures, is immoral. To be human means to have certain rights of man, and the Christian must be engaged until every man enjoys them.

The entire evening of our arrival in Montgomery was spent seeking to convince Justice Department officials of the need for providing guarantees, through arrangement with state authorities, that the aims of the Freedom Rides would be assured at the end of a requested "cooling off" period. If they were not, and a lull followed, surely renewed violence would attend the resumption of desegregated travel sometime later. Attorney General Kennedy had that day urged a temporary "return to normalcy," which meant of course a temporary return to the patterns of segregation.

"Why should Negroes always be asked to make the concessions?" we asked. "Why not allow free, unhampered travel during the moratorium period, allowing the white community to become accustomed to it? Or, if there are to be no Freedom Rides for a while, assure their right to resume freely at some mutually agreeable fixed date."

The officials were unable to make these guarantees that evening, the momentum for moving on was mounting, and the situation seemed

2 Since 1954, the non-discriminatory provisions of the Interstate Commerce Act of 1887 have increasingly been interpreted to mean what in fact they say. At any rate, is it unlawful to arrest whites and Negroes for, in effect, asking a private entrepreneur (the lunch-counter proprietor), even were he not operating in a bus terminal (as this proprietor was), to serve them on a non-discriminatory basis, whatever his past practices had been? Cf. Louis H. Pollak, "The Supreme Court and The States: Reflections on *Boynton* v. *Virginia*," California Law Review, Vol. 49, March 1961, No. 1, 15–55.

to demand a continued witness to our position. So we decided to push on for New Orleans by way of Jackson, Mississippi.

The rest is history. Accompanied by four Negro ministers who had come to see us off, Ralph Abernathy, Bernard Lee, Fred Shuttlesworth and Wyatt Tee Walker, we purchased our tickets for Jackson. Having sat down at the terminal lunch counter for a parting cup of coffee, we were arrested for breaching the peace—disorderly conduct and unlawful assembly. After twenty-eight hours virtually incommunicado and segregated in jail, each of the Connecticut group was released on a thousand dollars bail, provided by our students and colleagues, and was told to return for trial on June 16th.

Our consciences, kinsmen and colleagues all ask us, "Has anything come of all this?" The implications of the Freedom Rides are enormous, and my answer is a deeply convinced, "Yes, four central consequences have followed."

First, although the rides were not initiated by Martin Luther King, the riders, the moment they met violence, called on King to lead the proceedings, to quell the fury unleashed within the Negro community, and to represent the movement with Washington. His remarkable triumph as strategist and spiritual leader in this moment of adversity reinstates the principle of direct nonviolence as the pre-eminent, maximally effective device, except for the ballot itself, for achieving social change. His unbending gentleness means that the leadership remains in Christian hands, keeping at bay the violent extremists within the Negro community who, understandably frustrated, seek on occasion to rush, weapons waving, into the breach. King remains not only "a powerful symbol and a genuine person" ("The Burning Issue," May 29 issue) but the actual leader as well. As long as he leads, the country is spared that frightening prospect forewarned by Paton's Msimangu, "I have one great fear in my heart, that one day when the whites finally turn to loving, they will find we are turned to hating."

Second, from the pressure on the Justice Department during the rides and from the litigation following the rides, there will emerge a clear-cut statement once and for all forbidding segregation in public terminals. The Justice Department, under increasing pressure from at last aroused national leaders as well as the riders and the Negro community, has petitioned a ruling from the Interstate Commerce Commission stating clearly the ground rules for the free use of travel facilities. All local terminals that fail to comply would immediately have their licenses removed, and once these quite specific rules and regulations are spelled out, impressive fines could be levied for their violation. This ruling, which would hardly have been forthcoming without the rides (or certainly not so soon), will save thousands of dollars in court costs and speed up the process of desegregation by at least five years.

The other form that clarification of this issue will most likely take will be an injunction restraining police officials from interfering with integrated groups enjoying the facilities already assured them, in effect declaring that Federal statutes take precedence over unjust local segregation ordinances and laws.

Third, the morale of the Negro community has been boosted and the forces for nonviolent pressure have become more mobilized than ever. The Negro leadership has no illusions about the wholesale eradication within the next generation or two of prejudice, that deep-rooted personal matter of the heart. But they are bent on the elimination of discrimination in the public order perpetuated by ancient and inhuman laws.

King constantly distinguishes between desegregation and integration, the former a matter of law and society, the latter dealing with friendship, hearth and home. He insists that the present goal is desegregation, and that integration and the erasure of prejudice can come only by way of desegregation and the destruction of discrimination. The Freedom Rides have solidified that stirring in the land reflected in the sit-ins into a wave of quiet pressure that cannot be turned back. They have speeded up the process of desegregation, and pulled the Negro leadership, which through proliferation and native pluralism had threatened to become diffused, into one.

Finally, "the agony of the South" has at last been seen to be national in scope and everywhere to include Negroes. When we moderates spoke of "Southerner" we, too, long meant "Southern white." But no longer can the Negro's role in the "national agony" be overlooked nor his lawful claims as a citizen denied. My former kind of moderation only confirmed Orwell's biting observation that "We believe that all men are created equal, but some are created more equal than others." This will do no longer.

For us who went on the Freedom Rides there has resulted an identification and empathy with Negroes that we never knew before, and the realization that just such a sense of identification by our national leaders will be necessary if they are to understand this group on the move, and sense the heart of this world-wide social revolution. The Freedom Rides have dramatized this need and profoundly affected the lives of everyone involved.

The rides have to be understood, finally, as but one important act in an ever-accelerating drama. They confirm and support and are organically related to all the less publicized efforts for social and racial justice. They are a part of a movement that will stop short of nothing but full freedom.

June 26, 1961

Selma at First Hand

~~~⚬~~~

Wayne H. Cowan

"COME ON DOWN" was Martin Luther King's Macedonian call to shocked, irate Americans after Al Lingo's boys had brutalized a non-violent effort to march from Selma to Montgomery, Ala. Jim Dooley of metropolitan New York television commercial fame issues a similar invitation daily to come to Miami, but he has never met with a response to compare with King's. Not all who cared went, however; many stayed home and joined innumerable demonstrations across the country.

Once again the nation's conscience had been outraged, as it was by the police dogs, fire hoses and cattle prods of Birmingham. And when that happens the resulting action is bound to be powerful, both in its immediate witness and in its far-reaching effects. Not since the March on Washington had so many supporters of civil rights taken to the streets—North, South, East and West—to protest Governor George Wallace's and Colonel Al Lingo's joint denial of human rights by inhuman violence.

Johnson Hutchins, who taxied demonstrators back and forth in a Volkswagen Omnibus between Selma and the Montgomery airport some forty miles away, stated the issue simply—the right to vote. "I don't have any trouble getting into the county courthouse when I go to pay my taxes," he said, "and I don't see why they don't let us register to vote the same way. Instead they use our tax money to pay those troopers to beat our heads."

How did he explain the attack on the Sunday marchers? "I don't know . . . they seemed to go off their heads after those white people marched here on Saturday." He was referring to a group of eighty white Alabamans led by the Rev. Joseph Ellwanger, a Lutheran pastor serving a Negro congregation in Birmingham. Members of the group, which came from all over the state, returned on Tuesday to march again carrying signs indicating their point of origin (Huntsville, Tusca-loosa, etc.).

The town of Selma was tense as the last carloads of demonstra-tors arrived from the airport in Montgomery and Birmingham. Those who traveled from the former came in via U.S. Route 80 on which they were later to march. And they saw the scene of Sunday's atrocities—the sloping riverside where Sunday's demonstrators were chased by club-swinging mounted possemen. They also passed scores of cars oc-cupied by state troopers on the edge of town and more inside. The Negro quarter, particularly around Browns Chapel A.M.E. Church, was completely cut off from the rest of town. Motorcycle policemen barred all automobiles.

Browns Chapel is set in the midst of the George Washington Carver housing project, a series of relatively attractive, brick row houses interspersed by grassy strips. Many of the local Negroes milled in the street and on the sidewalk around it. The older ones appeared cowed, worn down by their years of near servitude. Those not quite so old could be heard to talk in newly discovered militant tones. The younger ones were more frolicsome—and fearless.

The latter had not been to school for almost two months, save for "freedom classes" in the churches. They spoke sharply of their principal, who would not allow teachers to leave the school dormitories to participate in the demonstrations. "He doesn't even know he's a black man," they complained.

Assembled on the playground near the rear of the church, the marchers stood or lolled on the ground in a warm springlike sun, unaware, by and large, of the Federal injunction against the march handed down by Judge Frank M. Johnson, Jr. For most of them it would not have mattered; a few, however, seriously debated what they should do. Only those inside the church—a small proportion of the total participants—were given instructions about the march and told how to protect themselves in case they were attacked.

Fortunately, as it turned out, communication was poor. (Even so, one veteran of the rights struggle termed it "the best organized demonstration the Southern Christian Leadership Conference has ever put on.") Had it been otherwise, a much greater and ultimately more dangerous *esprit de corps* might have developed. As it was, the group was rather subdued. Most of the activity consisted in the renewing of acquaintances on the part of the "outside agitators" and a mad scramble by Negro youths for some canned food (including tuna fish), which they proceeded to eat directly from the tins.

Every now and then word was passed down the assembled lines that the march would soon begin. Finally amidst a smattering of applause, Martin Luther King and other leaders took their places at the head of the line flanked by several hulking, beefy men in denim overalls who appeared prepared to throw themselves on top of King should it be necessary. Joining King in the front row was the Student Nonviolent Coordinating Committee's Executive Secretary, James Forman, wearing a heavy overcoat and carrying a hat so stuffed with newspapers that he could hardly get it on his head.

The march began. By this time few expected they were on their way to Montgomery—the destination was unclear. Slowly and somberly in low key it proceeded down the Sylvan St. sidewalk. A policeman stopped traffic at the corner, and the column turned and started down the almost deserted Water Ave. Tension mounted rapidly as the marchers proceeded past a number of ambulances, several of which looked like converted hearses. Inside several stores exhibiting "Closed" signs, groups of people stood behind plate glass windows and strained to see what would develop. It was like the film *High Noon,* as reporters and marchers alike searched alleys, doorways and rooftops for signs of impending trouble.

Up ahead at the corner of Broad Street something was developing. As the column approached the intersection it came to an abrupt halt and United States Deputy Marshal Stanley Fountain stepped forward, confronted King with the injunction, and then stood aside so that the march could continue. Reaching the crest of the Edmund Pettus Bridge spanning the muddy Alabama River, marchers caught sight of a wall of helmeted troopers. From the far end of the bridge the highway was bounded by troopers standing ten feet apart.

The marchers were stopped once again by Major John Cloud of the State Highway Patrol, who on "Bloody Sunday" had ordered his men to advance on the bewildered and helpless Negroes. The marchers and the troopers eyed one another at close range as King and Cloud carried on an almost inaudible dialogue while jets from nearby Craig Air Force Base streaked by overhead. In the middle of the prayers that followed, Cloud ordered all troopers from the highway—this sent a chill up the spine of at least one marcher who feared the way had been opened for an attack by the "rednecks" standing not too far behind the troopers. One minister later remarked, "It was the only time I ever prayed with both eyes open."

When the prayers were finished King did not accept the challenge that many observers believed was implicit in the opening of the highway by Major Cloud. Instead he led the demonstrators back across the bridge to town. As they turned around they sang in lively cadence. (They did not sing "Ain't Gonna Let Nobody Turn Me 'Round," as *The New York Times* reported.) "We love everybody," came their words; "we love George Wallace; we love the state troopers; we love Sheriff Clark. . . ."

The initial news reports indicated either that both sides had backed off or that King and his fifteen hundred followers—including a number of ministers, priests, rabbis, and what appeared to be the better part of the faculty of the University of Chicago Divinity School—had been turned back.

Viewed in any light the risks that King had taken were frightening. Had he not been able to control the demonstrators, the whole effort to affect the voting rights question favorably could have backfired. He wisely saw the folly of striking directly against the injunction; he recognized that his followers could not march to Montgomery without committing violence against the line of troopers. When several people near the front of the line insisted on continuing the march, his leadership was tested and recognized once again. And though his strategy was strongly criticized by some veteran campaigners and organizations within the civil rights movement, the risks inherent in any other course of action would have been far greater.

King had singled out Selma because he was confident he could dramatize to the nation the plight of its Negroes. The seat of Dallas County in the heart of Alabama's Black Belt cotton country, Selma had been ravaged by Northern troops almost exactly a hundred years ago. Scars of this defeat and Reconstruction bitterness still abide. Selma was the first city in Alabama to establish a White Citizens' Council.

Fewer than 350 of her 15,000 Negroes are registered to vote. During the first two months of the voting rights campaign three out of four Negroes were turned down while two out of three whites registered without incident. Against the "crippling legacy of bigotry and injustice," King set voting rights as the keystone for all other rights. "More than a badge of citizenship and dignity," he wrote recently, "it is an effective tool for change."

In light of the far-reaching legislation finally proposed by President Johnson to guarantee voting rights—now strongly supported by both parties in the Congress including certain prominent Southern leaders—it is quite evident that nonviolence has won another victory. Notice has been posted once again that time is running out for die-hard Southern reactionaries. The war against the willful denial of full rights to all our citizens is not finished, but a decisive battle has been fought— and the forces of darkness have suffered another stinging defeat.

Jimmy Lee Jackson (have we already forgotten his name?) and the Rev. James Reeb (who missed a ride to the airport in an already crowded car) are dead. Their murderers may never know justice, but these two have not died in vain.

April 5, 1965

Axioms for White Liberals

❧

Roger L. Shinn

AT THE END OF A summer that has changed irrevocably the racial situation in the United States we offer ten axioms for white liberals. We say axioms because they are the elemental assumptions for understanding and action in the new situation.

(1) The white man must recognize that he does not feel the pain of segregation as the Negro does. Those of us who take some pride in our efforts and sympathies have to reckon with the overpowering fact that we have not lived in black skins or borne the constant hostility of a dominant race. Even as we strive to become sensitive to the Negro's experience, we have to quit pretending that we understand his feelings or can speak for him.

(2) The white liberal can no longer set the strategy or timetable of progress. Increasingly Negro groups are charting their own courses. Whites for the most part do not devise the plans or select what they think are the wisest and safest actions. Faced with plans made by others, they decide to participate, resist or sit out the conflict. This does not relieve them of moral responsibility, but it changes the nature of some of their decisions.

(3) The time has come for liberal whites to quit praising Negroes as "nice people" who deserve to be treated better. Some Negroes are fine people and some are not. They are like any other ethnic group, except that they often show the special nobility or bitterness that comes from suffering injustice. The point is that they have rights to justice and opportunity because they are persons, not because they are a special kind of people.

(4) The race problem will be intensely frustrating until some grave economic problems are solved. The Negro's demand is more and more for jobs. But a lot of other people are also hunting jobs. General unemployment is no excuse for discrimination against Negroes; fair employment practices are urgent *now*. But the bitter fact is that improvement of Negro employment depends largely on generally improved employment. Most of America seems vaguely ready to recognize civil rights for all, but America is less ready to take the economic steps that are increasingly necessary.

(5) For the foreseeable future the white liberal will be troubled by an exaggerated racial consciousness among some Negroes, who will make demands that are hard to grant. The white man is in a poor position to complain. American society has conspired for generations to inflict upon the Negro the notion that he is visibly and ineradicably different. We cannot expect him to lose that sharp racial consciousness in a hurry.

(6) Similarly we may expect many Negroes to blame race for troubles that are not due to race. Everyone looks for some rationalization for his failures and frustrations. We have given the Negro a readymade rationalization that is valid nine-tenths of the time. We should not be surprised if he uses it the other one-tenth, when we (rightly or wrongly) are convinced it is invalid.

(7) We must expect Negro leaders sometimes to show the same

kind of intransigence from which they have suffered. So able and respected a leader as A. Philip Randolph is reportedly done with negotiation because it means compromise. "If I compromise," he says of his followers, "they'll picket me." Unwillingness to negotiate will make tough problems, but we must reckon with it.

(8) We can expect Negroes frequently to resent criticism, whether from whites or from their own spokesmen, including the justified criticisms that are part of normal social life. The Negro rightly complains that people who have never criticized Ross Barnett or Strom Thurmond become exercised over the political morality of Adam Clayton Powell. He may also become irritated when some of us who have long condemned the antics of Barnett and Thurmond point out the failings of Powell. In the poisoned racial atmosphere the ordinary give-and-take of public argument acquires a peculiar bitterness when directed against Negroes. Nevertheless some of the Negro's real friends, more concerned for honesty and the public good than for flattery, will risk misunderstandings and offer some criticisms to be tested in the arena of discussion.

(9) All generalizations, including those about the "New Negro," are suspect. Negro individuals show all the attitudes from fierce militancy to stolid apathy, from rank hostility to incredible good will.

(10) In so far as the white liberal actually shares in the life and cause of the Negro, he stands to gain an immensely more profound understanding of his colored brothers and of himself.

September 30, 1965

Maintaining Humanness in the Freedom Movement

࿇ ౿ ࿇

Malcolm Boyd

ANY WHITE MAN OR woman active in the freedom movement who is not a paternal do-gooder or dilettante is something of a Black Nationalist. This does not mean wanting Georgia or Montana or Arizona to be set aside as a black state restricted to Negroes. Nor does it mean black separatism or the Black Muslim approach. It does mean an honest recognition of the beauty of blackness and negritude, an understanding of African history, an awareness of Negro culture and history within the American heritage, and a dedication to help create a *new* society rather than simply welcome Negroes into first-class citizenship in the old. It is further understood that Negro contributions will be as fundamentally important as white ones in the new creation.

Yet the white person in the movement suffers severe identity problems. To many whites he is a "white nigger," while to many Negroes (particularly the majority who do not know him personally) he is "whitey" or a "white devil."

"Is a Dialogue Desirable Between Black and White?" was the title of a recent panel discussion. This focused sharply the *we—you* or *we—they* dichotomy as over against a *we* statement. This stems, of course, from white America's compulsive restrictions on Negro (and, therefore, human) freedom and its segregationist demands. It comes also from those endless community, church and women's meetings about "race relations" in which whites inevitably ask, and close the door by asking, "What is it that you people really want?"

During the recent Los Angeles rioting a Negro shouted, when he spotted a white man, "Let's get whitey." Another Negro retorted, "He's not a white. He's a priest." For this white priest, two masks stood between his humanness and that of the rioters.

Last May a number of Negro militants from Northern urban centers gathered in Washington to discuss goals and methods of organization. The host body was predominantly Negro, although a half-dozen whites belonged to it. When confronted by this handful of whites, one Negro from Harlem refused to go on with the conference unless it was firmly closed to *all* whites.

"It's okay for us to go to jail with you," came a response. "We can march on picket lines with you. But now are you telling us we can't sit down in this meeting with you?"

"Yes," the Harlem visitor replied. "That's the way it is." The conference went on without the whites, including the wife of one of the Negro leaders. Yet an Oriental woman, married to another Negro present, was permitted to take part.

Liberator, "the voice of the African-American," carried in its August correspondence section a communication that criticized "those so-called Black Nationalist intellectuals who find it terribly hard to be consistent with their militant . . . public postures when the doors to their bedrooms are closed." Such criticism of Negro leaders who are married to, or have relations with, white women is not uncommon. The letter continued:

> I'm a member of a new group of young nationalists who are in earnest, and who take Black Nationalism seriously. We are not interested in fiery rhetoric, clever intellectual forays, white communism, Islam, Christianity, Zen Buddhism or Bayard, nor in silly black homosexuals who write about other countries and talk about more marches on power-corrupted Washington. We see nationalism as purposeful and seriously involved in the destiny of black people and other people of color throughout a world devoid of the world's most impertinent bunch of bastards, the white race!

Yet I recall a prominent Black Muslim telling me, "I consider you more black than many blacks." (I am white.) He was referring to involvement in the struggle for freedom, rather than merely color, as his means of knowing a man; and he was being critical of the "black bourgeoisie" middle class.

If all United States "blacks" were made to comprise the freedom movement, it would undoubtedly die overnight. Many Negroes stand aloof from the movement for a variety of reasons, and a number of them frequently betray it. On the other hand, white blood along with black has nourished the movement's soil; and the battlelines, whether in Mississippi or Chicago, have consistently been interracial.

A woman who had not previously accepted any overt involvement in the movement was moved by the Selma crisis to carry a picket sign in a downtown Washington demonstration. She belonged to an exclusive Negro women's club and was told by one of her friends in that group, "You've embarrassed us, marching publicly with those beatniks and niggers."

Whites within the freedom movement (as contrasted with the less radical, more liberal civil rights movement) have generally supported, and even called for, Negro leadership. One of the most militant whites recently told me that he would only accept a job working for a Negro.

The background of this is, of course, the past domination by some whites of certain civil rights organizations, which resulted in the manipulation of such bodies by the power structure, white and black alike. This situation created the whole new set of problems that we are facing today. Los Angeles is a good example. There were middle-men by the dozen, but both the white power structure and the Negro middle class were tragically cut off from honest communication with the ghettoized mass.

In Mississippi last summer I talked at length with an elderly Negro man who has survived persecution and locally led the freedom struggle for a number of years. Someone close to him told me, "He talks to a white man just the same as he talks to a Negro." This is very unusual and daily becomes rarer. Acquiescence has become hostility, but neither can be described as a Negro's natural way of addressing another Negro.

Just as there are "colored whites"—persons who, although colored, think and live white—so are there "white Negroes"—whites who think and live black. But the black and white lines are hardening.

For example, I recall hearing a news broadcast in Alabama last July that reported the arrest of an alleged rapist. It identified him as a Negro, and identified the woman who had allegedly been raped as white. Images and reactions were immediately polarized. Whites saw the alleged attacker as guilty, depraved and deserving of serious punishment; Negroes (and whites in the movement) saw him as innocent, another pawn in the sexual mythology of the Southern white woman, a brother-scapegoat who deserved freedom and—just as immediately important—protection from the white police and "good" people.

Negroes who do not yet hate whites express the great need "for Negroes to get used to being with whites." They believe, therefore, that it is good for white student volunteers to work in the Deep South and in Northern ghetto slums. But a young, angry Negro community leader told a white co-worker, "The only way we can go is black. The movement's got to get blacker and blacker. Whites corrupt and bleed it."

I spoke with a young Black Nationalist in the Watts ghetto hours after the rioting subsided. He was twenty-one years old and had not finished high school. I asked him if he hated whites.

"I really don't hate the white man," he said. "I just want the Man to leave me alone. Just back up and keep his distance. I used to sit in school every day. A man there tells me Christopher Columbus discovered the New World. Another man says an Italian cat whose name began with 'V' did it. I don't know why the white man keeps confusing me. Blacks have been here for a long time. I want to hear something about *me*. But I can't find out."

What did he think about the rioting?

"It was the best thing that ever happened. You come to the Man and try to tell him, over and over, but he never listens. Why, the Man has always been killing. He first drove the Indians out. Now my arm's almost been bit off. I've got to bite back. The riot? There'll be more of the same until the Man opens up his eyes and says, 'We're going to give it to you because we're tired.' "

I asked if he had any white friends.

"A few whites I'll let know me. I know some whites who are okay. Others I can't have anything to do with. There's one white guy I knew at school . . . he *could* be a soul brother if he was black. I don't know any middle-class Negroes. Pride makes you rich. Material things don't matter. If a Negro is dressed well, the white man thinks 'that's one of those niggers who did all right.' So I never dress up."

He continued: "We just found out the white man has been killing the colored man with those birth control pills. He gave us birth control pills but he gave *his* women hormones so they could have quintuplets. The white man is trying to get rid of Indians and buffalo *and* black men.

"If the white man doesn't like me because of the color of my skin, why this Man-Tan? If the police chief considers us monkeys, why do his men proposition Negro women? The Beatles' haircut is long like ours used to be, so now we cut ours short. They try to get on the bandwagon and be like us. They try to sing like us. Everything we do, we do good. The black man is just great. Cassius Clay proved that."

What did he think should be done to improve the Negro's condition?

"A community organization might be right for us here. Not preachers or Toms or soul-saving sisters. The answer is the young black man. The old man can't help right now. No, we're not organized. You don't find a rat until you throw a piece of cheese out there. Then everybody's on the scene. My idol was Malcolm X. When he died I knew a brother was gone. But I didn't cry for him. If my mother fell down and died, I couldn't feel anything. I've got no tears for nobody.

"The police beat me on the head after they handcuffed me. I know hate isn't going to do any good. But I'm not going to love a white. Nobody can define love to me. I might want to make love to a white, but I can't love a white. And I'm tired of hearing that old thing about the good old Jesus Christ, how he walks on water, with his blue eyes and blond hair. The cross is a sign of death, that's all there is to it. Jesus Christ hung from it. The church people, with their Book, do you think they're going to tell me what's right and wrong? I want them to leave me alone. Preachers don't make sense. The Bible says, 'Do unto others as you would have them do unto you.' So?"

I asked another young Negro, a worker in community organization in Watts, how he felt about whites.

"The people have never been able to voice themselves," he replied. "They've been treated as a child by whites. So Negroes are biting the hand that feeds them. A dog will even bite his master after he's been beaten and kicked. When pain overcomes fear, a riot occurs.

"This wasn't a race riot. It was letting out a yell, saying, 'We're still living, we're here, you've got to let us live like you do.' If they don't hear, the whole world will rise up. All poverty areas are going to rise. What Negroes feel about whites is what has happened for the past five hundred years. A lot of whites are bound in the way of life they've lived for that long. They give what they want and when they want. They're used to having their own way. The Negro has been down so long. A lot of Negroes don't know how to get up, or even the advantages of getting up.

"I used to know some whites in high school. I was beat up by other Negroes time and time again because I swam in high school with a team of whites. 'I'm an individual,' I explained to colored as well as white friends. It wasn't easy. During the riot I fought. I fought when I was attacked by three policemen unduly and unnecessarily. You can't treat people like animals and expect them to act as citizens."

What leaders did he respect?

"The people out here, we believe in each other. 'I'm poor, brother, you're poor, brother.' The strong, the fearless are the leaders. The people were willing to follow Malcolm because he had words for them they could understand. The upper-class Negroes disliked Malcolm. Did Dick Gregory come and sit down with the people *before* the riot? Did Martin Luther King? These people didn't come in time, and they aren't respected. The parents have a respect for King because he represents their Master, their Creator. But youth can't understand nonviolence, turning the other cheek. They fear things they can't understand.

"This wasn't a riot. It was a movement of people who are tired and depressed, and don't have the leadership in themselves to show leadership. Martin Luther King has wrapped himself up in representing the people so much that he has lost his voice with the people. Instead of staying with the people, he has moved away. We don't want a black man the white man has built up to lead us. We know what we want."

One militant Negro organization (fifty per cent white in its membership) is setting up a "black-oriented" boys' club in Watts. "We're going to have a drill team named after a prominent Afro-American," one of the Negro leaders told me. "They will make their rank by learning Negro history or reading a book. It will be highly disciplined. One with girls will follow. We plan to have a Freedom House and a Freedom School for political education and economic cooperatives.

"We want to start by taking kids on trips," he continued. "We will expose them to something out of their environment. Take them to a company where they don't hire Negroes except to sweep the floors, and everything is all-white. Then we'll come back and discuss it. We'll have books everywhere. Politically oriented magazines and free books."

How does a white man react to "black-oriented" programs that are a part of the struggle in which he is a participant? One deeply involved white worker told me:

I find myself reacting in a number of situations in an anti-white way. This is because I'm closer in my everyday life to Negroes than whites. The whites with whom I come in contact frequently are

also in the movement. Other whites, who are opposed to the movement or indifferent to it, tend to regard me with suspicion. I'm
struggling to hold on to some kind of objectivity in all this. As a
white man among militant Negroes, I have to fight the tendency to
become masochistic. I mean, there's so much hatred toward whites
that I must absorb.

Black supremacy is, in my opinion, an idolatry. So is white
supremacy. People who believe in any kind of racial supremacy
tend to indulge in half-truths like the John Birch Society does. I'm
willing to say a person can live like that so long as I don't have to.
I think Pilate said the most "gospelish" thing of all when he said,
"What is truth?" I'm basically on the side of have-nots and anti
the haves. Well, most blacks are have-nots. Black America is, give
or take a little, have-not. White America is the biggest have in
history.

But one of the most important things for any white in the movement to overcome is the oft-noted sense of *noblesse oblige,* do-goodism or
working *for* "others." The more he can share in the lives of people with
whom he is working, the more sensitive he can become to the human
needs that are present, including his own.

A white man will not "become" a Negro, as a Negro will not "become" a white man. There is a considerable advantage in this. The white
man can continue to communicate with other whites in a way uniquely
established by racial and cultural ties, and a Negro can communicate with
other Negroes. Such persons become singularly important agents of communication—listening, speaking, reporting, interpreting, listening. Such
persons can often establish honesty in a given situation—black, white or
interracial—that might otherwise be marked by polite evasion, superficial
chatter and lies.

Last summer I donned a black mask to play the role of a Negro
shoeshine man in a play I wrote entitled *Boy*. A Negro wore a white mask
to portray a white man who brutalizes the Negro. We presented the play
throughout Mississippi and in parts of Alabama and Arkansas before
rural Negro audiences that, for the most part, had never set foot inside a
legitimate theater or seen a play. We often performed in community
centers or local churches in hundred-and-ten-degree heat.

The people were fascinated by the paradox of a white man's "playing" a Negro. They wondered, could he possibly *know* the role? And
some were thinking, what *right* did he have to undertake such a role? I
had to explain to audiences that I was not known simply as a white man,
but rather as a "white devil" or a "white nigger." I pleaded for humanness in the face of the forms of dehumanization that would destroy us.

My own feelings can change suddenly on the color spectrum. I can
react swiftly as anti-white or anti-black. It is always in a given context,

and it is not a color reaction so much as a reaction to a person or a situation. For example, I was very anti-white recently when I was shown an immense, quite vulgarly pietistic painting of the white Jesus—with long blond curls and eyes turned heavenward—that had been donated by a white church organization to an all-black community center in an embattled Negro ghetto. I wanted to shout, "Jesus wasn't white, he was a desert-tanned Semite." (In the play *The Community* a Negro asks, "Where was the white Christ when I was crucified by white Christians?")

I was very anti-black during a sit-in when the Negroes in our group subjected Negro policemen to a tongue-lashing that left them little dignity or humanness in front of a large number of whites. We were witnessing a public castration, and the sole basis of it was color.

I will never forget another time when I was anti-white. At a rather formal meeting a white man suddenly addressed one of the Negroes, "I want you to know that, despite your face being black, I know your heart is white."

Then recently in a tense situation in the Deep South where a few Northern white volunteers were working in the black ghetto, I felt anti-black as I noticed the whites were being shunned on all social occasions by the Negroes, who left them in a peculiarly painful isolation *as whites*.

The white man in the freedom movement, who is caught in the identity crisis between the prescribed roles of "white nigger" and "white devil," can never forget that he is not black, despite the fact that he has become something of a Black Nationalist. But it can be extremely helpful for him to remember he is human.

October 4, 1965

The New Rhetoric

VI

The Church's New Concern
with the Arts

❦

Amos N. Wilder

EVIDENCE OF a new interest in the arts on the part of the churches
appears on all sides today. At the level of the local church we note ex-
hibits of religious painting and sculpture, productions of modern plays like
those of Eliot and Christopher Fry, as well as initiatives with respect to
the dance and the pageant. The Riverside Church in New York City has
now for two years sponsored an annual anthology of poetry by college
writers, judges of which have included Marianne Moore, Richard Eber-
hart, and Mark Van Doren. Church bodies, local or regional, have also
organized series of lectures or institutes bearing on the modern arts. A

recent seminar in Religion, Drama and Literature at Drew University, held with the help of the Danforth Foundation under the auspices of the Commission on Literature of the National Council of Churches, attracted a good number of teachers of English. The lecturers included both theologians and distinguished artists. A significant venture last year was that of the New Hampshire Congregational-Christian Conference in association with Dartmouth College in providing a monthly series of lectures for pastors on such writers as Eliot, Kafka, Faulkner, and Camus. In many ways the churches are making amends for their shortcomings in this field.

It is certainly possible to be overly optimistic about such signs of interest in the arts on the part of Christians. It may well be that most of this interest is confined to relatively small groups. Matters like taste are hard to change. The re-education of the emotions is no doubt more difficult than that of the reason, if the two can be separated. The re-education of the imagination is still more difficult. Here, indeed, what is required is no less than a conversion. In his discussion of Catholic art in France, in *L'Art Sacré,* Père Régamey well documents the resistances to the significant new initiatives in ecclesiastical architecture and art, not only among the masses of believers but among Catholic intellectuals. He confesses quite desperately that the situation is all but hopeless, though the witness must still be borne. He cites encouraging examples of the reconciliation of those who were first scandalized, once they had actually become familiar with such new departures as the church at Assy or the chapel at Vence—familiar, that is, not by observation but by worship itself in these buildings.

Our hope for significant changes of attitude in this whole area must rest finally not so much on aesthetic instruction and "propaganda" in the good sense, but on the combination of this with profound cultural impulses today which affect the attitudes of men to faith and its forms. Revolutionary changes in life as a whole empty older symbols of their meaning, and men are ready then to respond to new symbols or new forms of old symbols that speak to the new situation.

More significant today than the church's activity in connection with the ecclesiastical arts is the deeper motivation which is revolutionizing the church's whole attitude to symbolic expression. Even those churches which we call liturgical, and which have maintained a positive attitude toward the arts, have recognized a new dimension in this area. The historical study of Christian art has quickened, and been quickened by, the new recognition of the importance of the symbolic element in religion and life. The historian of religion, generally, has learned to assign more significance to myth, ritual and art in the understanding of the world's faith. Psychology and anthropology have contributed their insights to the matter.

Thus the perceptive theologian today sees the arts not merely as

servants of the church in the sense of embellishments of worship or strategies for religious propaganda. Nor is he satisfied to set the arts, as an
inspirational resource, over against daily life, and to say that religion must
use the sources of the Spirit—meaning Beauty, Poetry and Imagination—
over against the prosaic and utilitarian world in which modern men live.
Here we have the idealistic fallacy. Such a dichotomy of prose and poetry,
of actuality and dreams, or of realism and imagination, is really an escape
philosophy. It disparages art and worship as mere consolations, and
surrenders over the actual life of men as, in effect, unredeemable. It
capitulates to the banishment of the arts and worship from a materialistic
world, from a rational-technological age.

The critics and lovers of art who everlastingly appeal to Beauty and
to the Spirit are always the first ones to reject a T. S. Eliot or a Faulkner, a Picasso or a Stravinsky; only much later, under the force of overwhelming evidence, to give them a grudging approval.

The theologian today recognizes that even the materialist lives not
by creature comforts, prosperity and success, but by his own symbols and
images, his own myths and rituals. He recognizes that the conflict today is
not between matter and spirit, but between two kinds of spirit; not between prose and imagination, but between a true and false imagination;
not even, finally, between ugliness and beauty, because what some would
call beauty and ideality cannot save.

What finally is important is the symbol and the kind of symbol, the
imagery and the kind of imagery, the myth and the kind of myth. For
symbols convey truth or error. They mediate illusion or reality. Sentimental symbols of aspiration, dreams and ideality may effect temporary
reflexes of beatitude or induce charmed states of euphoria, but this is
escapism. This is religious romanticism, and not true religion, much less
Christianity. At one time, it is true, Christian transcendentalism, like
Christian Platonism, incorporated a substantial core of the Christian view
of man and evil, so as to constitute a valid version of Christian theology.
But these strains of Christian idealism have been attenuated and washed
out in a great flood of religious and secular sentimentalism.

The best theology today, in its repudiation of a rhetorical religious
idealism, finds itself in agreement with a recurrent note in contemporary
poetry. Hebraic concreteness is more at home with modern verse than is
Greek Platonism. T. S. Eliot said of Henry James that he had a "mind so
fine, no idea [we add: no ideal] could violate it." The poets at least ask,
with Marianne Moore, for "real toads in imaginary gardens." The theme
which runs through the glorious celebration of the imagination in
Wallace Stevens is the same:

We keep coming back and coming back
To the real: to the hotel instead of the hymns

That fall upon it out of the wind . . .
              We seek
Nothing beyond reality. Within it
Everything, the spirit's alchemicana . . . [1]

              Not grim
Reality, but reality grimly seen.[2]

These things are said everywhere in Stevens. The "festival sphere" of the imagination, he says, begins from the "crude collops."

The poet Richard Wilbur recurs to a similar theme. Take, for example, his poem, "A World Without Objects is a Sensible Emptiness." The poem describes the alluring but accursed mirages of the goal of the mystic and the idealist. The poet is advised to turn back from the "long empty oven" of the desert to the real world and its homely objects: here is

              . . . The spirit's right
Oasis, light incarnate.[3]

A sound theological critique of the insipid idealism which prevails so widely still in Christian circles receives a notable reinforcement in the extraordinary book, *Mimesis,* by Erich Auerbach. This study of the contribution of Hebraic and early Christian realism to world literature in effect draws out the corollaries of the Incarnation for the aesthetic order. It constitutes a radical challenge to classical and humanistic axioms with regard to beauty and art, not in the form of an apologetic diatribe but rather of a masterly study in comparative literature. It becomes evident that the Hebraic-Christian concern with all humble and lowly and earthy reality in man and the world opens the way to the most significant life of the imagination. Here a Christian approach to art and symbol will rejoin much of the most influential artistic criticism of the last decade or two.

One may illustrate the new maturity in religious attitudes to the arts by noticing what has gone on in the theological seminaries in recent years. In times past, theological training was concerned, as indeed it always should be, with the professional and ecclesiastical aspects of the arts. The future minister was given, so far as possible, some introduction

---

[1] From "An Ordinary Evening in New Haven," in *The Collected Poems of Wallace Stevens.* Reprinted by permission of Alfred A. Knopf, Inc.

[2] Ibid.

[3] From *Ceremony and Other Poems,* Copyright 1948, 1949, 1950 by Richard Wilbur. Reprinted by permission of Harcourt Brace, Inc.

to his later responsibilities as one concerned with church music and hymnody, though even here he was often later at the mercy of his director of music. Some real effort was made in many seminaries to further his acquaintance with literature. There was here a dim carry-over of the ancient claims of rhetoric on the preacher. And indeed, the preacher should be, in the ancient sense, a grammarian, at home in letters, languages, eloquence and the classics. Both for his own spiritual culture and for the enrichment of preaching, courses were and are offered in English poetry as in the world's classics of devotion.

The new interest in the arts in the seminaries and among theologians contrasts sharply to the approaches mentioned. It is no longer only a question of the Sacred Lyre and the cultural and professional formation of the clergy. More urgent today is the whole question of imaginative vehicles, of symbolization, in religion. The semantic question in religious discourse is raised, and the whole problem of communication. Almost every department of theological study is involved at this level, and this means not only attention to the symbols and images of the Christian faith; it also means attention to the symbols and images and art forms of the contemporary world, as they are encountered in literature and the fine arts, but also in popular expressions, community rituals, social ideologies, and not least in the mass media of the time.

We realize better today that society lives by its myths, its favorable symbols; these are not idle or interchangeable. The Cross is not interchangeable with the Crescent or Lotus. The Cross is one thing, and the Swastika is another. The Sheaf of Wheat is one thing, and the Fascis is another. The "Battle Hymn of the Republic" is one thing, and the "Internationale" is another. The Lincoln Memorial is one thing, and the Tomb of Lenin is another.

Society lives by its symbols, and society represents a battleground of competing symbols. Sometimes they battle to the death. They signify sometimes a devitalizing stalemate within a family or nation of incompatible loyalties and banners: In France, the French Revolution and Catholic order; in our Southern states, ancient nostalgias and a genuine agrarian humanism—each with their evocative emblems.

Social responsibility and discernment require a clear perception of such rival myths and their power, recognition of such competing visions and rituals, ability to exorcize those that are malign, and to reconcile those that are benign. Society lives by its images, but its life is often stagnant and moribund where the living images fail. In either case, the church must recognize the situation. It is important to discern the real, activating myths of civilization from the formal clichés of political orators. A democratic society may proclaim its democratic dogmas, but the same society may be governed by undemocratic nostalgias and passions fed by obsolete dreams. The church itself may proclaim its Christian principles, but Christians may be ruled by sub-Christian imaginations.

Archibald MacLeish well states the importance of the myths of an age, what happens when they fail, and the responsibility of the poet, and, we may add, the believer, in renewing them.

> *A world ends when its metaphor has died.*
> *An age becomes an age, all else beside,*
> *When sensuous poets in their pride invent*
> *Emblems for the soul's consent*
> *That speak the meanings men will never know*
> *But man-imagined images can show:*
> *It perishes when those images, though seen,*
> *No longer mean . . .* [4]

The main point is that when we say Art, we say Image; and when we say Image or Symbol, we say Meaning, we say Communication. The arts, old and new, the fine arts, the practical arts and the popular arts, are peculiarly carriers of meaning and value in our society as in all societies. The church is learning that it cannot ignore such expressions of the society in which it lives. The encounter of the gospel with the world, whether in evangelism, religious education, apologetics, or theology, requires a deep appreciation of, and initiation into, the varied symbolic expressions of culture. It is in such manifestations at all levels that the moral and spiritual life of the age discloses itself.

The appreciation of the modern arts in certain church circles today is therefore one of the most important features of the whole situation. It is one aspect of the awakening of the churches generally to a better knowledge of the world about them. It is indispensable to the purification of the sacred arts. More important still, it will contribute to a new theological seriousness, a greater discrimination in the matter of Christian symbols. In some periods, Christians need to be awakened from their dogmatic slumbers; and this is still widely the case, for dogmatism destroys sensibility as the letter kills. But today it is widely true that the churches need to be awakened from their undogmatic slumber, in the sense that they have lost the sense of the fateful issues of good and evil, of salvation and damnation. This kind of salutory shock is provided by the modern arts, and not only by Christian but by agnostic artists and writers.

February 18, 1957

[4] From "Hypocrit Auteur" in *Collected Poems: 1917-1952*. Reprinted by permission of Houghton Mifflin Company.

William Faulkner: An Appreciation

❧

Julian N. Hartt

WILLIAM FAULKNER, THE MASTER storyteller of our time, died on July 6th. His greatest stories had long since been told. For a man who had contended with demons he made a quiet exit.

They are indeed great stories. He was moving toward the heights in *Sartoris*. He reached the pinnacles in *The Sound and the Fury, As I Lay Dying, Light in August* and *Absalom, Absalom!*; and then he created that splendid thing, "The Bear." These are the perfections of his achievement as a novelist. Thereafter, as our world plunged into the abyss of World War II, his stories took on a remarkable soteriological quality. Perhaps such creations as *Intruder in the Dust, Knight's Gambit, The Hamlet, The Town, Requiem for a Nun*, and *A Fable* reflect a growing sensitivity in Faulkner as moralist. He had become engrossed in making an affirmation ("Man will prevail!") to a world desperately needing affirmations it could credit and love. His art suffered from this admirable preoccupation. At the end—*The Mansion, The Reivers*—something of the old and wonderful narrational power flashes briefly again; but in *The Mansion* it is caught in the soteriological net, and in *The Reivers* it is overlaid with nostalgia—the original sin of the Imagination.

What is the greatness of the stories of the Thirties? They create, each in itself and each also in a grand cumulative effect, a legendary world; and they imbue that world with the feeling, passion and intelligibility of authentic history. They are, therefore, novels in the grand tradition, but they are also remarkably individualistic achievements.

Faulkner's individuality is exhibited, for instance, in his use of a folkloristic medium, quite as though he had reckoned (and rightly) as follows: It is possible to have real history only in the unconsciously artful devices of memory and speech habitually employed by people celebrating rather than reconstructing the past; or, if reconstructing it, doing so to see where and how a grand design was ruined and became ruinous —as Thomas Sutpen does in *Absalom*. So Faulkner's prime characters weave circumstantial detail with fanciful reconstructions into a marvelous fabric of speech, both internal and overt.

In the disclosure of the internal world, Faulkner does not slide off into stream of consciousness. The close-out soliloquy of Quentin

Compson in *The Sound and the Fury* illustrates the point: It is a firmly structured dialogue between Quentin and his father, between the guilt-charged present and the brooding past. The fated and fatal moment has a meaning, definite, consummatory and terrible: It is in guilt that men are of one substance with each other across the generations and across cultural differences. This, and not the superstitions and quasi-metaphysical notions of race, religion, etc., is the bond of unity.

But in his best stories there is nothing philosophically programmatic about this performance. Faulkner carries it off by cunning employment of the rhythm of folk speech—its musical beat and stress, its intonations, its silences, its complex interweaving of fact and fantasy, its rich conjunctions of comedy and terror. Faulkner has no equal in the mastery of a folkloristic medium. He chose and perfected it artistically because such speech is the prime medium in which the natural community expresses its central life—its code, its memories, its hopes.

That natural community is Faulkner's dominant theme. He is a regional writer certainly, but Yoknapatawpha County is not merely Mississippi—it eludes geographical and sociological confinement. His novels create this legendary kingdom in important and rarely superfluous detail —Oh wonderful Yoknapatawpha!—but the natural, richly particular community that he so artfully creates is also the one community embracing and constituting us all—Oh wonderful Mankind!

He shows us how paltry and thin is the history of the community when it is measured in the long roll of successive generations of a family on the land. Yet how deep, dense and rich is its story when its history is grasped as destiny, as deeds heroic and base, as honor loved, violated, and recompensed, as guilt incurred, communicated, accepted, and atoned. The "great families" had not been there long before the Civil War, and we learn how they achieved greatness—by trickery, luck and violence. So their legacy is tainted, damned and damning, and the great families peter or flame out, strangely and terribly recompensing outrage. So the community is under a curse; "doom" is the way to pronounce "destiny."

But Faulkner was not a conservative and monolithic tragedian. He shows us also the life-affirmers, the lovers of justice, as distinguished from the instruments thereof, and a people immune to the curse—unless fortuitously trapped by it—the Negroes. Eventually Faulkner's soteriological commitments persuaded him to tilt the scale to the side of these components of the community. Though the novels of the Forties mark a decline of his powers, there is something peculiarly instructive as well as deeply poignant in them.

In the towering novels of the Thirties he celebrated the whole community as the human reality. There are bad men in it—and I think Doc Hines, that pious monster, is the prize—but the worst they can do

does not destroy the community. In fact, the central and climactic violence in *Light in August,* the slaying of Joe Christmas, is very nearly
ritualistic: the blood of the victim forthwith becomes the imperial *presence* in and over the community, "of itself alone serene, of itself alone
triumphant." And in *The Sound and the Fury,* Jason Compson is undone
by his own cunning born of avarice and envy; but Faulkner brings this
off with strokes of comic device. In neither case does he enter the lists;
he does not lead a loud cheer for Providence. Instead, each of these novels
concludes on a comic note far from invocational.

Then a great change appears: Now he must show men acting of
prepense purpose and settled resolution to redress iniquity, to punish—
and not just to recompense—outrage. The evil Snopeses must be brought
low, and this cannot be left to the deliberate pace of the Higher Powers.
So Ratliff is transformed from an essentially folkloristic figure into a
moral hero; and Mink Snopes, whose earlier appearances in the trilogy
hardly promised such great things, becomes an avenging angel of the
Lord.

In other words, Faulkner came to preaching. *Requiem for a Nun*
is his most embarrassing sermon, worse than *A Fable,* which has some
moments of narrational splendor. Once he had been content to show
what it means to endure in the active, and not merely passive, mode, as in
the great yarn *The Old Man.* But now he had to preach that man will
prevail. I think this means that during the Forties and the Fifties
Faulkner was afraid of how the human story might very well turn out;
so he began to light candles in the darkness. If this is so, his last story,
The Reivers, is no great comfort, because it is an exercise in nostalgia
lightly seasoned with grave assurances that guardians of human dignity
will never be wanting. For this purpose, he reached all the way back to
the venerable cliché of the prostitute with the heart of unsullied gold.

I guess that Faulkner had some unsettling hunches about how
history is made and might end. But what he knew surpassingly well is
how history is told, not necessarily, and perhaps not very often, by the
people who do the great and terrible things in it, but certainly by the
people who—despite its terrors and deceits—love it and accept it, as it is
and as being all there is. (" 'I dont hate it,' Quentin said . . . 'I dont.
I dont! I dont hate it! I dont hate it!' ") For this splendidly communicated gift, Faulkner will be remembered with profound gratitude so long
as people read with profit novels of those peculiar pleasures of intensified
perception and chastened love.

August 8, 1962

Albert Camus: Political Moralist

⌁⌁⌁

William F. May

THE WRITINGS OF ALBERT CAMUS have had a decisive influence on the political convictions of many young Frenchmen. Yet he often sounds like a Christian moralist. In fact there is no better way of moving toward the center of his political convictions than by recognizing their theological dimension.

"The astonishing history evoked here is the history of European pride." With these words Camus introduces his eloquent study of the nineteenth and twentieth centuries, *The Rebel* (New York: Alfred Knopf, Inc., 1956). Camus writes scathingly "of the horizontal religions of our times," of the attempted deification of man that has plagued contemporary life. In the fashion of the Christian prophet, he pursues the moral pretensions of the French Revolutionaries, the pedantry and hypocrisy of the bourgeois world, the demonia of the fascists, and the messianic utopianism of the Marxists. In all these movements, Camus argues, man overreaches himself, pretends to one sort of divinity or another, but concludes by justifying the violation of man.

Further, in a manner reminiscent of the classical theologians, Camus links the cardinal sin of pride with a consequent dishonesty and murder. Every human absolute eventually contradicts itself and does so at terrible expense to the solidarity of the race. In honor of Justice, Law and Order the French Revolutionists unleashed a lawless terror. Although praising the formal virtues of honesty, conscience, and the dignity of work, the bourgeois class created social conditions that made the exercise of these virtues impossible. While declaring everything permissible in the name of a glorious Germany, Hitler led this very Germany to an impermissible, inglorious defeat. In deference to a future humanity, the Stalinist commits inhumanities that defer indefinitely the advent of the New Jerusalem. The results in each case are more than contradictions furnished by the turns and twists of events. There is a fundamental moral incoherence at the root of all these movements, as they lay an ax to their own principles and split open the race.

Camus' affirmations also have a familiar ring for moralists in Christian circles, especially those concerned with "proximate justice." Against the wild immodesty, contradiction and betrayal of human solidarity that ensues when men absolutize a particular group or future for man, Camus urges a passion for justice that is governed at every point by a sense of limits. He displays the essential double tension: The prophet's zeal for response to the abuse of man's dignity, with distrust for a zeal that denies all restraints upon that response. In every instance, Camus recommends a modesty, honesty and decency in political action that will honor the proximate character of justice; he recommends these persuasively by reflecting the discipline of these virtues in his own writing.

Yet the rejections and affirmations suggested so far are hardly enough to register Camus in the latent Church. Notoriously absent from "the history of European pride" is the sense that it is man who is prideful. Ideologies rather than men appear to do most of the overreaching of limits. Man is treated as the victim rather than the author of the ideologies that have dominated our times. In short, there is little sense of man as sinner. As might be suspected, Camus also shows little sympathy for "realism" in politics—an immediate corollary of the sinfulness of man for so many Christian moralists. He has little patience with those who counsel the use of force on the grounds that the world is not yet redeemed. Camus calls not for realistic action in the light of the sinfulness of man but for action on behalf of man as the relatively innocent victim.

And yet, admitting these distinctions, why not add a dash of pessimism and a pinch of realism and still recognize in Camus' study of pride a significant contribution to Christian anthropology? This is rather difficult, for at the very core of his whole thinking is the denial of God. Clearly denied in his doctrine of limited political goals is God, the Limiter. Although it is out of fashion amongst some theologians to take such a denial seriously, Camus, at least, asks us to consider it so. The denial of God informs the whole of his political thinking. Ultimately he makes it the basis for his rejection of realism in politics, and he places it at the origin of every virtue and every improvement in the human condition. To sense the weight and breadth of this conviction, it is worth returning again to his understanding of pride.

Christians have interpreted pride as the attempt on the part of the creature to play the Creator. In fact, Augustine once remarked that every sin is a grotesque mimicry of one of the perfections of God. Curiosity imitates God's omniscience; ambition seeks to duplicate God's glory; luxuriousness parodies the abundance of the divine life, etc. In sin, man perversely imitates God's virtues.

Camus also understands pride as the attempt to imitate God. Not his virtues, for God has none. But rather this single encompassing vice: God is a murderer. The proposition is simple and fully horrifying. If God exists and every man dies, God is the death-bringer. He is the one who places every man under the penalty of suffering and death. When all the cant, the prayers and imprecations are done with, this is the truth about God: He is the one who slays, the one who raises buboes in the groins of little children, the one who places all men under the penalty of the destruction of their flesh. Neither cult, nor ecclesiastical apparatus, nor theological ingenuity can obscure this fact. ". . . the order of the world is shaped by death" (*The Plague*, tr. Stuart Gilbert, London, Hamish Hamilton, 1948, p. 123), which inflicts upon man a never-ending defeat. In the light of this horrible fact, Camus does not summon man to atheism but to blasphemy. To deny God's existence is inaccurate. In a sense, he does exist. God exists as the destroyer. But to say "Hallowed be thy name"? This is unthinkable. In decency, man can only blaspheme the death-bringer, resist and desecrate his name. He is a ghoul, a chewer of corpses, against whom men ought to rebel. For God has transgressed a limit—human life.

Camus urges action then, *not* in the image and similitude of God, but action that bears witness to one's original manhood, a manhood that receives its outline in the original refusal to consent to God and his works.

Pride, on the other hand, is a human work of murder added to the divine work of murder, a human injustice that corresponds to the divine injustice, a transgression of limits.

The chief difference between God and man is that God offers no justification for his behavior; he is silent. But man does. In political life, he offers ideologies which attempt to justify murder. Reactionary ideology justifies unrestrained repression as a means of preserving good order and life. Revolutionary ideology justifies the use of every means—war, duplicity and murder—for the sake of a future life and order.

Camus opposes both on the grounds of the limit discovered in the original insurrection against death itself. All subsequent established orders and revolutions betray their origins when they resort to murderous means in their own right.

No more than Israel is permitted to forget her covenant with her God, or the Church her covenant in the blood of Christ, is the revolutionist permitted to forget his covenant in the blood that originally prompted his insurrection against death. In organizing itself for the future, a revolution must not forget its origins. Otherwise the revolution obscures its future goals and disfigures its face in the present.

Camus is clearly interested in recovering a form of sanctity in political life founded in a double refusal: The refusal of God and the refusal to be God. His rather spectacular theological criticism is directed to that end. He rejects political realism in both its conservative and revolutionary forms and summons man to a modesty, an honesty, and a decency that he believes to be within the reach of man—and certainly within the reach of Western man—as it recovers the best in the European revolutionary tradition. His argument against the pride of the realists concludes in a summons to sanctity.

Sanctity does not refer here to the possession of some moral perfection by hero or community, but rather to a politics of witness—political action that is luminous at every point to its origin. If need be, even the goal must be sacrificed for the sake of this witness.

> . . . revolution must try to act, not in order to come into existence at some future date in the eyes of a world reduced to acquiescence, but in terms of the obscure existence already made manifest in the act of insurrection.
>
> (*The Rebel*, p. 252)

Camus' saints are the revolutionaries of 1905 in Russia, members of the battle organization of the Social Revolutionary Party. These men, above all, were distinguished by a sense of limit. Kaliayev, for example, was willing to assassinate, but not when there were children in the carriage of the victim. Moreover, as testimony to the fact that not even such discriminate murder, strictly speaking, was justified, the revolutionary was prepared to atone with the offering of his own life. Camus, in a bitter note, distinguishes such rebels from the dominant realist tradition in the West by remarking,

> Two different species of men. One kills only once and pays with his life. The other justifies thousands of crimes and consents to be rewarded with honors.
>
> (*The Rebel,* p. 173, note 6)

Revolutionaries like Kaliayev, however, have always been criticized by the realists as being nihilistic. They live and die on behalf of an immediate witness, but they are irresponsible toward the future. They are ready to protest momentarily; they are willing to take their Hungarian holiday from tyranny. But soon the ecstasy is over, and they lapse by their ineffectiveness once again into the negative fraternity of the condemned. If one is limited to means that must bear immediate witness to one's origin and end, then there is little hope of success. And when a leader pays little attention to success, he purchases a glorious moment at great cost to his people. Renunciation of all concern with efficacy, in the long run, implies a practical acceptance of the world as run by those who avail themselves of force without restraint.

The whole art of politics depends upon the use of means that to some degree obscure origin and goal. Perhaps in the realm of art it is possible to achieve a work that is luminous in detail, that suggests an utter appropriateness in the use of means, but not so in politics. Unless one is willing to abandon the future, there is need for the use of force, indirection and even disguise in the present.

Camus does not entirely neglect this argument of the realists against a political ethic of immediate witness. He is not unmindful of the problem of power in politics. His savage attack on capital punishment, for example, is not an attack upon penal systems as such. His novel, *The Plague,* does not disparage the need for public structures of power. In *The Rebel* he shows himself sufficiently sensitive to the problem of political force to cast about for power groups that would furnish the material principle for his own ideas.

However, Camus is outspoken in his criticism of the absolute justification of the use of power. In Western culture absolute justification has been furnished by futurism—Christian and Marxist; therefore, Camus has levelled his guns against both. Conservative Christian futurism urged the acceptance of present abuse in the name of a supernatural tomorrow; Marxist futurism has encouraged revolutionary violence in the service of an earthly tomorrow. In both cases the means are justified absolutely; the present is a mere instrument in the hands of God or the Party. Camus insists that the *present* can never be considered raw material or instrument in relation to the future. Violence may be necessary, but it is never in the strictest sense of the word justified.

Beyond urging this restraint on the use of power, however, Camus also argues that the realists overlook different levels of power and efficacy. Camus suggests that there is an efficacy in sap, as well as in the tornado, that the realists are inclined to overlook. On this point, Camus has more in mind than the Western politician who has discovered that there are moral and spiritual, as well as military, forces and urges their full use. Rather he suggests an altogether different *relation* to power than that of use and manipulation. Here Camus' Mediterranean piety toward nature—and human nature—comes to the fore: Nature cultivated rather than manipulated, enjoyed rather than transformed, attested to rather than detested in the name of a more perfect fulfillment that lies ahead. When nature and human nature are looked at in this way, different levels of power and efficacy come into view.

Realists and futurists are doubly blind then—blind to suffering as they sacrifice the present to the future, that is, as they treat human nature and its powers like raw material that must be manipulated and transformed; but blind also to the creative possibilities of history itself, as they overlook different levels of efficacy and power.

Camus may be blind in his own way. We may not hold to his argument. We may surely note with some irony that his work has come out of a country in signal need of as much realism in politics as it can lay its hand on. But it is difficult to read Camus without having one's own vision corrected—particularly a tendency to farsightedness that causes one to overlook the evil and the summons to witness that lie near at hand. It is remarkable how easy it is to deal carelessly with the present, to charge off the whole of life to the interim needs of battle without witnessing to the origin of the war, to remain frozen in the present while serving some forgotten future thaw.

The Church militant has always recognized a danger in the Franciscan spirit. This journal was founded in concern with that danger. No doubt there is an even greater danger of Franciscanism in politics. But, no less than the Church, the political order is in trouble if there is no one around to insist on an immediate witness.

November 24, 1958

Wine of the Country—Sweet and Dry

Sidney Lanier

TWO REMARKABLE SERMONS ARE being preached daily in New York City. One is extravagant, vivid, sprawling across its subject with all the superficiality and sudden, stark shock of picture-magazine journalism; the other is slow, spare, taking its time to lay bare its mysteries with surgical precision. The first pleases its congregation because it is headlong, passionately engaged, colloquial; the second puzzles with a dry, private language as stylized as a dance. Each sermon is protestant but not Christian. Neither sermon is being preached in a church. Neither preacher is ordained, but after a glimpse of their vision no one would dare say they are not called.

The sermons are the Italian films *La Dolce Vita* and *L'Avventura*. The preachers are the vastly disparate Federico Fellini and Michelangelo Antonioni. The strangest fact of all is that these two men do not shrink from stating that they have a point of view, a personal comment, and a compelling need to make it known. This in an industry that is infamous for "sitting loose." Both have suffered financial discomfort as well as personal opprobrium for their presumption. They also share a common theme: The paralyzing emptiness at the heart of Western society, and its aimless, deathward drift.

Antonioni has said about his own film:

. . . I would say that [of his films so far] *L'Avventura* is the best. . . . Superficially, this film may look like a rather complicated and

225

perhaps mysterious love story. During the holiday trip, a girl [Anna] disappears; and the fact of this disappearance creates a gap which is immediately filled by other factors. For the missing girl's fiancé [Sandro] and her friend [Claudia] the search [for her] becomes a kind of sentimental journey, at the end of which they've reached a new and unforeseen situation. On one level, it could be a kind of thriller, with enough sophistication and enough weight to the characters to give it the pseudo-dignity of the psychological thriller . . . but *L'Avventura* has other ambitions. . . . I want to show that sentiments which convention and rhetoric have encouraged us to regard as having a kind of definite weight and absolute duration, can in fact be fragile, vulnerable, subject to change. Man deceives himself when he hasn't courage enough to allow for new dimensions in emotional matters—his loves, regrets, states of mind—just as he allows for them in the field of science and technology. . . . *L'Avventura* naturally does not pretend to have the answer to the disturbing questions it raises. It's enough for me to have posed them in cinematic terms.

(Sight and Sound, Winter, 1960–61)

And pose them he does, with a deceptive, uninvolved quality that finally strikes some viewers with the strangely delayed impact of looking at a clinical X ray of one's own fatal carcinoma. For some, the language is too muted, too special. To those who hear, he says that for many of us the old words stand for no reality, that men and women rarely communicate, "touch," except in anger or sexual passion; love, trust, fidelity are as outmoded and brittle as ancient pottery, in fact are similar relics of a time scarcely remembered. We are unattached projectiles hurtling obliquely past one another in infinitely empty space.

Antonioni uses space and distance as characters in his film: Barren islands in the flat, dark sea; empty landscapes; deserted towns. And bodies in space; moving boats seen or only heard; a train departing or rocketing along its track, or muttering and hissing in the distance; jets screaming over just before dawn as Sandro runs after Claudia. None of this is by chance. Unfortunately, even an alert viewer may miss a great deal, for such richly packed subtlety can be self-defeating.

The film ends at dawn after Sandro's senseless betrayal, on a small terrace in Taormina, as Claudia turns and walks a hundred thousand light years across the tiny terrace to Sandro, slumped on the bench, his tragic gift for self-betrayal yet again revealed. She touches him tentatively in pity, but the distance between them remains absolute. Their world has no bridges for such a gulf.

Unlike *L'Avventura, La Dolce Vita* will be a runaway commercial success. It will excite a plethora of reaction and comment until, like its Italian critics, we will cry *basta* ("enough"). It is a major film of remarkable power, and it speaks in the universal public language of gossip and scandal.

Its form is that of a "filmed newspaper" whose anti-hero, a mediocre gossip columnist, drifts weakly through a series of fantastic episodes of the sort that feed the tabloid presses of the world. There is no plot; we simply follow Marcello's chrome-plated flashbulb-lit slide down—down past the inner point of no return—to damnation. Marcello moves, through his fantastic goal-less pilgrimage, from following Christ dangling from a helicopter, to gawking at semi-nude bathers, to a homosexual night club, to a casual sexual encounter, to his mistress's attempted suicide, to an unreal encounter with a Hollywood star, to a fake miracle perpetrated by two far-from-innocent children and re-staged disastrously for television, to the humanist Steiner's cultural evening at home, to a visit from his father, to a self-consciously decadent party at the castle of a prince, to an argument and parting with his mistress, to Steiner's double murder of his children and suicide, to a tedious orgy, and to a denouement at dawn.

"The sweet life" is the ironic name for the whole spectrum of modern life that, vulgarized and exploited, offers no sure and fixed points of reference or commitment. It is a carnival without Lent. It is not just a bawdy slap at the excesses of an International Bohemia that lives by a cynical indecent exposure of itself to the highest bidder. Institutional Christianity is revealed as a hysterical fraud in which the faithful, asking for healing, get a miracle staged for television and are trampled in the ensuing chaos; rationalist humanism is sterile, and its safe haven of culture-worship is an obscene *trompe-l'oeil*.

The Steiner incident, which is the crucial episode of the film, shows Marcello that what he thought was enviably secure is actually fear-filled and self-destructive. It is a decisive rejection of intellectualism and aestheticism that, appearing to be wisely ripe, is actually rotten—more rotten than the sensualist and hedonist because it is a withdrawal from and a denial of instinctual life. After this episode Marcello is clearly doomed.

After a joyless orgy the film ends on a windswept beach in the gray light of dawn with Marcello no longer able to hear or respond to the invitation of the young girl (his lost innocence and hope) to join her. The sea-filled slough between them is too deep to be crossed. He turns and walks away toward the androgynous manikins gathered around a hideous deep-sea monster, symbol of what he and they have become. Fellini has shown us ourselves as swarming, coupling, credulous, fearful animals whose self-indulgence and abuse of freedom are leading us precipitately, inevitably, back beyond Eden, to the darkness of twenty thousand fathoms.

It is a film packed with energy and indignation, but it is not flawless. Aside from its need for editing, there is a quality that emerges on reflection, a quality that I can only call puritanical. It verges on the kind of prurience that is a familiar ingredient of American protest. There is a tendency toward dwelling on the grotesque and shocking beyond the point of reality to the edge of caricature. It is filled with a naïveté that is very American—middle-class American; De Sica called the film "provincial"—that sees sin as predominantly sexual, and always somehow ugly, dirty, and repulsive.

La Dolce Vita is a very moral film, perhaps too moral to be good. But the warm good intentions compensate for its tendency toward gaucheness. For the theologian, *L'Avventura* is closer to the heart of the matter.

If I had to choose between the two directors, I would more confidently put the analysis of the sickness of my soul in the hands of the monkish, inward Antonioni; as for Fellini, he could show me Rome by day and by night and share good talk over red wine till dawn and beyond, stopping together on the way home by some time-stained little church for a prayer, just in case.

May 15, 1961

The Gospel According to St. Matthew

~ ☙ ~

Tom F. Driver

PIER PASOLINI'S FILMED VERSION of the First Gospel, though by now much celebrated, has not yet received in this country its due measure of praise. Signor Pasolini, the Italian Marxist writer and film-maker, has produced in *The Gospel According to St. Matthew* a work of almost unsurpassed cinematic beauty and at the same time the first biblical film that embodies genuine faith. This double achievement no professed Christian of our time could have reached, for it has been born of a childlike astonishment at the moral holiness of the Christ, an attitude that centuries of cultural accommodation have all but destroyed in the Church.

In order to appreciate this extraordinary film properly, it is necessary to consider the nature of authentic speech, for the film presents us

228

with nothing other than that genuine Word of which theologians so frequently write but of which they seldom find examples toward which to point. The origin of this Word is quite outside human invention and control, but it could never be present in culture if there did not also occur authentic human speech, the marks of which can in part be identified.

The kind of speech that I am calling "authentic" recognizes no obligation to conform to accepted canons of style, beauty and rhetoric. At the same time it feels free to employ any styles and techniques that are useful in the course of its swift flight to its target. This quality in the speech of the early Church, as reflected in the New Testament, has been discussed by Amos Wilder in *The Language of the Gospel*. The earliest Christian speech, he says, "is naïve, it is not studied; it is extempore and directed to the occasion, it is not calculated to serve some future hour. This utterance is dynamic, actual, immediate, reckless of posterity; not coded for catechists or repeaters."

What Wilder says of early Christian speech is also to be said of Pasolini's film, which is certainly not coded for critics and is extremely difficult to review. It is great partly because it has so much in it that is unacceptable from a theoretical point of view. The music, for instance, is a hodgepodge of Bach, Mozart, Prokofiev, Webern, Negro spiritual and African Mass. Who would think that a director could accompany the scene of the visit of the Magi (itself an enormous cliché) with a solo voice (is it Odetta's?) singing "Sometimes I Feel Like a Motherless Child," and get away with it?

There are scenes, such as the Slaughter of the Innocents, that remind one of Brueghel the Elder; others, such as Christ carrying the Cross, that are reminiscent of medieval paintings; still others, such as the Garden of Gethsemane, that are like Edward Steichen in his romantic vein; and some, such as the shots of Mary's house near Nazareth, that look like documentary reportage. A few scenes resemble bad Sunday School illustrations; others, such as the walking feet of Satan in the desert, only a consummate artist could have imagined. The viewer is likely to resist the mixture of styles, the juxtaposition of the banal and the creative, until he realizes that the mixture is not a sign of ineptitude but of an utterance so authentic that it can afford to appear naïve.

The fragments of diverse styles and techniques that Pasolini uses are not, however, employed for their effect. He has understood that authentic speech is reckless in that it cares nothing for effect but instead drives single-mindedly toward the statement of its intent. And the greatest single strength of his film is that he has detected this quality in Matthew's Jesus.

For instance, after the temptations, Jesus walks on a lonely path toward Galilee. He meets a group of farmers who are carrying scythes and winnowing tools to their fields. Passing them, he says, "Repent, for the Kingdom of Heaven is at hand," and keeps on going. They stop and stare after him as if wondering whether he said what they thought he said. When Jesus gathers his disciples, he does not sit them down to explain his mission. Instead he talks while he walks, striding ahead of the group, tossing his words to the wind. Those in the rear have to run to catch what he says while they try to keep their footing on the path.

In this context all the statements of Jesus about people *not* hearing, about ears that remain closed, become immensely important. A line such as "Therefore I speak to them in parables because . . . hearing they hear not" ceases to be a riddle and points straight at the fact that to hear the Word is as much a matter of intent as to speak it. "He that hath ears to hear, let him hear."

And eyes to see. Many have commented on Pasolini's having filled his screen with a succession of interesting faces—from the opening shot, which is a close-up of Mary's face as Joseph looks at her in scorn for the unexplained pregnancy, through Wise Men, priests, Herods, lepers, soldiers, the Christ, and countless others. But even more than the faces one should remark upon the eyes. The characters in this film can hardly believe what they see. Rather, they cannot believe what they hear, and so they peer—those who are hearing at all—as if sight might lend credence to what the ears are telling.

In their turn, the eyes of those who view the film reach out as if to touch the screen (even when they would like to turn away), hoping perhaps that the next shot may explain or at least resolve the terrible tension created by the presence among men of the holy judgment that pours forth from the lips and eyes of Jesus. The latter, played by Enrique Irazoqui, a Spanish student, reminds one of a Byzantine Christ. His eyes survey and penetrate all, like the Pantocrator in the dome of the church at Daphni.

Pasolini's use of eyes is climaxed by a relentless gaze of the camera into the face of Mary as her eyes turn away from and return to the unbearable sight of her son among the crucified. Then the screen goes black. There is nothing at all to see. In the dark we hear these words:

> For this people's heart is waxed gross, and their ears are dull of hearing, and their eyes they have closed, lest at any time they should see with their eyes and hear with their ears and should understand with their heart, and should be converted, and I should heal them.

The film has many touches that could be regarded as "effects" but are instead simply the film-maker's attempt to make his audience see. At the trial of Jesus, the camera is among the spectators standing across the courtyard from the principals. Someone's head is in the way, and the camera moves first to one side and then the other in an attempt to get a clear view. We notice this touch of planned realism, but what deserves praise is that Pasolini refuses to make a style of such contrivance. Using the device once, he drops it and goes on.

Likewise, in a shot of the faces of soldiers waiting to attack the innocent children, the camera pans from one to another, overlooks a man in the second row, goes back to him and then passes on to the rest in sequence. It is what you might do in a home movie, and in a professional one it could be precious. Pasolini makes it tell and then discards it.

If this sort of thing merely served one's sense of immediate presence at the event, it would be at worst arty and at best irrelevant. That is not what happens. The film cares no more for historical reality than does a medieval mystery play. At the same time it is more deeply imbedded in historical actuality than any biblical film or play I have ever seen. I should say that it takes history for granted, which is the only way really to live in history.

I mean the film bypasses completely the "historical problem." Hollywood has not done so. The biblical films of Cecil B. DeMille, Samuel Bronston, George Stevens, *et al*, have been much touted for their historical accuracy. The studios hired expert consultants to achieve it. They have their reward. Pasolini, for his part, did only the obvious thing. He shot his film in black and white in southern Italy, where the Calabrian towns, countryside and early Renaissance buildings are obviously not Palestinian but are similar enough not to bog anyone down except those to whom "history" means imitation of the thing "as it really was." The costumes also are such as will do without making a fuss.

But best of all, Pasolini has refrained totally from embarking upon the cinematic quest for the historical Jesus. "Not enough human kindness in the portrait," several spectators say to me. "Read Matthew," say I. For reading Matthew is exactly what Pasolini did—shut up in a hotel room in Florence for a whole day so as to avoid the crowds turned out to see Pope John, and turning idly to the Bible in the room, and being struck dumb to read without interruption the Evangelist's account of a man whose moral holiness was such as to give one the uncanny sense that this impractical, unworldly, reckless, obsessive obedience to the pure demand of the unseen Father is what life, after all, is about. It was a shock of recognition, and out of it the film proceeded like a word born of startled comprehension.

Matthew gives the film its dialogue, all its scenes, its unconventional shape and its spirit. I, I, I! The first-person pronoun rings through the film on the lips of Jesus. Follow! Come! To me, me, me! God in Heaven, such a man is not to be borne! Obsessed. Angry. Gone, completely gone.

We could psyche him out if we had the means and the will to do so, but we have neither; for the address cuts through the person and through the performance and through the host of preliminary concerns we ought to have and do have about the film and about psychology and history and about what we will do tomorrow.

Follow him where? He is a man on the move, seldom at rest, and his destination is nowhere if not ultimate, and ultimate is not a place you can go. You can't follow such a man, and they didn't. We are Peter weeping. Yet we may also be Peter the inarticulate man imbued with speech.

One turns to Matthew and is reminded that nowhere in the film does Jesus say, "Come unto me, all ye that labor and are heavy laden, and I will give you rest." I do not remember his saying, ". . . my yoke is easy, and my burden is light." One remembers instead, "Woe to you, scribes and Pharisees, hypocrites!"

A few years ago, Peter Brooke removed the tenderness of Cordelia from his production of *King Lear*. As there is a theater of cruelty, I do not hesitate to say that *Il Vangelo Secondo Matteo* is cinema of cruelty. But what does that mean? Certainly not that the Christ of this film cannot be loved. Nor that in him is no redemption. It only means that Pasolini, as the one who utters a word, has not been instructed that we should hear at this time the message of comfort and rest. It means that this people's eyes are closed, their ears dull of hearing and that no opening is possible except through acquaintance with that in the Gospel which is cruel in its moral austerity.

I would not say this if I thought that the judgment that leaps from Pasolini's screen is simply that of a human temperament or an ideology. I think instead that it is the judgment of the holy. No doubt this is not the whole Gospel, not even the whole Matthew, but I think it is exactly that portion of the authentic Word that a man of our time may hear and speak.

June 16, 1966

Historical Analysis
and the
Continuing Crisis

VII

The Intellectual and
Moral Dilemma of History

❧

Hans J. Morgenthau

IT IS A GREAT PARADOX THAT nature is much more unambiguously susceptible to human understanding than is society past and present. That which man has not created and which it is beyond his power to create—the macrocosm of the stars and the microcosm of the cells and atoms—man can understand with an adequacy that points to the common source of both. How else explain the affinity between the cognitive qualities of the human mind and the laws by which the universe moves? Not only is man able to retrace and project into the future the movements of the natural bodies, but by virtue of that ability he is capable of recreating the forces of nature and harnessing them to his will. Nowhere, except in the contemplation of his suffering and hope, is man more triumphantly aware of his kinship with the Creator than in his cognitive and manipulative relations with nature.

In the world of nature, which he faces ready-made and which he leaves as he finds it, man proves himself a master of understanding, imitation and control. How different, how frustrating and humiliating is the role he plays in understanding and controlling the social world, a world that is properly his own, which would not exist if he had not created it, and which exists the way it does only because he has given it the imprint of his nature. Of this social world man can at best have but a partial and corrupted understanding and but a partial and ultimately illusory control. For the social world being but a projection of human nature onto the collective plane, being but man writ large, man can understand and maintain control of society no more than he can of himself. Thus the very intimacy of his involvement impedes both understanding and control.

The awareness of this paradox is, if I understand its intent correctly, the moving force of Reinhold Niebuhr's new book, *The Structure of Nations and Empires.* It is the *mega thaumazein,* the "great wonderment," the shock of incongruity, that according to Aristotle is at the beginning of all philosophy. That shock feeds on two basic experiences—one intellectual, the other moral—and both cast doubt on man's ability to find the truth about society. The intellectual experience is doubt about the meaning of history. What is unique and ephemeral in history and what is constantly revealing a repetitive pattern that lends itself to generalization about the past and future?

> . . . is there any consistency, any perennial pattern or permanent force in man's search for community? Is there a permanent pattern in the anatomy of community which may be discerned in such diverse communities as the tribe, the city-state, or the ancient or modern empire?

The moral experience is doubt about man's ability to grasp what meaning there is in history, given the involvement of his pride and aspirations in the historic process.

The intellectual difficulty that stands in the way of a theoretical inquiry into the meaning of history results from the ambiguity of the material with which the observer has to deal. The events he must try to understand are, on the one hand, unique occurrences. They happened in this way only once and never before or since. On the other hand they are similar, for they are manifestations of social forces. Social forces are the product of human nature in action. Therefore, under similar conditions, they will manifest themselves in a similar manner. But where is the line to be drawn between the similar and the unique?

This ambiguity of the events to be understood by a theory of history—it may be pointed out in passing—is but a special instance of a general impediment of human understanding.

"As no event and no shape," observes Montaigne, "is entirely like another, so also is there none entirely different from another: *an ingenious mixture on the part of Nature. If there were no similarity in our faces, we could not distinguish man from beast; if there were no dissimilarity, we could not distinguish one man from another.* All things hold together by some similarity; every example is halting, and the comparison that is derived from experience is always defective and imperfect. And yet one links up the comparisons at some corner. And so do laws become serviceable and adapt themselves to every one of our affairs by some wrested, forced, and biased interpretation."

It is against such "wrested, forced and biased interpretation" of historic events that a theory of history must be continuously on guard.

Nor are the untoward results of this dilemma of having to distinguish between what is typical and perennial and what is unique and ephemeral in history limited to the interpretation of past events. That dilemma affects gravely, and sometimes absurdly, forecasts of and planning for the future. In 1776, Washington declared that "the Fate of our Country depends in all human probability, on the Exertion of a Few Weeks." Yet it was not until seven years later that the War of Independence came to an end.

In February 1792, British Prime Minister Pitt justified the reduction of military expenditures and held out hope for more reductions to come by declaring: "Unquestionably there never was a time in the history of this country when from the situation of Europe we might more reasonably expect fifteen years of peace than at the present moment." Only two months later the continent of Europe was engulfed in war. Less than a year later Great Britain was involved. Thus was initiated a period of almost continuous warfare that lasted nearly a quarter of a century.

When Lord Granville became British Foreign Secretary in 1870, he was informed by the Permanent Undersecretary that "he had never, during his long experience, known so great a lull in foreign affairs, and that he was not aware of any important question that he (Lord Granville) should have to deal with." On that same day Prince Leopold of Hohenzollern-Sigmaringen accepted the Crown of Spain, an event that three weeks later led to the outbreak of the Franco-Prussian War.

The day before World War I broke out, the British Ambassador to Germany disparaged the possibility of war in a report to his Government. Franklin D. Roosevelt thought toward the end of his life that the great political issue with which the postwar world would have to deal would be Anglo-Russian rivalry, with the United States playing the role of mediator.

These difficulties, inherent in the nature of things, have been magnified since the eighteenth century by a philosophic tendency to identify a particular historic phenomenon with a particular social situation and to draw from this identification the conclusion that by doing away with the social situation one could eliminate an undesirable historic phenomenon. Conversely, by generalizing the social situation one could generalize a desirable historic phenomenon as well. Thus the conviction arose that war was a by-product of either the autocratic or the capitalistic organization of society. Therefore the destruction of autocracy or capitalism would of necessity usher in the abolition of war; conversely, the universal triumph of democracy or of communism would usher in universal peace.

Similarly and more particularly, imperialism has been identified, and by no means only by Marxists, with capitalism, from which identification the logical conclusion was drawn that the end of capitalism would signify the end of imperialism as well. The very existence of power relations, the inequality of the strong and the weak, the mastery of the former over the latter, the differentiation between ruler and ruled was attributed by nineteenth century liberals to autocratic government and is attributed by contemporary Marxists to the class structure of society.

All these identifications have one fallacy in common: The confusion between the perennial and the ephemeral, the typical and the unique in history. Our society in particular, with its underdeveloped sense of historic continuity and its penchant for social innovation, finds it hard to accept the underlying regularity and typicality of the historic process. If you accept these qualities of history, you must submit to its laws and try to learn from them; you are foreclosed from treating each new historic situation *de novo,* as a unique occurrence to be disposed of by one radical action similarly unique. On the other hand, if you do not accept these qualities of history and are free to transcend the limitations of tradition and disregard the counsels of ancient wisdom, your social inventiveness is limited, if it is limited at all, by nothing but elemental common sense and common prudence.

Philosophy, tradition and individual experience have predisposed us for the latter attitude. The great problems of history with which we must come to terms tend to appear to us not as members of a chain organically tied to the past and growing into the future, but as cataclysmic interruptions of the normalcy of peace and harmony, occasioned by evil men and evil institutions. Let us do away with those men and institutions, and we will have solved not only this particular historic problem but the problem of history itself. We are, as it were, in flight from history, and whenever history catches up with us, as it did intermittently before World War II and has done continuously since, we endeavor to gain our freedom from it by obliterating in one great effort the issue that blocks our way.

The vanity of these endeavors is attested to by their consistent failures. It is one of the great contributions of Professor Niebuhr's book to demonstrate through the analysis of historic phenomena the fallacy of this approach to historic understanding and political action. The demonstration is made by fitting the imperialism, universalism and utopianism of communism—the overriding historic phenomenon of the age—into a pattern of empire that was not established by communism but of which communism is but the latest manifestation.

The roots of that pattern reach back to ancient Persia and Babylon. The pattern is clearly visible in the character and claims of the Roman and Chinese empires and fully developed in the two Christian and the Islamic empires of the Middle Ages. The articulation of both the similarities and dissimilarities—but particularly the former—between the great empires of the past and the imperial structure and claims of communism illuminates both the historic and contemporary scene.

The tendency to disparage the perennial and typical in history and to dissolve the historic process into a series of disconnected disturbances, unique and ephemeral, disarms contemporary man in the face of a phenomenon that is truly unique: The ability for universal destruction that man has received from nuclear power. This ability has introduced into the relations among nations a radically novel factor. Qualitatively speaking, it is the only structural change that has occurred in international relations since the beginning of history. For nuclear power has radically altered the relations that have existed since the beginning of history between the ends of foreign policy and violence as a means to these ends.

These relations have traditionally been by and large of a rational nature. That is to say: The risks run and the liabilities incurred through the use of violent means were generally not out of proportion to the ends sought. A nation calculating these risks and liabilities could rationally conclude that even if it should lose, its losses would be tolerable in view of the ends sought. A nation acted very much like a gambler who could afford to risk a certain portion of his assets and was willing to risk them in view of the chances for gain provided by taking the risk.

This rational relationship between the means of violence and the ends of foreign policy has been destroyed by the availability of nuclear power as a means to these ends. For the possibility of universal destruction obliterates the means-end relationship itself by threatening the nations and their ends with total destruction. No such radical qualitative transformation of the structure of international relations has ever occurred in history, and the radical nature of the transformation calls for correspondingly radical innovations in the sphere of policy.

Yet, paradoxically enough, a civilization that likes to see novelty in history where there is none, by dint of its distorted historic perspective seems to perceive but dimly the genuine novelty with which nuclear power confronts it. A society that is almost enamored by social innovation for innovation's sake faces in virtual helplessness a situation that requires—not for the sake of a traditional national interest but for the survival of civilization, if not of mankind itself—an extreme effort of bold, innovating imagination. Thus history threatens to avenge itself for having been misunderstood in thought and abused in action.

Faced with this mortal threat to their survival, both the United States and the Soviet Union have fallen back upon a time-honored yet thus far ineffectual remedy: Disarmament. Are the chances for disarmament better now than they were in the past? The answer to that question depends again upon what one considers the perennial and ephemeral factors in history to be.

One school of thought holds that the possibility of disarmament is predicated upon the preceding or at least simultaneous settlement of outstanding political issues that have given rise to the armaments race in the first place, and that the threat of nuclear war has not materially affected this perennial functional dependence of disarmament upon a political settlement. Another school of thought assumes that the threat of nuclear war has radically altered this traditional relationship, which was perennial only in appearance but was in fact dependent upon certain ephemeral factors no longer present today. It also assumes that the desire to avoid nuclear destruction provides today an incentive for disarmament that invalidates the conditions upon which disarmament was predicated in the past. The question whether or not the novelty of the nuclear threat has actually reduced what seemed to be a perennial principle of statecraft to an ephemeral configuration poses again the dilemma that casts doubt upon our understanding of history and renders hazardous our political action.

The other great dilemma upon which Professor Niebuhr's book centers is the moral dilemma in which history involves man. That moral dilemma results from the ineradicable tendency of man to claim for his position in history more in terms of moral dignity than he is entitled to and to grant his fellows less than is their due. Hamlet implores the Queen in vain:

> . . . Mother, for love of grace,
> Lay not that flattering unction to your soul,
> That not your trespass, but my madness
>   speaks.

For the position of the actor on the political scene is of necessity morally ambivalent, and that ambivalence, in conjunction with the logic inherent in the political act, inevitably corrupts his moral judgment.

The political actor seeks power, that is to say, he seeks to reduce his fellow man to a means for his ends. By doing so, he violates a basic tenet of Western morality: To respect man as an end in himself and not to use him as a means to an end. Both the contradiction between the political act and morality and the logic of the power relation itself compel the political actor to make it appear as though his striving for power and the exercise of it, far from violating morality, were actually its consummation. That appearance is achieved by clothing him and his act with a moral dignity they do not deserve and by depriving the object of the political act of at least some of the moral dignity he deserves.

Politics and morality are reconciled by the latter being bent to the requirements of the former. The political actor now can proceed with a good conscience, being assured of his moral superiority and the moral inferiority of the object of his power. He can also proceed with a determination maximizing his chances for political success; for he will find it hard to convince himself that, in view of the difference in moral qualities between himself and the object of his power, he has not only a moral right but also a moral duty to rule. As Tolstoy put it in the epilogue to *War and Peace:*

> When a man acts alone, he always carries within him a certain series of considerations that have, as he supposes, directed his past conduct and serve to justify to him his present action and to lead him to make projects for his future activity.
>
> Assemblies of men act in the same way, only leaving to those who do not take direct part in the action to invent consideration, justifications and projects concerning their combined activity.
>
> For causes, known or unknown to us, the French begin to chop and hack at each other. And to match the event, it is accompanied by its justification in the expressed wills of certain men who declare it essential for the good of France, for the cause of freedom, of equality. Men cease slaughtering one another, and that event is accompanied by the justification of the necessity of centralization of power, of resistance to Europe, and so on. Men march from west to east, killing their fellow-creatures, and this event is accomplished by phrases about the glory of France, the baseness of England, and so on. History teaches us that those justifications for the event are devoid of all common sense, that they are inconsistent with one another, as, for instance, the murder of a man as a result of the declaration of his rights, and the murder of millions in Russia for the abasement of England. But those justifications have an incontestable value in their own day.
>
> They remove moral responsibility from those men who pro-

duce. the events. At the time they do the work of brooms, that go in front to clear the rails for the train: they clear the path of men's moral responsibility. Apart from those justifications, no solution could be found for the most obvious question that occurs to one at once on examining any historical event; that is, How did millions of men combine to commit crimes, murders, wars, and so on?

Professor Niebuhr lays bare the mechanism by which morality clothes politics with undeserved dignity and politics transforms morality into an instrument of political domination. It is particularly fascinating to observe how this mechanism operates in the relations between the great imperial and religious structures. The religious structures become imperial in performance and the imperial structures become religious in pretense. Typically, it is politics and imperium as its more dynamic manifestation that transform and corrupt morality and religion, and it is much rarer for morality and religion to reform and spiritualize politics and imperium.

The moral dilemma of history, like its intellectual counterpart, is existential. They can be mitigated but not resolved. Both grow out of the nature of man and of history as man's creation. In history man meets himself, and in his encounter with history he encounters again, magnified into superhuman proportions, the fallibility of his intellectual understanding and moral judgment that prevents him from completely understanding and adequately judging both history and himself.

February 8, 1960

Utilitarian Christianity

❦

H. Richard Niebuhr

IN RELIGION AND SCIENCE there is a constant conflict between the devotees of pure endeavor after truth and the seekers after immediate, tangible results. For the latter, truth is a pragmatic device by means of which men are enabled to gain satisfactions as biological and temporal rather than as rational and eternal beings. For the former, truth—abstractly in the case of science, concretely in the case of religion as "The Truth"—is an intrinsic good. Devotion to it does have consequences for the biological and temporal being, but to seek it for the sake of these consequences is self-defeating. Pure science and pure faith believe that the secondary satisfactions come only by way of indirection. The secret of atomic structure is not found by those who want to win victory in war or cure diseases; the secret of the kingdom of God is not revealed to those who are anxious for their lives, for food and drink, for freedom from want and fear.

In the present crisis of mankind, however, all emphasis seems to be placed on utilitarianism in both science and religion. How science is responding to the complex situation in which it finds itself is not our immediate concern here. In religion, to which we want to direct our attention, the growth of the utilitarian spirit is an alarming phenomenon. Utilitarianism seems to mark not only the attitude of the political powers that use religion for the sake of social control and transform it to suit their purposes, but also the attitude of many who oppose them. The utilitarianism of the Japanese war party in its employment of Shintoism is one thing; the pragmatism of the American military government in dealing with that Shintoism is another thing; but they are both utilitarian and pragmatic. The instrumentalism in matters of religion which characterizes communism and national socialism differs from the instrumentalism of the resistance movements and democracy; but in both instances we are dealing with a utilitarian use of religion in the service of non-religious ends. The utilitarianism of an individualistic period, which promised men that through faith they might gain the economic virtues and wealth, differs from the pragmatism of our social climate of opinion, in which religion is used as a means for gaining social order and prosperity; but they are both utilitarian and equally remote from the love of God for his own sake and of the individual or social neighbor in his relation to God. The use of religion for the sake of healing mental illness differs from its use in the effort to heal physical diseases; but in either case religion, the worship of God, is a means to an end.

Recently the social form of this utilitarianism has been given high sanction in an official statement made by the Federal Council of the Churches of Christ in America. Addressing the Christians in America on the subject of *The Churches and World Order,* the Council not only recommended many helpful steps which might be taken in the direction of the much desired goal of peace and order, but put its recommendations within a theological setting that is almost completely utilitarian. Doubtless there are overtones and undertones of another spirit but the major idea is a thorough social pragmatism. "Our first task," the report declares, "is to demonstrate that our Christian faith can enable all men to enjoy a fullness of life which not only equals but surpasses that which any other faith can accomplish." "Fullness of life" may mean many things; but what is meant here appears from the fact that it is something which other faiths also offer in an inferior or equal manner and that it is elsewhere declared that "our dedication . . . is to the progressive realization of the dignity and worth of man in every area of life— political, economic, social and religious." It is the sort of fullness of life that will amount to "a demonstration of the practical application of our faith" and which will therefore bring into being a world "responsive to that faith." The general idea is very clear: Men in our time desire some things very much—escape from suffering war and other disaster, freedom and a sense of their dignity, abundance and peace. These values they may have if they will turn to the Christian faith, if they will repent and lay hold of the sources of spiritual power that Christianity offers. The church will also benefit, for the demonstration that Christianity can provide these goods will cause men to turn to it.

Similar ideas are being voiced in numerous church statements and in the writings of Christian theologians. Christianity offers an alternative to communism, it is said, as a way of organizing the economic life. Christianity, another maintains, gives us the key to the problem of justice in our time, enabling us to know what is due to every man and how to give it to him. Christianity, it is argued, shows us how we may have not only a durable but also a just peace. Christianity has the answer to all the human problems that arise in man's quest after health, peace, prosperity, justice, joy.

Why there should be such a development of theological utilitarianism at any time and especially in our time we can readily understand. There is a reason in the faith itself. Its paradox of the losing and finding of life, of the addition of all other things if the kingdom of God is sought, has always tempted men to lose life for the sake of finding and to seek the divine rule for the sake of food and clothing. This temptation becomes especially acute when long cherished values are imperiled. Men beset by anxieties are likely to seek mental peace through worship since they discovered in earlier experience that it was a by-product of a devotion that had no ulterior purpose but was directed to the eternal glory. In the decline of a culture, the revival of the religion which gave life to that culture is sought for the sake of staving off death, though the civilization had been a by-product of religious concern. When individual liberties are threatened men tend to cultivate the sense of duty to the transcendent for the sake of which they originally fought for those liberties. One can also easily understand why religious utilitarianism in our time should be dominantly social, since our greatest concern is for the preservation and ordering of a social life that is threatened with anarchy and since our greatest sufferings arise out of our social disorder. There is another reason for the rise of this social, religious utilitarianism—the apologetic one. Christian faith is so much faith and so little sight that its adherents are always seeking for some demonstration which will prove to themselves and others that it is true, though the demonstration is bound to be somewhat beside the point—like most miracles—proving not truth but utility, and exhibiting a power which may be that of God, but may also be that of faith itself, or of spiritual forces somewhat less than divine.

Though one can understand the reasons for the rise of this Christian pragmatism, it remains a dubious thing, giving birth to all sorts of skeptical questions. Will the church be able to live up to such promises? Is there any warrant in its history or in the nature of its faith for the assurance that it can, if men will follow its teaching, guarantee them peace, the end of suffering, escape from disaster, the realization of human dignity and worth in politics and economics as well as in religion?

There is little basis in history for the promise that this religion sincerely followed will bring fullness of life to its adherents in the sense that theological utilitarianism intends. The Jewish people, more faithful than any similar group in the keeping of the moral laws they share with the Christians, more assiduous in the practice of repentance, more diligent in forgiveness, have indeed survived to this day and so demonstrated in a fashion the social relevance of their faith; but it would be difficult to describe the sort of existence the Jewish race has enjoyed as "fullness of life." The Christian church cannot maintain on the basis of its own record that it has made a notable contribution to the peace of the world. It has rarely if ever been at peace within itself, and the wars of the nations it has most deeply influenced have equalled and surpassed in frequency and in destruction those waged by societies dominated by other faiths. It is easy to say that Christians have fought so much not because they were Christians but because they were not good Christians, but this is a dubious argument since there is no indication that men can now be more sincere in their practice of Christianity than in the past, and since Christianity makes men deeply concerned about values for the sake of which they sacrifice peace. Historically there is no ground for the assertion that faithful adherence to Christian faith reduces suffering. It leads to the alleviation of the sufferings of others, but through the operation of sympathy and compassion, of asceticism and the sense of sin to the increase of suffering among Christians.

If there is not much ground in history for the assurances of theological utilitarianism, there seems to be less ground in the structure of the faith itself. If Second Isaiah, the book of Job, and the New Testament were dropped from the constitution of the church it might be possible to maintain that the biblical doctrine is one of prosperity as the consequence of virtue, but how shall one rhyme the ideas about the suffering service of Israel and the story of the cross with the assurance that faith leads to fullness of life? It can't be done except by means of reference to another sort of experience than is contemplated in statements about "fullness of life"; it can't be done without reference to a resurrection. On the other hand the effort to translate Christian faith into a socially useful force entails the suppression and transformation of some vital elements in it, just as the effort to make it serviceable to individualistic success in the era of early capitalism entailed the deformation of the Reformation into the sort of thing that Tawney has described for us.

All this does not mean that Christian faith has no social applications or a relevance to the crisis of our days. It does mean that these applications and this relevance must stem from its own imperatives and not from the wishes and desires we entertain apart from the faith. It does mean that the effort to recommend Christianity as a panacea for all the ills from which man suffers and thinks himself to suffer is erroneous and disastrous; it does not mean that Christians are not bound to seek for ways and means of alleviating these ills. It does not mean that repentance does not bear social fruits; it does mean that repentance practiced for the sake of such fruits is a bad kind of magic.

To take the last point first: Christian faith calls for a complete change of mind, not because repentance is socially effective, or individually effective for that matter, but because the mind is out of harmony with reality. Repentance is called for not because we shall suffer or because civilization will perish if we do not repent, but because others are now perishing for us and because we are attacking the very son of God, or God himself, in our endeavor to escape suffering and to maintain our civilization at any cost. Repentance is called for not because we have chosen false means to the achievement of our ends but because our ends themselves are idolatrous. A repentance which leaves ends uncriticized and which is motivated by the desire to escape judgment in history or beyond history is a far cry away from that change of mind which the gospels present. But such radical repentance, though it is not designed to be socially relevant, may have social consequences. It may lead to that sort of disinterestedness which is able to deal with the questions of politics and economics objectively and helpfully just because it does not take them too seriously, just because it has gained a certain distance from them. It may lead to that situation in which men are able to think the new thoughts which the crisis of the times requires and which they cannot think so long as they remain bound by the passion of this—worldliness.

A Christianity that is not socially utilitarian still has social relevance because its imperatives direct it to work in society. It is imperative for such a Christian faith to remember and to realize the dignity of every man as an eternal being, in his political and economic relations as well as everywhere else, though that realization may involve the sacrifice of dignity on the part of Christians and the Christian community. Imperative Christianity does not ask whether the love of neighbor will bring forth a society in which all men will love their neighbors; it acts in hope, to be sure, but love and justice are its immediate commands and not its far-off goals. It does not condemn the abuse of atomic power because we have thereby imperiled our future but because we violated our own principles. It does not believe that social virtue will be rewarded by length of life but that "no evil can befall a good man"—or a good nation —"in life or in death."

Such a non-utilitarian faith does not undertake to show that in the Christian gospel we can find the solution to all the problems of human existence any more than that we can find in the Scriptures answers to all the questions we raise about the world of nature. It does direct its followers to seek by means of all the intelligence they can muster to find out what to do to alleviate distress, to heal physical and mental disease, to order the vocations and to distribute justly the goods men produce. In consequence the social measures of such faith have nothing peculiarly Christian about them. The Christian setting in which they are conceived and practiced does not become tangibly or visually evident. There is nothing here to which one can point and say, "This is the demonstration of what Christianity can do for man." For every such measure will be only a demonstration of what disinterestedness can do, and Christians will participate with men of many other faiths in carrying them out.

In a world where the power struggle has taken precedence over every other concern, where every group is interested not only in doing good but in seeing to it that it gets credit for doing good, and where good is being done for the sake of power, the church, as church, must surely feel called upon to go about its work with quietness and confidence, abjuring utilitarianism and the defensiveness that goes with it.

July 8, 1946

The Quest for Christian Imperatives

F. Ernest Johnson

IN THE ISSUE OF THIS MAGAZINE for July 8, H. Richard Niebuhr presents a challenge that should have the serious attention of every Christian. He indicts "utilitarian Christianity" or "Christian pragmatism" for making religion a means to social and personal ends—good ends, to be sure, such as social order and mental health, but ends that are not the "intrinsic good" of religion. The recent pronouncement of the Federal Council of Churches on *The Churches and World Order* is given as an illustration of putting ethical recommendations in "a theological setting that is almost exclusively utilitarian." The word "utilitarian" is used, of course, in its historical sense, not with any crass connotation.

That Mr. Niebuhr has described an actual tendency in Protestant Christianity can hardly be questioned. It is to be hoped that his article will be made the basis of much study and discussion, for it has far-reaching implications. Many may attempt a refutation of the critique by reference to the biblical dictum, "By their fruits ye shall know them." But this is rather too facile. The ethical relevance of Christianity is not called in question, nor the usefulness of social and moral criteria in testing the genuineness of religious profession. The point is that the attempt to validate Christianity itself by reference to its ethical results, actual or hoped for, runs counter to the historic belief in the absolute imperatives of the Christian religion, which stand independently of all consideration of the objective consequences of their acceptance. As a proposition, that is hard to dispute, whatever inference may be drawn from it.

No doubt the tendency to base the Christian apologetic on pragmatic grounds is more characteristic of liberal than of orthodox Christianity. Indeed, it is implicit in all "value theories" of religion. To be sure, evangelical Protestantism has fostered it by its emphasis on the subjective aspects of religious experience. After all, to make "inner peace" an end in itself is not different in this respect from making world peace an end in itself. Nevertheless, it is in liberal theological circles that the "value" apologetic to which Mr. Niebuhr objects has become explicit. The social gospel, whose distinctive feature is the application of the Christian ethic to the structure of society, has undoubtedly encouraged this trend, not because it is "utopian"—an accusation that is only partly true—but because it stresses the developmental as against the consummatory aspects of the Kingdom of God. Its focus is historical and hence it engenders objective criteria.

It should also be noted that this tendency is accentuated in a time of social crisis, such as the present. An odd paradox results. "Crisis thinking" operates against "crisis theology." Total war, cultural disintegration, and atom bombs focus attention on impending disaster rather than on that "critical" encounter between man and God which is quite independent of the vicissitudes of history. The perennial human "predicament" is overshadowed by imminent historical tragedy. Even orthodox theologians tend to reinforce the Christian apologetic by reference to objective perils.

246

But merely to point this out is to raise questions rather than to answer them. Granted that Christian imperatives have an absolute character, supported by a transcendental faith, how are these imperatives to be identified? Consider the issue of pacifism, which has stirred so deeply the readers of this journal. No one more than the earnest pacifist Christian affirms the absoluteness of the Christian ethic and the duty to act in scorn of consequences. And how does the non-pacifist Christian answer him? Not merely by proclaiming that it is the will of God that tyranny be resisted, but by what he regards as a realistic analysis of historical forces. If his analysis had resulted in a rational conviction of the historical efficacy of nonresistance as an ethical force, would this not radically affect his interpretation of the will of God? To affirm the absoluteness of a Christian imperative is one thing; to be convinced as to the content of that imperative is another. How can we escape resort to some pragmatic test in the effort to discover the will of God?

Admittedly, the Christian ethic is all too commonly watered down by the infusion of purely secular criteria. But is it a mark of secularization to seek validation of the Christian enterprise by reference to objective criteria which point to the realization of spiritual goals? How else can a Christian apologetic to the non-Christian world be constructed? The church cannot escape judgment by the world on the basis of ethical effectiveness. On the negative side, this is too patent to be ignored. If, for example, Protestant Christianity is accused of deepening class cleavage, or if Catholic Christianity is accused of reenforcing fascist tendencies, the necessity to meet the challenge is instantly felt. Can we exclude the converse of this principle: The authentication of Christianity by reference to the "fruits of the Spirit"? Who among us has not on occasion seized upon the German Confessional Church's resistance to Nazism as having apologetic value?

These questions defy any attempt at simple categorical answers. Perhaps they call for a reexamination of this word pragmatism. We all recognize the pragmatic (judgment-by-consequences) basis of practical decisions. The pragmatist who consistently identifies "truth" with the "consequences of its being true" is a *rara avis*. Much of the current "social pragmatism" reveals an ethical dynamic that could not be generated through total preoccupation with "process." Rather, it suggests an inexplicit faith in the ordering of human affairs that puts "long-run" outcomes beyond hazard. Perhaps if this faith were rendered more explicit, and if the implications of "absolute imperatives" for Christian practice were clarified, the conflict between historic and "utilitarian" Christianity would be less acute.

September 5, 1946

On *The Deputy*

⧦⧦⧦

Martin Niemöller

VERY SOON AFTER THE TEXT of *The Deputy* was published in Germany, it became the center of an agitated and passionate discussion that is still going on. For the moment, even in the midst of the first rather sensational reactions, it seems as if this discussion will grow in depth and importance. This must and will happen, since the early reactions have failed to solve one of the basic underlying problems raised by the play.

The first question that has not been convincingly answered is whether or not the facts have been considered and presented rightly or whether this has been done in such a way that the result must be contested as one-sided and distorted. This problem will have to be left to the historians and their research, which may take considerable time. Certainly the cacophony of approving and of contradicting voices has not been suitable for bringing about any adequate clarification. Besides, they have been so loaded with all sorts of insinuation that the facts nearly disappeared in the face of questions about the author's person, his motives and his intentions.

The answer to this first question may remain in doubt for some time to come, but the real question deserves to be heard and to be taken seriously. That the Roman Catholic Church and her highest representative did not find the way to identify themselves and their life with the Jews and their indescribable fate—which leaves the impression that Christianity here refused to follow its Master, to deny itself and to take up its cross—is a reproach that calls upon *all* Christians and *all* Christian churches to examine themselves. It must be admitted that the Protestant churches in Germany have also fallen victim to their self-interest. This is true of even the Confessing Church, which at least tried to resist Hitler's demands and threats.

As early as the fall of 1933 the Pastors' Emergency League claimed the Christian right to give religious instruction to Jews, to accept them by baptism into their church fellowship and to treat them as legitimate members. Now *The Deputy* makes it clear that even this attitude did not express anything more than the Church's own interest, and had no regard for the human beings outside the Church who happened to be Jews.

So the non-Roman churches have no right to excuse and to acquit themselves of Rolf Hochhuth's reproach that they have behaved inhumanly. There was one occasion in 1937, if I remember rightly, when the Confessing Church, through its Council of Brethren, sent a memorandum to Hitler with a bitter complaint not only against anti-Christian but also against anti-humane measures of Nazi offices and organizations, in which the treatment of Jews was sharply criticized. Unfortunately this document was never published.

If the Christian churches were to become aware of their self-centeredness and recognize their fundamental duty both to identify themselves with and to love all fellow-beings for whom their Lord and Savior died, then the wide attention given to *The Deputy* would have borne ample and blessed fruit. For this reason we ought to be grateful to the author, who certainly has written his play not in order to offend or to insult but to warn and to help.

And this leads to the second question raised by the play, which also has not found a clear and unanimous answer: Was it really necessary to recapitulate all these events at this time, more than thirty years after they occurred, and set the world aflame? Many people think that everybody knows what happened and that we are able by now to draw our own conclusions from it.

But this certainly is not true of the younger generation in Germany. Only two or three years ago a West German newspaper reported that a young boy who had left school and was just beginning his apprenticeship claimed, when asked about Hitler, that he never had heard that name!

Now surely this part of history belongs to every curriculum in German schools. But many of the teachers were party members and don't like to be reminded of those days and their own shortcomings, and they are afraid of being questioned by their pupils as to their behavior in Hitler's Third Reich. Other teachers prefer to pass over this whole era because they know that any conversation at home may result in new difficulties between parents, who for the most part sided with the Nazis, and their children, who may lose the last bit of respect for parental authority when they discover what happened.

And the newspapers have not written much about the Nazi days during the last fifteen years because nobody is interested in a past that is full of immoral and criminal acts, done or provoked by a criminal and immoral government that nevertheless had the support of nearly one hundred per cent of the population.

For these reasons, the new generation in Germany has not received any real information and is lacking a very important perspective that they need to influence and direct the decisions they will be called upon to make. Since they cannot learn about it in school and since their knowledge is so fragmentary, any genuine and honest information must be welcomed. The present danger is not that a new form of Nazism or fascism will arise, but that this coming generation will not succeed in recognizing the connection between the Nazi catastrophe and the state of mind that led to it, which in a new spirit of militarism and nationalism may once again become disastrous.

In view of this danger Hochhuth's play must be acknowledged as something helpful, because it will arouse some real interest in the younger generation and has, in fact, already done so. The Christian churches should also learn from this play; its criticisms of the Christian egoistic self-interest should not be repudiated but accepted and turned into a sincere self-examination and an incorruptible reflection on the churches' calling and duty. The churches are called upon not only to preach humanity to sinful, that is inhuman, beings, but to live it and thereby to bear witness to the life and saving power of their Lord and Savior, Christ Jesus.

March 30, 1964

Nazism and Communism

Karl Barth

This letter was written by Professor Barth in response to criticism from Germany that he did not seem to be applying the same standards in opposing communism that he applied to Nazism in 1938. At that time he wrote a significant letter to Professor Joseph Hromadka in Prague, asserting that opposition to Nazism was a service to Christ.

YOU THINK IT WOULD BE ADVISABLE if I stated expressly why I do not want the logic of my letter to Hromadka applied to the present East-West conflict, why I do not find the present situation analogous to that of 1938. One could put the question even more clearly: Why do I not write to my West-German friends today what now would apply to the Russians in the same way that my letter then applied to the Nazis? I shall try to give you my answer:

(1) The Hromadka letter in 1938 was written in the days of the Munich settlement. It was sent to Prague where the decision was being reached, as to whether the world outside of Germany would tolerate German aggression. On the 30th of September in that year I wrote in my diary: "Catastrophe of European liberty in Munich." I stood alone

with this interpretation. "Realism" meant in those days the acceptance of the situation created by Hitler. Thanksgiving services were held in all the churches, including those here in Switzerland, for the preservation of peace. Six months later Hitler had violated this infamous accord of Munich. A year later he was in Poland—and the other consequences followed. If the "Czech soldier" [of whom Barth spoke in the Hromadka letter] had stood and had not been betrayed by the West, the Russians would not now be standing at the Elbe. That is when the die was cast. That is when the East-West problem arose. And that is when Europe and Christendom slept. . . .

I do not know when and how and to whom I would now direct a similar letter. A situation in which everything depended upon a yes or no decision has not subsequently developed. The determination, whether rightly or wrongly motivated, to resist Stalinist Communist aggression is the common policy of the West. Its intensification through a Christian word is superfluous. On the question no one sleeps today. On the contrary, one notes rather a nervousness, hysteria and fear which is not conducive to the highest form of determination. The Christian word today would have to be that we ought not be afraid. But such a word ought not be shouted. It can best be expressed in the way one lives and remains silent, particularly since so much is being said, both helpful and foolish. . . .

(2) In the Hromadka letter I called, in the name of the Christian faith, for resistance to the armed threat and aggression of Hitler. I am no pacifist and would do the same today. The foe of Czech and European freedom proved in those days again and again that his force would have to be met by force. . . . The peace at any price which the world, and also the churches, sought at that time was neither human nor Christian. That is why I "shouted" at that time. . . .

The present Russia is not the peace loving nation it professes to be. It claims to be menaced, particularly by the Anglo-Saxon powers. I cannot understand the reasons for this fear though I have tried to remain receptive to its arguments. It is obvious that Russia assumed a threatening attitude immediately after the conclusion of the war.

I must admit that if I were an American or British statesman I would not neglect preparations for a possible military defense. . . . But all this is being done in the West today without any specific Christian word or warning being necessary. . . . Today the Christian duty lies in another direction. Today we must continue to insist that war is identical with death in the sense that it is inevitable only when it has happened. In 1938 war was an actuality, but it could have been nipped in the bud with the right kind of determination. Russia has not created a similar situation today. It has not presented anyone with an ultimatum or committed aggression. (I do not hold it responsible for Korea.) There is no evidence for, and much evidence against the idea that it wants war. There are still means of avoiding war. Until they are exhausted (as they were exhausted in 1938) no one in the West has the right to believe in the inevitability or the desirability of war or to meet Russia as Hitler had to be faced. We do not face the glorification of war and we must, therefore, express our resolution to oppose communism without falling into fear and hatred or into war-like talk and action. A war which is not forced upon one, a war which is any other category but the *ultima ratio* of the political order, war as such is murder. . . . Every premature acceptance of war, all words, deeds and thoughts which assume that it is already present, help to produce it. For this reason it is important that there be people in all nations who refuse to participate in a holy crusade against Russia and communism, however much they may be criticized for their stand.

Finally we cannot emphasize too strongly that the most important defense against communism consists in extension of justice for all classes. In the event of war we must be prepared to face an army of millions of well equipped soldiers who will be convinced (from our standpoint, wrongly) of the righteousness of their cause and who will be prepared to give everything in the battle against the "criminals" (they mean us). Could one say as much for the armies of the so-called free world? Mere hatred of communism and Russia will not suffice us. The masses of our people must have experienced the value of our freedom in such a way that they would be willing to give their life for it. . . . Of course communism might triumph without war if its worser values appeared better to the masses of the Western world than what we offer in the name of democracy. In France this seems to be the case. Whoever does not want communism (and none of us do) had better seek for social justice than merely oppose it.

(3) On the question which you put to me on the remilitarization of Germany: One must not confuse this question with the general problem of pacifism, nor with the general question of the defense of the West. It is not logically correct to demand that anyone who disavows pacifism and believes in the defense of the West should also favor German re-militarization. I will give you a few reasons why I regard this as a unique problem. . . .

In the first place, I do not have the temerity to ask the German people, who have been bled white in two wars, to make this sacrifice again. A normal survival impulse must persuade the German people to refrain from this sacrifice.

In the second place, I regard it as impossible to expect of the German people that they arm for a war that is bound to be a civil war for them, in which Germans will be arrayed against Germans.

Thirdly, it does not seem to me to be morally defensible to tell a nation that one has sought to demilitarize to the point of denying it the use of tin soldiers as children's toys, that its salvation now depends upon preparation for another war.

Fourthly, it seems clear to me that the remilitarization of Western Germany might be the spark in the powder barrel with which the West, and Germany in particular, ought not to play.

In the fifth place, it is not at all clear to me how the western strategists propose to defend Germany between the Elbe and the Rhine, which might mean that a German army is expected to sacrifice itself at the Pyrenees after leaving their families in Germany.

In the sixth place, I believe that the positive defense against communism has a special significance for Germany. Has enough been done for the exiles, for the unemployed and the homeless, and for the return of war prisoners that communism might not be drawn into Germany as a sponge draws in water, despite the present rejection of it in Western Germany?—As a German I would be inclined to say, we cannot do this for we are otherwise engaged.

Finally, I ask a question hesitantly because I will risk the ill-will of Germans: Would it not be bad policy to have a German army, with all that goes with a German army in the European situation? History has proved that if an Englishman or a Swiss puts on a uniform that is not the same as when a German puts one on. The German becomes a total soldier too easily and too quickly. In common with many Europeans I would rather not see the re-emergence of the German soldier. And even if I were a German, and perhaps particularly if I were a German, I would rather not have his re-emergence, not even when the peril from the East is considered.

February 17, 1951

The Nuclear Dilemma

John C. Bennett

I FIND IT HARD TO UNDERSTAND why so little is said within the Church, or outside it, about the moral issues that are involved in the possibility of nuclear war. We hear a great deal about the extent of the destruction;

we hear especially about the threat to ourselves. One wonders why we don't hear more about the possibility of our becoming destroyers on a vast scale. Is it because we are so sure that if we are firm and show no moral hesitation about the use of nuclear weapons, there will be no war and hence no such moral problem? Is it because this whole matter is regarded so fatalistically that it is assumed that there is no real question of choice? Is it because, from the days of obliteration bombing in World War II, we have been convinced that, once war has started, all moral questions must be subordinated to strategic questions, and any degree of violence is permitted if it can be expected to make victory more likely?

In recent months there seems to have been a progression in the positions that are widely accepted. First, many of us have accepted the idea of nuclear weapons as a deterrent designed to prevent their use. Second, we seem to have moved to the recognition that, if a nuclear attack were initiated by another nation, we would retaliate with nuclear weapons. This was no more than carrying out the logic of the first position, and yet it presupposed the possibility of the failure of deterrence, a possibility that those who hold the first position may not really take seriously. The idea of nuclear retaliation raises moral problems that have not been given enough attention. These problems may be reduced to some extent if it is assumed that the retaliation would be directed against the striking power of the enemy and not against populations; also, a retaliatory strike might seem to be a mere response to an action of another and involve a minimum of freedom.

Third, *many Americans are making a great moral leap from the acceptance of the inevitability of such a retaliatory strike to the sanctioning of the initiating of a nuclear war in response to something less than a nuclear attack,* perhaps in response to a provocative political act or perhaps as a result of frustration in the course of conventional military operations. Critics of the Administration are calling for a clearer manifestation of the will to initiate a "nuclear exchange" (an extraordinary phrase to obscure the realities to which it points). Hanson Baldwin recently wrote about the distress felt by officers of the Air Force in Europe because of the tendency of the Government to emphasize the use of conventional weapons in the event of a conflict over Berlin and to go very far to avoid the "nuclear exchange."

We often hear that we must be ready to initiate nuclear war in order to preserve our honor, in order to be true to moral commitments. But our honor, our faithfulness to our commitments, our willingness to die for our beliefs do not depend upon our will to initiate a nuclear conflict. For us to attack the cities of Russia would be a great atrocity. No moral commitment can oblige us to perpetrate such an atrocity. But it would be almost as evil a deed to take the step that might initially involve the use of tactical nuclear weapons, knowing that it would be almost sure to result in the total conflict in which we would be both the destroyers and the destroyed.

I realize that there are so many possible contingencies that experts on strategy cannot predict what would happen if the more limited nuclear weapons were used. It is significant that Professor Kissinger now has greater doubt about the likelihood of our being able to limit nuclear war (*The Necessity of Choice,* Harper, 1960, pp. 82-83). Is there not also great danger that West Berlin itself might be an early victim of the very conflict fought to save it? Limited nuclear weapons in the crowded territory of Central Europe might seem quite unlimited to the inhabitants.

The whole discussion of nuclear war—discussion chiefly of strategy and degrees of destruction rather than of the moral issues involved—is confused by the tendency to assume that though there would be millions of casualties, perhaps scores of millions, the survivors could still emerge from their shelters and re-establish a free nation dedicated to Western values. Herman Kahn's book, *On Thermonuclear War* (Princeton University Press, 1960), is in many ways a great intellectual achievement, but it seems designed to promote this blindness concerning the indirect and more intangible effects—the moral and emotional effects of nuclear war.

Walter Lippmann is more convincing when he says that such a war "would be followed by a savage struggle for existence as the survivors crawled out of their shelters, and the American republic would be replaced by a stringent military dictatorship trying to keep some kind of order among the desperate survivors." Indeed, we might even desire that such a dictatorship would be established in view of the prospect of neighbors shooting one another to defend their shelter space and their food supply.

I think that Professor Hans Morgenthau, the dean of political realists, is sound when he says that there is a fundamental error in Kahn's optimism, which "lies in the assumption that the moral fiber of a civilization has an unlimited capacity to recover from shock" (*Commentary,* Oct. 1961, p. 281). Morgenthau believes in the nuclear deterrent, and he would not advocate surrender to the Russians; but he disavows the illusions that cause many people still to speak of nuclear war as a means of defending Western values and as having any positive meaning.

There is another aspect of our initiating nuclear war that should also be considered. This decision would be ours, but the effects would be disastrous for many people who would have no part in it. We make so much of free choice and yet, in a moment of choice on our part, we might determine the fate of whole nations that are little more than bystanders in the present conflict between ourselves and the Soviet Union. Not only would they, too, have many casualties, but they might have their social systems overturned as effectively as by a Communist revolution, and they might lose the reality of freedom or the opportunity to achieve it.

Furthermore, because of our political and strategic judgment in one moment in history, we would be imposing the genetic effects of nuclear war on future generations. Those who know most about these effects seem to be the most worried, although there is so much that is unknown or indefinite that it is difficult to cause either the public or those who must make decisions to take them seriously. Indeed, Herman Kahn goes so far as to say that it is an advantage that the effects of nuclear war will be spread over many generations because no one generation could bear the full brunt of it (*On Thermonuclear War*, pp. 48-49). This is a ghastly argument. We are certainly the last generation that could use it, for the cumulative effect of several nuclear wars would be too much for the toughest strategists to contemplate!

What are the implications of this discussion for policy? I realize that the dilemma is a terrible one for persons who have the responsibility to determine policy. They inherit a situation that contains the results of the fateful errors of many years. Senator Fulbright is certainly right in seeing the errors that have been made on both sides of the conflict over Berlin.

There may be subjective satisfaction in prescribing for the Government a consistent solution, whether it be unilateral nuclear disarmament or a one-sided kind of toughness that, on principle, refuses all concessions to Communists. But I cannot share any such satisfaction. I believe that we have a responsibility to do what we can to preserve a military balance in the world, that it would be a great disaster if the Communist world had a monopoly of nuclear power.

In the present juncture the combination of firmness and flexibility emphasized by President Kennedy is right, though both words are capable of endlessly varied interpretations. There are those who say that we should emphasize firmness because they believe that this would prevent the Russians from making any moves that might actually provoke war. These persons seem to have an amazing sureness that nuclear war would be prevented in this way. They avoid all discussion of the moral dilemma, so great is their sureness. But such rigidity would merely preserve a situation that is explosive in itself, and it would be tied to a policy that, because it looks toward a united Germany allied with the West, must always be unacceptable to the Russians and hence provocative.

A further problem arises from the fact that the will on our part to initiate nuclear war may make escalation from conventional operations to all-out nuclear war more likely. There is risk in any policy. But we have a responsibility to look at all the risks and not merely at the one risk—that the Russians might gain some advantage.

The chances are that we will outlive this crisis, and what may seem most difficult to plan or to do in the midst of a grave emergency may have more meaning in terms of a longer future. The radical reorientation in the thinking within our Government, involving a shift away from reliance on nuclear weapons to forms of military power that can be more readily kept limited, will probably have a chance to broaden the possibilities for action open to us. There may be time for some of the optimistic illusions about nuclear war to be deflated—I hope on both sides of the Iron Curtain.

Certainly, the discussion of the religious and ethical meaning of our decisions in this area would go on. Many Catholic theologians and moralists have adapted the traditional conception of the "just war" to the idea of a limited war in the nuclear age. It has seemed to me for some time that Protestants, with the exception of the pacifists and nuclear pacifists, have tended to be silent. It is time now to think again about these issues and to break the silence.

Kenneth W. Thompson

NO ONE WHO COMBINES SCIENTIFIC KNOWLEDGE with moral imagination rests easily in the present crisis. The specter of fifty- or one-hundred-megaton bombs wreaking havoc over a sixty-mile radius, and exceeding the damage of all the bombs dropped in World War II, imposes a cloud of anxiety over all our lives. The moral destructiveness for those who use and those who suffer these weapons is enormous. If "Thou shalt not kill" is a mandate from which men are seldom exempt, how much more restrictive should be the law "Thou shalt not annihilate."

Yet there is some sophism in the claim that taking many lives is morally more offensive than killing one man. War in terms of any ultimate moral judgment is evil; by any absolute standard it is as wrong to bomb a city with cannons as it is with atomic bombs. We distinguish in international law between combatants and non-combatants, but this distinction is often breached in conventional war as well.

By relative standards, war is judged by another set of criteria. Some wars are "just wars"; a defensive war is more acceptable than a war in which we strike the first blow. Most of the rules about "just," defensive, or legitimate wars are difficult to apply in the thermonuclear age. War, we are told, no longer serves a rational purpose; its consequences—for victor and victim alike—outweigh any possible advantages.

Since war has lost its rational purpose, most of the rational and moral discussion has concentrated on the prevention and limitation of war. If cynics and idealists agree on the immorality of nuclear war judged by any objective standard, the grounds for protest by the moralist are less compelling. Yet moralists share a rich tradition of protest. Even given the consensus concerning the morality of nuclear war, many of our more sensitive humanists and religious writers insist that an ethic of war today must be an ethic of protest. Yet an ethic of restraint, limits and silence may well be more relevant.

I doubt that many Americans, or most children of Western civilization, have any illusions about the moral infamy and destructiveness of nuclear war. One example may serve to illustrate this point. Following World War II, our negotiators failed to achieve agreements with the Russians. Early in the postwar period, when negotiations reached an impasse, each side was tempted to condemn the other and retreat from the bargaining table. Recently, I have noted that, even following major breakdowns in serious negotiations, neither side has been prepared to abandon negotiations. They have observed in private—and sometimes in public—that the stakes were too high, that the hazards of thermonuclear conflict were so great that the parties must not give up on chances at the conference table.

If the prevailing view of nuclear warfare, in any absolute terms, is the same for militarists and moralists alike, the greatest role for the moralist may not be one of moral protest. Contemporary society may not need the moralist to instruct it on the gravity of nuclear conflict. The uniqueness of his contribution in warning men of the dangers may not be that which he claims for it.

The disturbing quality in Dr. Bennett's approach lies in its revival of past illusions shared by Protestants and humanists alike. In my view, Dr. Bennett runs the risk of neglecting the sage counsel of Archibald MacLeish, who during World War II distinguished between the pure and the responsible. The pure are those who protest war and conflict; the responsible are those who seek to limit, deter or restrain nations who might go to war. Under present circumstances, if we announced our intention never to use thermonuclear weapons, we could invite precisely the consequences Dr. Bennett most fears. For the one lesson of the cold war is that Soviet advances have been checked only through the use of countervailing power—with power being defined in broad moral and material as well as military terms. If we announce when and how we will use or not use the power available to us—if the past is any guide—the Soviets will move to exploit our declaration.

Once we are clear about the limits and restraints of force, the moral burdens of remaining silent on what we will do or not do are considerable. We may have sacrificed the cause of the rebels in Hungary when we announced we would not intervene. With this reassurance, the

Soviets turned to a strategy of terror and intimidation. If we declare we shall not use thermonuclear weapons except in the ultimate defense, we have assisted the Soviet Union in plotting a campaign of expansion and imperialism. They will know in advance the limits they face and the broad area within which they can pursue their cause. It may call for greater moral resources than we can muster, more self-discipline than we are capable of to set ourselves limits of military strategy and then remain silent in the face of an ever expanding foe.

I would prefer the moralist to master a strategy of restraint, silence where policy dictates, and self-discipline rather than merely to protest with all right-thinking men the grave hazards of the nuclear age. A strategy of restraint would support limited goals, conventional military strategy, limited accommodation, probing for possible agreement. I see this as far more constructive than a strategy of moral protest.

Paul Tillich

THE BEST COMMENT I CAN MAKE on John Bennett's paper is contained in the following theses. I prepared them originally for a recent discussion with Dean Rusk, Max Freedman, Henry Kissinger, and James Reston on Eleanor Roosevelt's television program, "Prospects for Mankind." I am glad to publish them in connection with John Bennett's congenial article. [Editor's note—Dr. Tillich's theses were discussed by James Reston in his regular column in *The New York Times* of October 25.]

(1) Ethical problems underlie all political considerations. They become predominant when the political situation puts alternatives before the statesmen that cannot be escaped by compromise. They must anticipate them, even while negotiations aiming at compromises are still going on.

(2) The ethical problem is not, as in discussions with older forms of pacifism, the rightness or wrongness of power-groups using force. The negation of this right, I am glad to say, did not come up in the present conversations. The primitive identification between personal and social ethics was hardly noticeable. But there are social ethics; and the question of their principle must certainly be asked. It is, as I call it, creative justice —a justice whose final aim is the preservation or restitution of a community of social groups, sub-national, national or supra-national.

(3) The means for reaching this aim must be adequate to the aim: Negotiation, diplomacy, war (if necessary), a peace that not only

does not destroy but also makes a new community possible. War occurs when a social group feels attacked and decides to defend its power to exist and the ultimate principles for which it stands (e.g., democratic freedom in this country).

(4) The decision to enter a war is justified only if it is done in the service of creative justice. Each such decision, however, is not only a political and military but also a moral risk.

(5) In the light of the aim of intergroup justice, a war fought with atomic weapons cannot be justified ethically. For it produces destruction without the possibility of a creative new beginning. It annihilates what it is supposed to defend.

(6) In the present situation this ethical principle lends to the following political-military preferences:

> (a) Defense—political and military—not only of its power to exist but also of its ultimate principles for itself and those who adhere to the same principles and who are likewise threatened, is a clear, ethical demand.
>
> (b) If such defense is in particular situations impossible with conventional weapons (as it would be in the case of Berlin and perhaps parts of Western Europe), even then this does not justify the use of atomic weapons; for they would not be means of defense but of mere destruction of both sides.
>
> (c) Nevertheless, atomic armament is justified because it shows the potential enemy that radical destruction would take place on his side as much as on the other side if he attacks first with atomic weapons.
>
> (d) For the American strategy this means that no atomic weapon can be used before the enemy uses one, and even then not for "retaliation" but in order to induce him not to continue their use. (Practically, the very existence of atomic weapons on both sides is probably a sufficient deterrent.)
>
> (e) If this includes—as it very probably does—a temporary military retreat in Europe on our side (by no means a total surrender), this is a most ordinary phenomenon in most wars and can be redressed by the arrival of the total Allied military power.

(7) This suggestion makes, on the basis of ethical principles, a sharp distinction between the atomic weapons of total destruction (including the tactical atomic weapons) and the so-called conventional weapons, which can be directed against the enemy army and its bases. Of course, the atomic weapons remain in the background, but our awareness of the social-ethical imperative must prevent us from ever using them first again.

November 11, 1961

The Survival of the Free Society

⤳ ♡ ⤶

Adlai E. Stevenson

IN A MATTER OF DAYS we enter a new decade. Just as a hundred years ago, on the eve of the Civil War, we entered the decade of the Sixties that proved decisive to our republic, so in this century we are entering the same decade—on the eve of trials equally decisive. Therefore it seems to me not a time for uncritical self-congratulation but for critical self-examination. Shaw wrote: "The more things a man is ashamed of, the more respectable he is." Well, I don't think we are as respectable as we like to think.

I don't think we are shocked by the gross inadequacies of our schools, or by the fact that our scientific achievements lag behind the Russians'. I don't think we are ashamed or really much concerned about our decaying cities, about our neglected resources or the infirmity of our defenses, or about the implications of the growing disparity of living standards between the rich and the poor nations, or that America's stature in the world has been declining while the crisis is mounting.

And, finally, in the face of the most powerful and dangerous challenge our capitalist economic system and our democratic political system have ever confronted, I have seen little awareness of the public responsibility of private power.

But the steel strike dramatizes the fact that we are at the end of an era. Everybody is agreed that this cannot happen again, that the public interest is the paramount interest, and that irresponsible private power is an intolerable danger to our beleaguered society.

Our American tradition has been to disperse power and trust to luck to make power responsible. James Madison, in the *Federalist* (No. 10), found safety from factions in having a great many of them, fighting over a large territory. But in order to have any confidence that if enough centers of power contend they will make one another responsible, we must attribute to Providence a greater interest in the welfare of the American people than either our history or our merits would seem to justify.

The time has come for us as a people, as a community learning together, to learn how to assume conscious control of our destiny. If a society is to be free and just, all power in it must be made responsible. We are certain of this when it comes to governmental power. When the Constitution was framed, government and the individual were the only

261

two entities in society. Government was the one with the power. Now other centers of power may have a more direct and drastic effect on the individual and on the life of the country than any eighteenth century government could have hoped to have. This raises new constitutional questions. Where private groups—like big business and big labor—are performing public functions, they must be held to public responsibility. And one may forecast with some certainty that the Supreme Court will increasingly hold them to this responsibility.

But are the alternatives always between governmental control and letting private power run wild until it is checked by collision with other private powers?

And if private power is to be made responsible, we shall have to look to the centers of power, like the business community, to bring about this result. Businessmen will have to get over their neurosis about government, for government has a positive duty to see to it that business is directed to the common good. The same is true of labor. To the extent to which labor and management see to it that their activities are directed to this end, direct intervention in their affairs by government may be avoided.

But in September it proved necessary—for the first time in our history—for government to establish controls over the internal affairs of the labor unions—their constitutions, their elections, the administration of their offices—because of the irresponsibility of a comparatively few labor leaders. This was a failure not just for the unions, but for democracy. The system is weaker today than it would have been if labor had done for itself what government has now had to do for it.

And now there is this bitter, stubborn failure of private responsibility in the steel industry. Although the public has been barred from knowing what is going on, it now appears that the crucial issue is not wages, but rather the handling of the problems arising from automation. And apparently both sides are insisting on virtually absolute control over these decisions, without regard to the cost to the country.

The basic failure was far deeper than the fact of the strike itself. Thoughtful men who have championed collective bargaining as a keystone of a free economy are now voicing concern about its capacity to cope with the problems of the technological revolution—at a time when America cannot pay the price of nationwide stoppages in its basic industries.

By the end of January—unless earlier settlement is reached—the country will again be exposed, with no protection, to a steel strike. And in the spring the question will be whether the railroads will be operating or not.

The impression created around the world by the spectacle of such failures in our vaunted democratic capitalist system is lamentable. I suspect the country will no longer accept this state of affairs. And if there are more stoppages Congress may be expected to reflect the public temper in legislation, which would not only stop strikes but might stop or seriously cripple collective bargaining too. The most likely prospect would be some form of compulsory arbitration, limited to the case itself.

But it is now apparent that the emergency disputes provisions in the Taft-Hartley Act do not work and that a new and reasonable law is needed.

I hope you will forgive my speaking of this last point in personal terms. "I told you so" has always seemed to me a demeaning phrase. But with your indulgence I want to quote from a speech on Labor Day, 1952, in Cadillac Square in Detroit, by a then candidate for President:

> "New methods must be found for settling national emergency disputes . . . .
>
> "We cannot tolerate shutdowns which threaten our national safety, even that of the whole free world. The right to bargain collectively does not include a right to stop the national economy . . . .
>
> "All the Taft-Hartley answer boils down to is that in national emergency disputes employees shall be ordered to work for another 80 days on the employer's terms . . . .
>
> "What we need is a . . . law that will provide for investigation and reporting to the public on the issues involved, one that will provide for more effective mediation between the parties . . . . [Because these emergency cases are always different] the Congress should give to the President a choice of procedures when voluntary agreement proves impossible: seizure provisions geared to the circumstances; *or* arbitration; *or* a detailed hearing and a recommendation of settlement terms; *or* a return of the dispute to the parties . . . ."

If there is excuse for this anecdotal intrusion it is only in the fact that I would propose today substantially what I did then—except a little more so.

The "choice of procedures" approach still seems to me the right one. I think of it as essentially a mediation approach but with real teeth in it, with the opportunity afforded for effective assertion of the public interest, and—if I may use the term here—with the inclusion of an "insurance policy" covering the possible risk of mediation failure, with the public named as the beneficiary.

I would add one proposal to my 1952 suggestion: The President should have authority to convene a special public board—a Board of Public Responsibility—well in advance of the strike date in any key industry, perhaps as listed by Congress. The Board would meet with the parties to the dispute; it would express the public interest to the parties, keep the President advised, and perform whatever mediation functions appeared advisable. Its effectiveness would be immeasurably enhanced by the parties' knowledge that the Board's final responsibility— if its efforts at mediation should fail—would be to recommend to the President what further action should be taken. The possible forms of this further action, the "choice of procedures," would include, to avoid any party's confident reliance on being "taken off the hook," the possibility of *no* further action—assuming the situation permitted this.

With such a law it is likely that no case would ever get to the final stage requiring the ultimate Presidential action. But if it did—if the parties were unable or unwilling to resolve their dispute, to exercise responsibility consonant with their power—then I would see no reasonable objection to requiring that the dispute be taken out of their hands entirely; that the President be authorized in that case to require in one form or another that production be continued while the dispute was resolved by process of reason rather than by subjecting the economy to grievous injury.

I have no illusions about this proposal. It will be objected to on the ground that it intrudes the government into these cases at too early a stage. I think not. It was one thing to expect the public to accept the results of collective bargaining when that result represented the "decentralized decision making" of a thousand different sets of negotiations. But with the development of industry-wide bargaining, decisions affecting the entire economy are made by a small group of men sitting at a single table, and the public has no alternative to accepting those decisions. I think it is entitled to be represented at that table in the restricted sense I have suggested.

Also it will be said that this proposal involves a denial of the rights of labor and management to strike and to shut down a basic industry. It seems to me that this, too, is a legitimate and necessary implication of the decision to resort to industry-wide bargaining. The greater the power, the larger the responsibility. When the public is denied alternative sources of supply it is entitled to demand that the supply not be shut off. It was in a similar context of labor-management strife that Mr. Justice Brandeis once said: "All rights are derived from the purposes of the society in which they exist; above all rights rises duty to the community."

All these changing circumstances demand fundamental changes in the collective bargaining process. They will mean, I suspect, increased use by labor and management of various forms of continuous bargaining, in place of the present practice of concentrating all bargaining in the brief periods just before old contracts expire, while a strike bomb is set and ticking.

Finally, let me repeat and emphasize the importance of the fact that our economy and the society it serves will be weaker by whatever degree it is necessary for government to intrude upon the settlement of labor-management disputes in order to make private power responsible.

But I wish our failure to display to a watchful, skeptical world the fullest wisdom and responsibility of democratic capitalism was confined to labor-management relations.

Increasingly in the past eighteen months I have become puzzled by the rising chorus of fear about this great and powerful economy. When a $500,000,000,000 annual income is in sight; when we have the highest per capita income in human history; when we have weathered three recessions without a decline in consumer income; when catching up with American productivity has even become the—curiously un-Marxist—goal of our rivals, the Russians—our leaders tell us we can spend on space research only half what we spend to store a single year's surplus crop. They also tell us we cannot afford to spend proportionately on education what the Russians spend, on welfare what the Scandinavians spend, on arms, I'm told, what the Chinese spend. We have half the free world's gold, and only twice since 1945 have we had an adverse balance in our international payments; yet we attach with panicky haste the "Buy American" strings to our loans while asking everyone else to end their trade restrictions.

What is one to make of it all?

On the one hand, we are the wealthiest people in history; on the other we teeter on the edge of bankruptcy. With goods fairly running out of our ears, we moan about the dangers of inflation.

When our political and business leaders warn us that we are "spending ourselves into bankruptcy" they have only one kind of spending in mind—public spending derived from tax money or official borrowing. Nobody cries "reckless spending" when perfectly good office buildings on Park Avenue with years of life ahead of them are pulled down to make room for new ones carrying higher rents and higher profits. The charge of spending is hurled indeed against attempts at the other end of the same avenue to pull down ghastly tenements and rehouse families with the elements of human decency. There is no outcry about business expense accounts that equal in a year what a primary school teacher can earn in a decade. Who asks what cost to our economy day by day is added by including in the cost of every product the packaging and persuasion to buy what in many cases people do not really want?

Where, then, is the waste? Surely not in the public domain.

In short, what the prophets of bankruptcy and collapse really mean is that all government expenditures must be held to a minimum while the flood of private consumption goes up unchecked, even if the consumption is of marginal human value. There is more here than a matter of priority and value. For it is precisely in the public domain that the Communists present their most dangerous threat. To refuse to meet the challenge in the area of government spending is ideology in reverse. Unless we are prepared to spend not what we can "afford" but what we need in such areas as defense, economic aid, education and basic research—to name only the four chief areas of Communist challenge—it is not just our free enterprise system that we are putting in jeopardy, it is the survival of free society itself.

I think we are evading this issue. I think we have underrated the Soviet challenge. Their atom bombs came long before we expected. Sputnik was an ugly surprise to us. Now they have pinned their colors to the moon, and even sent us photographs of its back side. Four years ago I often warned about the implications of rapid Soviet economic growth. It makes no difference that prominent politicians—not of my party!—broadly hinted that I might be a disloyal American. But it does make a difference if we are still making the mistake of under-estimating our rivals—perhaps as an easy escape from the disagreeable fact that public spending, far from falling, very probably ought to increase; that taxes, far from falling, may have to be higher, at least until disarmament or an accelerated rate of economic growth gives us adequate resources.

The point is that business carries a heavy share of the burden of foresight, understanding and leadership not to put the last least triviality of private spending ahead of public needs in priority and esteem. Public spending in defense and research must have priority because survival depends upon it. Public spending on education, on health, conservation and urban renewal must have priority because the dignity and grace of our free way of life depends upon it.

And there is another priority—the question whether as a community, we, the wealthiest society known to man, can keep our spiritual self-esteem and offer the poor underdeveloped countries an alternative to communism as a method of economic modernization.

Regardless of the Communist competition in these areas, we have to go no further than the Christian basis of our nation's ethic to know how this issue will be decided. While we double and treble our standards of life, the meager living of nearly half our fellow men on this planet threatens to diminish further. For example, between India's annual per capita income of sixty dollars and our own, which is about two thousand dollars, the job is already as great as the gulf between Dives and Lazarus, and it is growing wider.

Now that Asian attention is riveted on the President's journey, how incalculable might be the effect if we were to choose Delhi to announce a new and sustained Western effort to aid world growth and world investment. For in India live nearly half the inhabitants of the emergent areas.

I have talked to you leaders of a great essential business about our failures because I have seen little sign of any challenging, positive approach to the great problems of our time. In the most radical and revolutionary epoch of man's history, our dominant concerns seem almost wholly defensive. We are not spurred on by the positive opportunities of world building and nation building inherent in our position as the most fabulously endowed people mankind has ever seen.

On the contrary, our foreign policy is dominated by fear of communism, our domestic policy by fear of "inflation." Economic assistance programs have been sold chiefly as a means of checking the Communists, never as our creative part in extending the technological revolution to the rest of mankind. The spur to our exploration of the solar system and scientific research has not been our restless desire to extend the boundaries of human knowledge. It has been irritation with the Russian achievements. Interest in greater excellence in education flared up not because we want every free citizen to exercise to the full his innate talents and capacities, but because our rivals are producing more scientists and technologists.

So let us assess our needs—our need to maintain equality of military strength until controlled disarmament takes its place, our need for better education, our need for wider research, a greater thrust into outer space, our need for decent cities where segregation and delinquency give ground in the wake of redevelopment and renewal, our need to conserve our national resources, above all, water.

All these needs—domestic, foreign and military—will cost more money, at least until we can make some progress with disarmament. But keeping the budget down isn't as imperative as keeping our heads up.

I think our needs could be covered by existing tax rates at higher levels of economic growth. But I am sure that if our political leadership defines the tasks with clarity and conviction, we will approve what is necessary to fulfill our national purpose whatever the sacrifice—higher taxation in years when the private economy is running at full stretch, for instance, budgetary deficits in times of slack, restraint upon wages and profits to slow down inflationary pressure, less emphasis on private rights and more on public responsibility.

But the recompense will be to see American society once more the pacesetter in human affairs, to see freedom once more the great challenger on the human scene. For this, surely, is the crux. An attitude of unadventurous conservatism cannot stand for long as the creative image of freedom. I tremble for our future—and for the world's future—if growth, thrust, initiative and the vast new frontiers of science are felt to be the prerogative of Communist discipline and drive, if "the shot heard around the world" has been silenced by the shot around the moon.

Today not rhetoric but sober fact should bid us believe that our curious combination of complacency and apprehension, of little aims and large fears, has within it the seed of destruction first for our own community and then for the larger hope that, as science and technology bring the nations inescapably together, freedom, not tyranny, will be the organizing principle of the society of man.

January 11, 1960

Notes on Contributors

KARL BARTH has been the major force behind the revival of Protestant theology in this century. His personal war against Hitler is history, and his multi-volume *Dogmatik* is a theological landmark.

JOHN C. BENNETT is co-chairman of the *Christianity and Crisis* Editorial Board and president of Union Theological Seminary. He has contributed significantly to Protestant thinking on international affairs, communism, Catholicism and church-state relations.

DIETRICH BONHÖFFER, a young theologian of great promise, was martyred by the Nazis for his participation in a plot against the life of Adolf Hitler. His writings have greatly influenced recent theological thought.

MALCOLM BOYD is an Episcopal priest who has been deeply involved in the freedom movement and is a veteran of many civil rights projects in the South. He is the author of *Are You Running With Me, Jesus?*

HERBERT BUTTERFIELD, the distinguished British historian, is master of Peterhouse College at Cambridge University. His books include *Christianity, Diplomacy and War* and *Christianity and History*.

WAYNE H. COWAN is managing editor of *Christianity and Crisis.* A former missionary to Japan, he has written for *Commonweal, The Christian Century, America* and other journals.

HARVEY COX, a member of the Editorial Board, teaches at the Harvard Divinity School. He is the author of the best-selling book, *The Secular City,* in which he combines his theological and cultural interests.

DENIS DE ROUGEMENT, a well-known Swiss writer, is the author of *Love in the Western World* and *The Devil's Share.* He is President of the Congress of Cultural Freedom.

TOM F. DRIVER has been staff reviewer for *The Reporter, The New Republic* and *The Christian Century.* A member of the Editorial Board, he teaches at Union Theological Seminary.

LANGDON GILKEY, one of the more astute younger American theologians, teaches at the University of Chicago Divinity School. He is the author of the recently published *Shantung Compound.*

ROBERT C. GOOD, who coordinated President John F. Kennedy's task force on Africa, is now United States ambassador to Zambia.

JULIAN N. HARTT teaches philosophic theology at Yale Divinity School and is the author of *Lost Image of Man.*

WAYNE C. HARTMIRE, JR. is director of the California Migrant Ministry. He worked closely with those engaged in the 1965 grape-pickers strike in Delano, California.

F. ERNEST JOHNSON, a member of the Editorial Board through-out the twenty-five years, is professor-emeritus of Teachers College, Columbia University. He has been deeply involved in the work of the Department of Church and Economic Life of the National Council of Churches for many years.

SIDNEY LANIER is president and a founder of the American Place Theater in New York City, which offers opportunity for American writers to develop their dramatic talents.

EDWARD B. JOLLIFFE, Queen's Counselor, is a Canadian lawyer who was born in China of missionary parents and attended West China Union University. He last visited Communist China in the late Fifties.

JOHN DAVID MAGUIRE, by profession a theologian, teaches religion at Wesleyan University and serves as chairman of Connecticut's Advisory Committee to the United States Commission on Civil Rights. He is also a member of the Editorial Board of *Christianity and Crisis*.

JACQUES MARITAIN, now retired from his teaching post at Princeton University, is perhaps the outstanding Roman Catholic philosopher of the past generation.

WILLIAM F. MAY heads up the newly founded Department of Religion at Indiana State University. A contributing editor, he is presently writing a book about the seven deadly sins and others.

HOWARD MOODY is minister of Judson Memorial Church in New York City. His efforts for political and social reform and his work with the artistic community have been reported in *Esquire* and other journals.

HANS J. MORGENTHAU is a professor of political science at the University of Chicago. His articles have appeared in many journals and he is the author of *Politics in the Twentieth Century*.

REINHOLD NIEBUHR, theologian and political philosopher, is known to a wide audience through his prolific writing in articles and books, including *The Nature and Destiny of Man* and *Man's Nature and His Communities*.

THE LATE H. RICHARD NIEBUHR was considered by many to be a theologian's theologian. For many years he served on the faculty of Yale Divinity School. His books include *Christ and Culture* and *The Kingdom of God in America*.

MARTIN NIEMÖLLER, German U-boat captain in World War I, and later a fearless critic of the Nazi regime who was imprisoned from 1937 to 1945, is president of the Evangelical Church of Hessen-Nassau. He is also one of the seven presidents of the World Council of Churches.

ALAN PATON is probably best known as the author of *Cry the Beloved Country*. A South African, he has displayed unusual integrity and courage in opposing his nation's policies of apartheid.

LISTON POPE, a member of the *Christianity and Crisis* Editorial Board for a number of years, teaches social ethics at Yale Divinity School. He is the author of *Millhands and Preachers* and *Kingdom Beyond Caste*.

STEPHEN C. ROSE recently joined the staff of the World Council of Churches in Geneva, Switzerland. Founder of the journal *Renewal,* he is also a member of the Editorial Board of *Christianity and Crisis.*

ST. HERETICUS is a regular *Christianity and Crisis* feature. Robert McAfee Brown has made it his life's work to bring the satiric Saint's writings to a wider public.

ROGER L. SHINN, an Editorial Board veteran, is dean of instruction at Union Theological Seminary. He has written on political and social questions as well as theology. He is the author of *Tangled World* and edited *The Search for Identity: Essays on the American Character.*

THE LATE ADLAI E. STEVENSON, twice-defeated candidate for President and a Governor of Illinois, will always be remembered as one American who tried to talk sense to other Americans.

M. M. THOMAS, the journal's contributing editor for Asia, is director of the Christian Institute for the Study of Religion and Society in Bangalore, India. He is also secretary for Church and Society of the East Asia Christian Conference.

KENNETH W. THOMPSON has taught political science at the University of Chicago and Northwestern University. A member of the Editorial Board, his articles have appeared in many journals. He is the author of *American Diplomacy and Emergent Patterns* and *Christian Ethics and the Dilemmas of Foreign Policy.*

THE LATE PAUL TILLICH came to the United States to teach at Union Theological Seminary after clashing with the Hitler regime. He later taught at Harvard University and the University of Chicago. His *Systematic Theology* is a prerequisite for an understanding of modern Christian theology.

AMOS N. WILDER is now retired after many years of teaching New Testament at the Harvard and the University of Chicago divinity schools. An editorial board member for more than ten years, he has written frequently about literary subjects, including the book *Theology and Modern Literature.*